W9-AHR-587

NATIONS OF THE MODERN WORLD

CEYLON	S. A. Pakeman *Formerly Professor of Modern History, Ceylon University College. Appointed Member, House of Representatives, Ceylon, 1947–1952*
MODERN INDIA	Sir Percival Griffiths *President, India, Pakistan and Burma Association*
MODERN IRAN	Peter Avery *Lecturer in Persian and Fellow of King's College, Cambridge*
JAPAN	Sir Esler Dening *H.M. Ambassador to Japan, 1952–1957*
MALAYA	J. M. Gullick *Formerly of the Malayan Civil Service*
PAKISTAN	Ian Stephens *Formerly Editor of* The Statesman *Calcutta and Delhi, 1942–1951* *Fellow, King's College, Cambridge, 1952–1958*
SOUTH AFRICA	John Cope *Formerly editor-in-chief of* The Forum
SUDAN REPUBLIC	K. D. D. Henderson *Formerly of the Sudan Political Service and Governor of Darfur Province 1949–1953*

TURKEY	Geoffrey Lewis *Senior lecturer in Turkish and Fellow of St. Antony's College, Oxford*
THE UNITED STATES OF AMERICA	H. C. Allen *Commonwealth Fund Professor of American History, University College, London*
YUGOSLAVIA	Muriel Heppel and F. B. Singleton

NATIONS OF THE MODERN WORLD

TURKEY

TURKEY

By
GEOFFREY LEWIS

THIRD EDITION

FREDERICK A. PRAEGER, *Publishers*
NEW YORK · WASHINGTON

BOOKS THAT MATTER

First Published in the United States of America in 1955
by Frederick A. Praeger, Inc., Publishers
111 Fourth Avenue, New York 3, N.Y.

Second Edition, 1960
Third Edition, 1965
Second Impression (corrected) 1966

Library of Congress Catalog Card Number: 65–14182

Printed in Great Britain

TO

J. and A. C., C. and I. O., and J. R.
with gratitude and affection

Preface to Third Edition

THE REVOLUTION of 27 May 1960 made it desirable to carry out a major revision of the book and this has now proved possible. I was an eye-witness of the revolution and my experience is similar to that of eye-witnesses of earlier revolutions in Turkey: public rejoicing that tyranny was dead, followed by a long period of disillusionment because the millennium had in fact not arrived. But I have learned never to despair of the Turks; they have an almost British talent for muddling-through and a self-respect that will one day lead them to the heights of which Atatürk dreamed.

G. L. L.

OXFORD *1964*

Note to Second Edition

THIS EDITION incorporates a large amount of additional material, as well as corrections. My thanks are due to the many readers who have written to give me the benefit of their special knowledge.

It has not always been possible to make the full alterations in the text, so that extensive footnotes have been added throughout. Chapter 28, 'Economic Policy and Overseas Trade', is supplemented by the first part of the new Chapter 31, entitled 'Postscript 1959'.

G. L. L.

OXFORD *1959*

Preface to First Edition

WHEN I WAS invited to contribute a book on Turkey to Benn's Nations of the Modern World Series, I was offered the choice of writing a completely new work or revising the volume written by Professor A. J. Toynbee and Mr Kenneth P. Kirkwood for the same series and published in 1926.

To do justice to all that has happened in Turkey during the last quarter-century would naturally have involved a drastic recasting of the earlier work. If all that was required was the addition of new facts and the deletion of those which had diminished in importance through the perspective of the years, revision might have been the obvious choice. But revision would also have involved pruning the observations and conclusions of my predecessors and grafting on the results of my own recent visits to Turkey. A close study of the book persuaded me that one could not hope to bring it up to date without inevitably ruining the flow of its argument and distorting the carefully-drawn pattern of history which it presents.

This book then is new, but it is not to be regarded as rendering obsolete its earlier namesake: Toynbee and Kirkwood's *Turkey* will always hold an honoured place on the student's shelves. On one point only do I disagree profoundly with my predecessors, and that is the quotation from Thucydides which introduces their book:

> "I shall be satisfied if my narrative is favourably received by readers whose object is exact knowledge of facts which have not only actually occurred, but which are destined approximately to repeat themselves in all human probability."

For it seems unlikely that the events leading up to the foundation of the Turkish Republic and its progress along the hard road to democracy can ever be duplicated between now and Doomsday.

. . . . .

It is one of the oddities of scholarship that, although there is no shortage of narratives written by British travellers in Turkey from the sixteenth century onwards, very few British orientalists have devoted themselves to Turkish studies. Until recent years, therefore, the field was left open to the non-specialists, who did not permit their ignorance of the language, history and institutions of Turkey to deter them from writing books about it. This they contrived to do by the device of treating the Turks as they would a non-human Act of God, an impersonal entity which any historian was entitled to discuss, as he might discuss the Fire of London or the Krakatoa Eruption. The Turks were not a people, with a cultural tradition of their own; they were a troublesome appendix to European history, they were a thorn in the flesh, they were the Eastern Question.

During the last few years, political and military cupboard-love have helped to increase Western interest in the Turks, and this has resulted in a more realistic appraisal of the achievements and potentialities of this hitherto under-rated people. Inevitably, however, the balance has swung the other way. Even a few years ago, a journalist, called upon to supply a half-column about Turkey at short notice, would have filled it out with a few references to the prevalence of veiled women. In like circumstances today, he will refer to the absence of veiled women. Both pictures are false.

The purpose of the present work is to convey an impression of what has been going on in Turkey of recent years, and what the Turks are like, with enough information about the past to make intelligible the present. The book is in two parts: the first and longer tells the story of the Turkish Republic down to the present day; the second describes some aspects of the modern Turkish scene.

At the end of the Preface will be found a note on the Turkish alphabet, which has been used for Turkish words and names. I have to own to some inconsistency: words familiar to English readers are left in their Anglicized form, and this principle is extended to the familiar spelling 'Istanbul', although most Turks spell it with a dotted I. The reader will notice that I also use the old name 'Constantinople': when dealing with Turkish history, sometimes the one name seems more appropriate, sometimes the other. For fluctuating between 'Smyrna' and 'İzmir' I have no real excuse. 'Smyrna' comes more naturally but the influence of N.A.T.O. is giving currency to 'İzmir'; the latter will probably prevail and only figs will keep alive the memory of the old name, just as the time-honoured English names for 'Ankara' and 'Thailand' survive in the wool of the one and the twins and cat of the other.

I gratefully acknowledge my indebtedness to the works of Professor Paul Wittek, Dr Tarık Z. Tunaya and Professor Enver Ziya Karal. I wish also to thank Dr Berna Moran and Bay Nejat Sönmez, for their prompt and helpful replies to my queries.

G. L. LEWIS

OXFORD *1955*

NOTE ON THE TURKISH ALPHABET

MOST OF THE consonants have much the same values as in English, and the vowels as in Italian, with these exceptions:

c is pronounced like *j* in 'jam'; *ç* like *ch* in 'church'; *j* is pronounced as it is in French; *ş* is like *sh* in 'shop'; *ğ* is silent in standard Turkish, serving only to lengthen a preceding vowel; *g* is always hard, as in 'get'.

Dotted *i* is like *i* in 'bit', undotted *ı* like the *i* in the non-U pronunciation of 'Cyril' or the Missourian's pronunciation of the first vowel in 'Missouri' (the corresponding capital letters are respectively *İ* and *I*); *ö* and *ü* are pronounced as in German. A circumflex accent over a vowel denotes a slight *y*-sound between it and the preceding consonant; thus 'coot' would be written *kut* in Turkish letters, but 'cute' would be *kût*.

Contents

PART II

Map

PART ONE

Chapter 1

The Ottoman Empire

THE EARLIEST home of the Turks was somewhere between the Tien Shan Mountains and the Aral Sea. Between the sixth century, when they left it (guided, according to ancient legend, by a grey wolf), and the time of their irruption into the Arab empire, they had come under the influence of several faiths: Buddhism, Manichaeism, Judaism and Christianity. All of these had, at various times and in various regions of Asia, seduced them from their ancestral religion, an animistic worship of the sky, earth and water. Yet no other creed had for them the lasting appeal of Islam. Its intrinsic suitability as a faith for fighting-men is obvious: the demands which it makes are few; the rewards which it promises are great, particularly to those who die battling 'in the Path of Allah'. But what must have had even more weight with the Turks who came over to Islam in such numbers during the tenth century, was the fact that acceptance of Islam automatically conferred citizen-rights in a vast and flourishing civilization. A passage from al-Beruni (*d.* 1048) is worth quoting in this context:

> In his *Geography*, Ptolemy fixed the latitude of places remote from Greece solely by hearsay, for in those days those lands were ruled by mutually warring peoples, so that to travel unmolested was impossible. But now the world has changed: the domain of Islam has spread over all the regions, from the borders of China in the far east to the Spanish frontier in the far west; from Abyssinia in the south and from India, to the Turks and Slavs in the north. In all these broad lands, the various peoples which formerly nurtured feelings of enmity for one another have now united in God-given amity.

The 'amity', however, was at best a participation in a common religion and culture; politically, the world of Islam in the tenth century was rent by faction, besides being beset by external enemies.

The Turks found the situation well suited to the exercise of their warlike gifts. There is an Arabic tradition, put into the mouth of the Prophet, which runs thus: 'God Almighty says, "I have an army which I have named the Turks. Whenever I am wroth with a people, I unleash the Turks upon them." ' In 1055 Baghdad was seized by the Turkish horde known as the Seljuks, after a famous chief who was the ancestor of their ruling family. Establishing a great empire in south-west Asia, they continued their westward drive. Within sixteen years they had defeated the armies of Byzantium at Manzikert (1071), and six years later they were installed in Nicaea.

But the future did not lie with the Seljuks. The expansion to Nicaea was not the work of the regular Seljuk forces but of semi-independent bands of Ghazis, Warriors for the Faith. As far back as the ninth century we begin to hear of bodies of 'Volunteers' in Khurasan and Transoxania, men whose only means of livelihood was to war against the unbeliever and who were now the support of the authorities and now their bugbear. It is profitless to discuss whether they were inspired more by the hope of plunder than by religious zeal; what is certain is that they were sworn to fight to the death against the infidel, wherever they might find him. There are records of many such Ghazi organizations which carved out kingdoms for themselves. When this happened, although the main body might settle down to enjoy their conquests, yet always there were some who, finding no place in a settled society or remaining true to their vows, left their brethren to their inglorious respectability and themselves went on to advance still further the frontiers of Islam.

Such were the men who, almost against the will of the Seljuk Government, extended the Seljuk dominions in the eleventh century, and such, too, were the men who followed Ertuğrul 200 years later, out of Central Asia into north-western Anatolia. It is with the coming of Ertuğrul that Ottoman history begins, for he was the father of Osman,[1] the first Sultan of the dynasty which was to hold sway for six centuries.

Ertuğrul and his 400 horsemen were by no means the first Ghazis to establish themselves in Anatolia. By this time the Seljuk power was crumbling before the inroads of the Mongols, who had already made themselves masters of Persia and Iraq. In the west of Anatolia various bands of Ghazis were ensconced in independent principalities, owing at most a nominal allegiance to the Seljuks or their Mongol overlords, who held the interior. What was it that

[1] 'Osman' is the Turkish pronunciation of the Arabic '*Uthmān*. It is likely that his original name was 'Tuman' or 'Otman' (whence 'Ottoman') and that this was equated with '*Uthmān* by popular etymology (H. A. Erzi, *Türkiyat Mecmuası* 7–8, pp. 323–326).

distinguished Ertuğrul's band from all the others, so that his descendants ruled an empire which endured until the present century, whereas the very names of Menteşe, Saruhan and the rest of the Ghazi states of Anatolia are now scarcely known except to the historian?

The official myth of the Ottoman chroniclers was that Ertuğrul and his men belonged to the noblest of the Turkish tribes and were born for conquest and command. This explanation is clearly inadequate, but once the Ottoman power was firmly established we could hardly expect the chroniclers to perpetuate the real story. For emperors, unlike ordinary men, are privileged to choose their ancestors, and the leader of a band of miscellaneous adventurers is not the most suitable ancestor for an emperor.

What assured the unique success of Ertuğrul and his followers was that they had settled close to the frontier of Byzantium, the weakest spot in the walls of Christendom. From all the Muslim east came Ghazis to join them in battling for the Faith against the unbeliever; Turks, led on by the vision of what was becoming a rarity in Asia: a rich land unplundered by Mongols. The greatest prize, Constantinople, resisted the Turkish onslaught till 1453, by which time the Ottomans held most of the Balkan peninsula and all but the south-eastern quarter of Asia Minor.

A word must be said against the assumption that the capture of Constantinople was the work of barbarians from the steppes of Central Asia, and that darkness fell when they took the city. This, though once axiomatic in western Europe, was wrong on every count. The Turks were far from being barbarians before the conquest, as anyone can testify who has visited that jewel of a city, their old capital at Bursa. Nor were they fresh from Central Asia. The Ottomans had been near neighbours of the Byzantines for over a century before the conquest, and the cultural exchanges had been considerable. And not only the cultural exchanges; many an Anatolian Greek had a Ghazi for a son-in-law. The second Sultan, Orhan, and one of his sons had both married Byzantine princesses. The empire of the Comneni at Trebizond managed to survive the greater Greek empire by eight years, because of the matrimonial alliance between the reigning family and Uzun Hasan, the Turkish ruler of Persia. More than one Byzantine emperor had enlisted Turkish aid against his rebellious subjects. The friendship between Andronicus, son of John V Palaeologus, and Savcı, son of Murad I, had been intimate enough for them to conspire to murder their respective fathers and seize their thrones. The barrier between Greek and paynim was not so impassable in the fourteenth and fifteenth centuries as it may now seem to us.

At the zenith of the Turkish power, in the seventeenth century, the Ottoman dominions included the Balkan peninsula, the Crimea, Iraq and the western shores of the Persian Gulf, Syria, Palestine, western Arabia, Egypt, Libya, Tunisia and Algeria.

Some idea of the extent of the Ottoman power is conveyed by the tremendous fanfare of titles used by Süleyman I, known to Europe as 'The Magnificent' (1520–1566):

> 'I, who am Sultan of the Sultans of East and West, fortunate lord of the domains of the Romans,[1] Persians and Arabs, Hero of creation, Champion of the earth and time, Padishah and Sultan of the Mediterranean and the Black Sea, of the extolled Kaaba[2] and Medina the illustrious and Jerusalem the noble, of the throne of Egypt and the province of Yemen, Aden and San'a, of Baghdad and Basra and Lahsa and Ctesiphon, of the lands of Algiers and Azerbaijan, of the region of the Kipchaks and the lands of the Tartars, of Kurdistan and Luristan and all Rumelia, Anatolia and Karaman, of Wallachia and Moldavia and Hungary and many kingdoms and lands besides; the Sultan Süleyman Khan, son of the Sultan Selim Khan.'

Although the details of the acquisition, administration and eventual loss of these vast territories are irrelevant to our present purpose, certain features of the Ottoman Empire must be described, as being essential to a full understanding of the Turkish background. They are: (*a*) the Caliphate, (*b*) the Ulema, (*c*) the Sublime Porte, (*d*) the *Millet* system, (*e*) the *Devşirme* and (*f*) the Capitulations.

(*a*) The Caliphate

'Caliph' is the English form of the Arabic *khalīfa*, 'successor', which was first applied to the Prophet's devoted follower Abu Bakr (*d.* A.D. 634), who succeeded Muhammad as political and military chief of the Muslim community. He inherited also the Imamate, the privilege of leading the people in prayer. The prophetic function he did not inherit, for it was personal to Muhammad, 'the Seal of the Prophets', and could not be passed on. The Caliph was in no sense the spiritual head of the community; certainly the possession of the Imamate did not make him

[1] i.e., the former Eastern Roman empire.
[2] The shrine at Mecca.

so, for that office is not sacerdotal. Later Islamic theory makes the Caliph the Defender of the Faith, responsible for giving effect to the *Şeriat*,[1] the sacred law of Islam. For practical purposes the Caliphate came to an end in 1258, when the Mongols under Hulagu sacked Baghdad, the seat of the Abbasid dynasty[2] of Caliphs. But for three centuries before that date the Caliphs had been for the most part puppets in the hands of their Turkish military commanders. In 1261 the Mamluke Sultan of Egypt, Baybars, installed a scion of the Abbasid house as Caliph in Cairo, wishing to legitimize his own rule by appearing as the protector of the titular head of the Muslim community, the living symbol of the unity of the Faith. The shadow-Caliphs continued to grace parades through the streets of Cairo and to confer diplomas on new Sultans until the Ottoman conquest of Egypt in 1517. From that time on the Ottoman Sultans were the only dynasty who could have put up any serious claim to the Caliphate. None of the Sultans, however, made much play with the title (the reader may have noticed that it is not included in the list of Süleyman's designations) until Abdülhamid II. Later we shall see how Mustafa Kemal abolished the Caliphate, thus putting an end *de jure* to the institution which had been deprived of its power *de facto* by other Turkish commanders a thousand years before him.

(*b*) THE ULEMA

Ulema is the Turkish form of the Arabic '*ulamā*' 'sages'. As a technical term, it was applied collectively to the religious functionaries of every grade, from the humblest schoolmaster to the chief justices of the great cities.

Until the mid-seventeenth century the Ottoman Empire exhibited a feature characteristic of nomad states: the Sultan led his armies in person and his ministers accompanied him on campaign, leaving deputies in the capital. At the same time the Ottoman Turks were Muslims; instead of the tribal code of behaviour which had governed their ancestors' lives, they were subject to the *Şeriat*, of which the Ulema were the custodians, teachers and interpreters.

At the head of the hierarchy there formerly stood the *Kazasker*, the Judge of the Army, so called because he accompanied the Sultan on campaign. After the *Kazasker* came the *Şeyhü'l-İslâm*, the chief mufti (jurisconsult) of the Empire. In 1480, probably

[1] Arabic *sharī'a*.

[2] With the fifth Caliph, the powerful Mu'awiya (661–680), the office had become hereditary. His Umayyad dynasty was supplanted by the Abbasids in 750.

because of jealousy on the part of the Grand Vizier, Sultan Mehmed II curtailed the powers of the *Kazasker* by restricting his authority to the European provinces and appointing a second *Kazasker* to be chief of the Ulema in Asia. By the time of Süleyman I, the *Şeyhü'l-İslâm* had become head of the hierarchy, above the two *Kazaskers*. The power of the office varied according to the character of the incumbent: often the interpretation of a point of law was dictated by a knowledge of the sovereign's requirements, but there is no lack of examples of a courageous stand by a *Şeyhü'l-İslâm* against a Sultan desirous of riding roughshod over the sacred law.

(*c*) THE SUBLIME PORTE

The Turkish term *Babıâli* ('High Gate') was originally applied to the house of the Sultan's chief minister, the Grand Vizier, wherever that might be situated. In the mid-seventeenth century the name was transferred to the official residence which was then assigned to him, adjacent to the Palace. As the administrative work of most departments of State was carried out at the *Babıâli*, under the Grand Vizier's eye, the rather pompous translation 'Sublime Porte' came to be synonymous, for Europeans, with the Ottoman Government. In the closing years of the Sultanate, the *Babıâli* housed, besides the Grand Vizierate, the Ministries of the Interior and of Foreign Affairs.

(*d*) THE *MILLET* SYSTEM

The Prophet Muhammad regarded himself as the messenger chosen to bring God's Word to the Arabs, as others before him had been chosen to bring it to other peoples; he was the last of a series of prophets, and by his coming the work of his predecessors was completed and confirmed, not invalidated. Hence the Islamic ordinance that non-Muslim monotheists are not to be molested, so long as they behave themselves and pay their poll-tax. This policy proved its worth when the Arabs swept out of Arabia to win a vast empire at lightning speed; for they could never have ruled and exploited their new possessions without the help of the original administrators.

Like the Arabs before them, the Ottomans generally had the wisdom to let well enough alone. Members of the various *millets*—religious communities—among the subject peoples, were largely left to their own devices (for a notable exception see (*e*) below) under the supervision of their religious leaders, who were responsible to the Government for the good behaviour of their flocks, the settling of their disputes and the collection of taxes from them.

This system was not new to the former subjects of Byzantium. Rabbi Benjamin of Tudela, who visited Constantinople about 1170, records that every (Jewish) community was under the supervision of an *ephor*, appointed by the Government. Jewish tribunals administered Rabbinic law and the civil power gave effect to their judgments.

The Ottoman conquest in 1453 did not alter this state of affairs: the same Chief Rabbis who had held office under the Byzantine emperors continued to administer their people under the Sultans. The Oecumenical Patriarch was recognized as head of the *Millet-i Rum*, the 'Community of the Greeks'; indeed, it was the Conqueror himself, Mehmed II, who invested George Scholarios as Patriarch Gennadios II, a few days after the Turkish entry into the city.

As most of the commerce of the Empire was in the hands of non-Muslims, who also had a near-monopoly of medical knowledge, the authorities found it expedient not to make their lives a misery. The Government might even intervene to protect a *millet* against an unjust head: a particularly interesting example is seen in this order of Murad IV (1623–1640):

> The Armenian community have petitioned my Threshold of Felicity, making known the following facts: it has been their custom, from the Conquest down to the present time, that on the days when they congregate in their churches to celebrate their vain rites, everyone puts money into a plate according to his means, and this money is collected and used to help the weak and infirm among them. Their present Patriarch, in addition to taking the customary taxes specified in his diploma of investiture, has acted unjustly by demanding money out of the collections made as described above, as well as what he calls 'fruit-tax' on the orchards attached to their churches. I hereby order that the Patriarch be not permitted to transgress the established custom, the sacred law and my imperial command, by demanding more than the customary taxes specified in his diploma.

To nineteenth-century Europe, the Ottoman Empire appeared as the persecutor of non-Muslims, but such repressive action as was taken was aimed at the nationalist aspirations of the non-Turks. It is worthy of note in this connection that the Ottoman department which dealt with the heads of *millets* was the Ministry of Foreign Affairs. Religious persecution as such was of rare occurrence.

In the nineteenth century there came a change in the Muslim Turk's attitude towards his non-Muslim fellow-subjects, as we shall see, but in the old days, while the self-confidence of Islam was still unshaken, the prevailing spirit was one of tolerance. Sometimes, indeed, the authorities had found it necessary to remind non-Muslims that in the eyes of Islam they were second-class citizens, but the frequency with which such reminders were issued shows that the regulations were not too rigorously enforced. Here is a typical decree, dated 1631:

> Whereas it is a matter of religious importance that the infidel community should not ride on horseback or wear sable coats or Frankish brocade . . . but should be humble and lowly in their style of dress, it has come to my august hearing that for a long time this has been neglected and that the infidel and Jewish[1] communities have, with the connivance of the authorities, been going about the streets on horseback and in fine clothes . . . and they and their women are more imposingly dressed than the true believers. I hereby order that this practice must cease.

It is clear from this and other decrees of a like tenor that the authorities were deferring to narrow religious opinion and that these periodic attempts to put the infidels in their place did not arise from governmental prejudice.

About the end of the seventeenth century we find a large number of orders relating to complaints from the Armenian and Orthodox Churches about Roman Catholic missionaries who were busy among the population; an Armenian priest was sentenced to the galleys for 'corrupting the Armenian community and trying to win them over to the Frankish religion', and at the same time a number of people were arrested for 'causing a mischief by altering the text of certain books and printing the altered versions and circulating them among the Armenians'. At the request of the Orthodox Patriarch, certain priests were banished for 'making changes in the established rites and persisting in the Frankish persuasion'. We hear of 'Frankish priests wandering the provinces in disguise, corrupting the Orthodox, Armenian and other Christian sects and trying to turn them aside from their old beliefs'. It is easy to see why the Government was so much opposed to Catholic missionary activity; a *millet* with its head out of reach of the Ottoman power was not to be encouraged. Nowadays there is a survival of the old attitude, in the Republican law whereby the head of each religious community must be a Turkish citizen. Athenagoras I, who was elected Orthodox Patriarch in November

[1] The Christians, being more numerous, were the 'infidels' *par excellence*.

1948, was obliged to renounce his American citizenship before taking office.

In modern Turkish *millet* is used to mean 'nation', but the word has not yet lost its older sense. If you tell a Turk that your *millet* is *İngiliz*, he will assume not only that you have a British passport but also that you are a member of the Church of England.

(*e*) THE *DEVŞİRME*

Devşirme means 'collecting' and is the term applied to the compulsory recruitment of Christian boys for training and eventual employment in the civil and military service of the Empire. The majority of the Ghazis who won the first victories for the House of Osman in Anatolia were cavalrymen. The need for an infantry force was soon felt, however, when the Turkish advance brought them against cities which had to be besieged, and when the occupied territories had to be garrisoned and administered. For although the Ghazis were efficient instruments for conquest, they were not the sort of men to submit to discipline or the boredom of garrison duty far behind the front line. The first recruits to a standing army were young Turks, who were given smallholdings which provided them with a living in peace-time, and who were paid a regular daily rate when called out for war. But as their numbers proved inadequate to the needs of the expanding Empire, recourse was had to a new device. According to Islamic law, the sovereign is entitled to one-fifth of all booty seized in warring against the infidel. So one in five of all the Christian boys taken prisoner in the campaigns in Europe were chosen to be slaves of the Sultan, the others remaining the property of their captors, to employ or sell as they pleased. The Sultan's fifth were put to work, either on the horse-transports that plied between Lapseki and Gallipoli across the Dardanelles, or as apprentices to Turkish farmers in Anatolia. When they had learned Turkish and had become familiar with Muslim ways, which might take as long as ten years, they were admitted to the *Yeniçeri*, 'New Troops', anglicized as 'Janissary'.

This system worked well until the disastrous defeat of Sultan Bayezid at Ankara in 1402, at the hands of Tamerlane, who dismembered the Ottoman possessions among the sons of Bayezid. It was the youngest of these, Mehmed I, who began the work of reassembling the divided territories, and the task was completed by his son, Murad II, who resumed the drive into the Balkans. But the hiatus in the conquests in Europe had meant the cutting-off of the supply of Janissaries, so in Murad's reign the *devşirme* system was inaugurated.[1] At irregular intervals of three to five years levies took place of unmarried males between the ages of eight and twenty, from the Christian population of Rumelia. Later the system was extended to other Christian communities, including those of Albania, Greece, Belgrade, Serbia, Bosnia and Hungary. The purpose was not simply to strengthen the army, but also to bring about the gradual Islamicization of the subject peoples and to integrate them within the Ottoman State. To achieve this end, a highly selective code of rules was laid down for the guidance of recruiting officers. The principle was that every recruit should be unspoilt, unsophisticated, raw material, his mind a *tabula rasa*. Orphans who had had to fend for themselves were not taken, nor were boys who knew some Turkish, or were married, or had a trade, or had spent some time in the big cities: Istanbul, Bursa and Adrianople. Jewish children were exempt, because most Jews were engaged in business.

On arrival at Istanbul the *devşirme*-boys were formally admitted into Islam: they raised their right hands and recited the profession of faith, the Arabic words meaning 'I testify that there is no god but God: Muhammad is the messenger of God'. They were then circumcised. Some writers have stated that the boys were not forced to accept Islam, a view which is accurate rather than true. The recruit to a modern army is not forcibly dressed in uniform, nor is he forcibly vaccinated; he submits to these assaults on his individuality because he realizes that they are a part of his new life and does as the rest of his intake are doing. One wonders, indeed, how many *devşirme*-boys had any comprehension of the meaning of the Arabic formula they were told to repeat.

The inhumanity of this systematic kidnapping of children from their parents (although it was forbidden to take an only son) is too obvious to need underlining. Yet there is ample evidence to show that while many who were eligible for the *devşirme* wished that they were not, others, who were ineligible, tried hard to be included among the levies. An exception to the rule that only Christian boys were liable to the *devşirme* was constituted by the Poturs, Muslim Bosniaks descended from certain Christians who had accepted Islam when Mehmed II conquered Bosnia, and had been permitted by him to volunteer for the service of the Imperial palaces. When drafts of Potur boys were on the march to Istanbul,

[1] The possibility of an earlier origin is suggested by V. L. Ménage in his article DEVSHIRME in the new edition of *Encyclopaedia of Islam*. For the juridical basis of the institution see Paul Wittek's article 'Devshirme and Sharī'a' in *Bulletin of the School of Oriental and African Studies*, 1955, pp. 271–278.

especially rigorous precautions were taken to prevent other Muslim boys from adding themselves to the convoy. Again, Süleyman I is reported to have said, after listing the peoples—Russians, Persians, Gypsies and Turks—from whom boys were not to be levied: 'If any officer recruits any of these, either for a bribe or at someone's request or because of the intervention of people in high places, and adds them to the number of my loyal slaves, may the curse of God and the hundred and twenty-four thousand prophets be upon him.'

For the *devşirme*-boy was starting out on a road at the end of which lay many of the highest offices of state, promotion to which was by a combination of seniority and merit. Theoretically, the only high positions open to free-born Muslims were in the religious hierarchy of the Ulema; civil and military rank was the prerogative of the Sultan's Christian-born slaves.

This state of affairs persisted until the middle of the seventeenth century, when public opinion brought about the break-down of the system and opened the doors of the Imperial service to free-born Muslim Turks, although the *devşirme* continued sporadically till the early eighteenth century. Thereafter the old type of State servant, cut off from his family and having no means of advancement in his new life except winning the favourable attention of his superiors, was replaced by men who owed their appointment to, and based their hopes of promotion on, unblushing nepotism; a development which hastened the Empire on its downward path.

(*f*) The Capitulations

The idea of absolute national sovereignty is of even more recent growth than the idea of nationhood. Over fifty years before the Ottoman conquest there was a Turkish community in Constantinople, with its own Muslim judge administering Muslim law. The Byzantine emperors had also granted privileges to the Venetian and Genoese merchants resident in the city, which Mehmed the Conqueror confirmed. For in those days it was not regarded as a derogation of sovereignty to let foreigners be ruled by their own laws. Consular authorities were responsible for the good behaviour of their nationals.

The first capitulations, to use the term in its general modern acceptance, were those granted by Süleyman to the French in 1535, when he concluded that offensive and defensive alliance with François I which scandalized Christendom. The autonomy which the French merchants in Turkey thereby obtained, together with the respect shown them by the Turks as representatives of the

Sultan's new ally, soon caused other European Powers to forget their distaste and to seek similar concessions for themselves: Austria in 1567, England in 1592.

Under the capitulations, foreigners were not subject to Turkish law; they paid no taxes, their houses and business premises were inviolable, and they could be arrested or deported only by order of their own Ambassadors. Disputes involving foreigners were settled by the consular court of the defendant, according to the law of his own land. Non-Muslim Turkish subjects in foreign employ could also be given this privileged status, by a diploma conferred by a consular authority.

In the old days, when Turkey was still a power to be reckoned with, and the foreign communities were small and almost exclusively mercantile, abuse of these great privileges was rare. By the mid-nineteenth century, however, Pera, the European quarter of Istanbul, had become the refuse-pit of Europe. All manner of undesirables were sheltering under the capitulations, confident that their own countrymen would back them against the Turkish authorities any day. The fact that the capitulations had been originally granted by a Turkey at the zenith of her power, as a gesture of good will and to encourage trade, was forgotten; they were regarded as an acknowledgment by the Ottoman Empire of its own decrepitude, of the foreigner's right to laugh at its laws. In this attitude to the capitulations we have the clearest indication of the depths to which the Empire had sunk.

Chapter 2

The Decline of the Ottoman Empire and The Beginnings of Modernization, 1683–1839

THE DECLINE of a great empire is a process to whose beginning a date is not easily assigned. The year 1683 has been chosen, as it was then that the Ottoman armies were forced to abandon the siege of Vienna, and the symptoms of decay appeared for all the world to see. The Ottomans, for so long victorious, could not comprehend the reasons for their failure: they put the blame on the treachery of their former ally, John Sobieski, on the incompetence of the Turkish commander, on anything but their own blindness in ignoring the advances made by the West. Young and vigorous nations had emerged in Europe, fired by new ideals, equipped with new knowledges and techniques, while the Ottoman Empire was marking time.

But the beginnings of the decline are to be sought over a hundred years before, in the golden days of Süleyman the Magnificent. For Süleyman sat so securely on his throne that he forgot how his ancestors had won that throne: he ceased to be a Ghazi and became an Emperor. The Ottoman Empire was doomed from the moment that its leaders lost sight of their *raison d'être*. For a time they enjoyed the fruits of their ancestors' conquests and then suddenly they found themselves on the defensive. They had been betrayed by their contempt for the West, which was based partly on centuries of military superiority, partly on the Muslim tendency to see non-Muslims as 'abject infidels' (to use an expression favoured by Ottoman historians), necessarily inferior to the followers of the one true faith.

The retreat from Vienna was the first of a series of setbacks which culminated in the loss of Budapest to the Austrians (1686) and was interrupted in 1699 by the Treaty of Carlowitz. But this brought the Turks no lasting security; on the contrary, the Austrian success had shown Russia that the grey wolf was losing his teeth. An almost unbroken succession of defeats revealed to the Sultans a glimmering of the truth, but as yet they saw no further than the superficial fact that somehow they had lost their ancient military supremacy; the only remedy they envisaged consisted in superficial military reforms.

Mustafa III (1757–1773) laid all the Turkish misfortunes at the door of the Janissaries, corrupt, pampered and undisciplined, zealous only in guarding their privileges. He saw no hope of reforming them, but his pessimism did not prevent him from doing his best to check the decline. At his request, the Hungarian Baron de Tott, who had entered the Ottoman service as an artillery instructor, founded an Imperial School of Naval Engineering and taught in it himself. Yet nothing better illustrates the Turks' complete lack of understanding of the real sources of Western superiority than the fact that this same Sultan attributed the Prussian victory in the Seven Years' War to efficient staff-work on the part of Frederic the Great's astrologers.

The Russo-Turkish War of 1768–1774 did nothing to awaken the Ottoman Government to a sense of reality; a year or so after the humiliating Treaty of Küçük Kaynarca which ended the war, the 600-strong artillery unit which de Tott had created and trained was disbanded on grounds of expense. But the French had perceived the serious implications of the Ottoman inability to check the Russian advance, and sent military experts to help reorganize the Turkish Army. Their efforts, however, were frustrated and the Grand Vizier Halil Hâmid Pasha, who had welcomed them, was dismissed, as Sultan Abdülhamid I (1773–1789) suspected him of plotting against the throne.

Selim III, who became Sultan in 1789, during the ruinous war that had been provoked by Russia's seizing the Crimea, was one of the most enlightened members of the House of Osman. Although it is his military reforms that have attracted most attention, he was not so narrow-minded as his father, Mustafa III, who had regarded the Janissaries as the root of all evil. For Selim was not blind to the anarchy that reigned among the Ulema, the hierarchy whose leaders had the power to veto any measure which they regarded as contravening the sacred law. The *medreses*, their training-schools, were without discipline, and the teaching in them was antiquated. High office could be bought; only in the great cities were learning and ability necessary qualifications for judgeships. Even at best, graduates of *medreses*, however much they might know of the theoretical bases of Muslim law, were totally ignorant of the world about them. In the first year of the new reign, during discussion of a proposed treaty with Prussia, the

Kazasker of Rumelia, the second in rank in the hierarchy, asked, 'What's this place Prussia they're talking about?' Another of the great men present enlightened him: 'It's what they call Brandabork. It was once an Austrian duchy but it has gradually grown in strength, so that now it's the equal of Austria and Moscow.'

As soon as the Treaty of Jassy gave the Turks a breathing-space, Selim consulted various Ottoman statesmen about means to restore the Empire to its former greatness. Some were in favour of reforming the Army on Western lines. Others suggested a return to the code of laws promulgated by Süleyman, over 250 years before, which would surely bring back the glories of his reign. The former counsel accorded more with the Sultan's ideas, and experts were invited from England, France, Prussia and Sweden. A small force of soldiers was raised and not only trained but also dressed in European style. Some of the Ulema, horrified, declared, 'God will begrudge His aid to a Sultan who dresses the Army in frock-coat and trousers and sets Franks at the head of them.'

Selim was not impressed by the disapproval of the Ulema. During the war, he had written on the margin of a memorandum in which he was asked to sanction further payments for the reciting of prayers for victory, 'I should think the prayers are not being read with devotion, or else we haven't hit on the right people for the job, otherwise some result might be visible. Very well, let the payments continue for another six months. What can one expect from prayers said for money?' But he would have been wiser not to underrate the religious opposition.

The *Nizam-ı Cedid*, the 'New Order' which he planned, embraced the whole administration of the Empire. The details of it are now of academic interest only; Selim and his handful of supporters were not strong enough to fight against the entrenched forces of the old order. Incited by the Ulema, the people of Istanbul rose against him in 1806. The new troops were defeated by the Janissaries, and the *Şeyhü'l-İslâm* pronounced it lawful to depose the impious Sultan. He could have summoned the loyal troops of the Danube garrison to aid him, but would not risk opening the door to the Russians. It is fitting, in this book whose theme is the new Turkey, to praise the memory of Selim, martyred for his belief in the destiny of his country, a man whose worst fault was that his courage outrun his prudence.

The first reformer who had anything to show for his pains was Mahmud II (1808–1839). On his accession he found that there were no bounds to the insolence of the Janissaries, triumphant at having annihilated Selim's supporters. Mahmud bided his time until popular feeling turned against them, the comparatively small Army of Egypt having crushed a Greek revolt which the Janissaries had totally failed to quell. In the June of 1826 the Janissaries were blown up in their barracks, an event known in Turkish history as 'The Auspicious Incident'. The Sultan then set to work to raise a new army, thus putting the cart before the horse, an error Selim had been wise enough to avoid. Muhammad Ali, ruler of Egypt and the Sultan's nominal vassal, refused to help in the organization of the new army, having his own plans for the future of the Ottoman Empire, plans in which a strong Ottoman Army played no part. The Sultan would not ask for assistance from France or England, who had supported the Greeks in their rebellion. Prussia alone sent military instructors, thus laying the foundations of the friendship which has since been fostered by every German government down to our own day; a friendship which goes much deeper with the general run of Turks than the ancient official friendship for France.

The Prussian instructors, however, could not work miracles; the Tsar took advantage of Turkey's lack of a seasoned army to continue the century-old Russian advance into the Balkans. The escape of Greece from Ottoman hands, through the armed intervention of England, France and Russia, and its emergence as an independent kingdom in 1830, gave new hope to the nationalists in Turkey's other European possessions. Revolts broke out in Serbia and Bulgaria. The decrepitude of the Empire being once again laid bare, Muhammad Ali cast off all pretence of allegiance to the Sultan and invaded Syria. His son Ibrahim led an army into Asia Minor, which was turned back from its rapid advance on Istanbul only by the landing of a powerful Russian force on the Asian shores of the Bosphorus. The price was paid in the Treaty of Hünkâr İskelesi (8 July 1833) which gave Russian shipping the freedom of the Bosphorus and Dardanelles, while denying the same right to other powers except with Russian approval.

Other manifestations of Mahmud's zeal for reform were more successful. A school of medicine and a military academy were opened, as well as a number of secondary schools. Primary education was made compulsory. One hundred and fifty students were sent to Europe. A postal service was established, the foundations of a nation-wide police system were laid and pamphlets were distributed to teach the people the essential facts about infectious disease. The ancient practice of replenishing the Treasury by confiscating the property of officials and private citizens was abolished. It was ordained that the various types of male head-dress were to be replaced by the fez, a move which aroused great resentment but no serious opposition.

This apparently trifling innovation, which seems to have been enforced only in the case of soldiers and officials, is of great importance: it was a manifestation of the Sultan's desire that his subjects of various faiths should be no longer distinguishable by their attire. The traditional Muslim tolerance, based, as we have indicated, on contempt for the benighted adherents of other creeds, was to be replaced by a true equality of religions. Mahmud is reported to have said, 'Henceforth I recognize Muslims only in the mosque, Christians only in the church, Jews only in the synagogue. Outside these places of worship I desire every individual to enjoy the same political rights and my fatherly protection.' Circumstances were not favourable to the fulfilment of this startlingly anachronistic policy.

Since the turn of the century there had been an enormous increase in the import of European goods, particularly of textiles, which led to serious unemployment in the native textile industry. The middlemen in this trade were, as they had always been, non-Muslims. Though Turkish subjects, they were protected by the European Powers and rapidly became a privileged and wealthy class, whom the commercially backward Muslims were neither able nor willing to regard as brothers.

These people appear as a new type in nineteenth-century Turkish literature, the Levantine or 'Freshwater Frank' (as opposed to the saltwater variety, who came across the sea from Europe), who created 'a new Istanbul, Greek in its cafés and grocers' shops, French in its fashions, English in its coats, German in its beer-houses, Italian and Spanish in its music, Turkish in its watchmen and porters'.

This divergence between theory and practice, this increasing liberality towards the minorities on the part of the Government, coupled with a growing antipathy towards them on the part of the people, outlived the Ottoman Empire.

Chapter 3

The Period of the *Tanzimat*, 1839–1876

TANZİMAT, 'Regulation', is the name given to the programme of reform that was inaugurated in November 1839. Its architect, Mustafa Reşid Pasha, was a well-read and far-sighted statesman who had served as Ottoman Ambassador in Paris and was anxious to save his country from the doom that had overtaken the French monarchy. The Imperial Rescript proclaimed by Reşid in the Gülhane Court, with great pomp and ceremony, was a charter whereby the Sultan abdicated a portion of his authority in favour of the Council of Judicial Ordinances, which was henceforth to have the power to make laws, subject to the Sultan's approval. No one was to be punished without a public trial, and Muslims and non-Muslims were to receive equal treatment before the law. Legislation was to be introduced to end 'the traffic in favours and appointments, which is one of the chief causes of the decay of the Empire'.

Some historians have declared that the purpose of the *Tanzimat* was to deprive the Christian Powers of an excuse to take the Sultan's Christian subjects under their protection. This view represents only a part of the truth: Reşid and his coadjutors were intelligent enough to see that if nothing were done to remove the grievances of the subject peoples the Empire might crumble into ruin even without foreign interference. But certainly Reşid was at great pains to sound foreign diplomats about the probable effect of the Charter on European public opinion, and rather envied Muhammad Ali the approbation with which liberal thinkers in Europe had hailed his Egyptian reforms.

Yet the *Tanzimat* was still-born; it 'stopped at the doorstep of the Sublime Porte'. Good intentions were not enough; however much European liberals might applaud this manifestation of a genuine desire for reform on the part of the Ottoman statesmen, public opinion in Turkey was hostile. For as yet the only educated class of any size among Muslim Turks was that of the Ulema, who in the main saw no reason for altering the *status quo*, although they deemed it prudent to pay lip-service to the ideals of the *Tanzimat*, being indeed singled out in the Charter for a special threat of punishment in the event of their obstructing the reforms.

Despite the lack of a single word about education in the text of the Gülhane Decree, the years following its promulgation saw a remarkable advance in liberal thought in Turkey. Schools were built, by the generosity of enlightened individuals, although the State gave no financial help. An ever-growing number of scholars and officials visited Europe, and returned full of enthusiasm for the institutions they had seen there. True, this enthusiasm often betrayed them into a mere imitating of outward forms: factories were planned and even built with no source of skilled men to operate them; there was talk of founding a university, although there were no graduate teachers available.

During the reign of Abdülaziz (1861–1876), whose unwisdom and extravagance brought his country to the verge of disaster, the beginnings were seen of the movement to which European writers have given the name 'Young Turks'. In June 1865 the Society of New Ottomans was formed secretly in Istanbul. Its members numbered only 245, but most of them were men of influence. The prime mover was the great writer and patriot Namık Kemal. Two princes, the future Sultans Murad V and Abdülhamid II, were among those who followed its discussions. The main aim of the Society, whose members were pledged to strive, *inter alia*, for the betterment of the Christian subjects of the Empire, was to transform the Government into a constitutional monarchy. Its programme was based on that of the Carbonari, a secret Italian revolutionary society.

Although the Society was disbanded in 1872, its former members continued to work for a constitutional regime. They saw the reward of their efforts, short-lived though it proved to be, in 1876, when Abdülaziz was deposed. His policies had united almost the whole people in opposition: the advocates of reform who saw him as an incorrigible despot, the armed forces who were weary of the endless chain of defeats his reign had brought, even the Istanbul mob and many of the Ulema, who resented the conciliatory attitude adopted towards Russia by his favourite the Grand Vizier, Mahmud Nedim Pasha. His nephew Murad V reigned in his stead for only three months before his mind broke down; he was succeeded by his younger brother, Abdülhamid II.

Chapter 4

The Era of Absolutism, 1876–1908

ABDÜLHAMID was brought to the throne by the great liberal statesman Midhat Pasha, on the express condition that he set up a constitutional administration. Shortly after his accession, he appointed Midhat Grand Vizier, and on 10 December 1876, promulgated the Constitution, which had been drafted by Midhat, Namık Kemal and Ziya Pasha. Clause 113, the first of the Miscellaneous Clauses, after laying down the conditions under which the government could proclaim martial law, continued: 'It is exclusively within the competence of H.M. the Sultan in person to expel and to exile from the Guarded Domains of the Empire any persons whom reliable investigation by the police shows to be impairing the security of the government.' Once safely enthroned, Abdülhamid invoked this provision, whose dangerous potentialities the drafters of the Constitution seem to have overlooked, and exiled the courageous Grand Vizier (5 February 1877). To quieten the well-justified fears of his subjects, the Sultan went ahead with the arrangements for the creation of a Parliament, consisting of an Upper House and a Chamber of Deputies, which he opened on 19 March 1877.

The following month Russia declared war, the ostensible provocation being the atrocities committed by the Turks in crushing the Bulgarian revolt of 1876. The Sultan chose to blame this fresh disaster and the ensuing defeats on the Parliament, which he therefore closed on 13 February 1878.

The thirty years of absolutism which followed form a period without precedent in Ottoman history. The deposition and subsequent suicide of his uncle, Sultan Abdülaziz, had preyed on Abdülhamid's naturally suspicious mind, arousing in it a pathological anxiety for the safety of his person and his throne. He organized a network of spies and informers who were encouraged, and handsomely paid, to denounce those who might be conspiring against his rule. He would never dispense with the services of any whose information proved false, for fear of inhibiting future denunciations. Kipling's *The Old Issue* might have been written with Abdülhamid in mind:

> He shall break his Judges if they cross his word;
> He shall rule above the Law calling on the Lord.
> He shall peep and mutter; and the night shall bring
> Watchers 'neath our window, lest we mock the King—
> Hate and all division; hosts of hurrying spies;
> Money poured in secret, carrion breeding flies.

Yet outside the political sphere he seems to have had no objection in principle to any reforms which did not threaten his own security; thus he permitted the opening of secondary schools in most towns of the Empire, and in his day the number of Teachers' Training Colleges was increased from one (founded in 1848) to thirty-one. But all educational institutions came under an ever more rigorous control, particularly in the latter half of his reign, when his suspicions and anxieties had advanced to the point of mania. It is not without significance that he forbade the publication of medical works dealing with insanity. Literature and history lessons were removed from school curricula, as offering too great opportunities for the spread of revolutionary ideas. Their place was filled by Muslim jurisprudence, scholastic theology, Koran interpretation and ethics, for the Sultan clearly believed that good Muslims do not make dangerous revolutionaries.

It is less clear whether he was sincere in his insistence that the decline of the Empire was due to the decay of religious feeling, but certainly this view was general among Muslims in his day. The nineteenth century had already witnessed the eclipse of many Islamic dynasties, brought about by the steady advance of the Christian Powers into India, Central Asia, Egypt and North Africa. Apart from the Ottoman Empire, Persia and Morocco were almost the last surviving strongholds of Islamic political power, and the position of these three states was far from secure. Among the educated Muslims who saw and bitterly resented this fact, the conviction was spreading that in order to restore the greatness of the Muslim world it was necessary for all Muslims to unite and to turn back to their Faith, while at the same time taking all that the West had to teach them in the way of science and techniques. Abdülhamid was lavish in his subsidies to those who preached this thesis, for if Islam were ever to unite, it could unite only round the person of the Caliph. The title to which his ancestors had paid so little regard suddenly became a potent weapon in his armoury. In this policy he was given unbounded encouragement by Prussia, for reasons which must be explained in a brief digression.

In 1875, dismayed at the rapidity of the French recovery from the losses incurred during the Franco-Prussian War, Bismarck sounded Britain and Russia about their probable attitude in the event of a renewal of hostilities. Both countries replied in terms which left no doubt of their active opposition to the course he contemplated. With this road closed, Prussia's attentions swung eastward, towards the Ottoman Empire, whose incorporation in a Greater Germany had been one of von Moltke's dreams. The dream now seemed capable of realization.

Turkey's long period of decline, with its well-nigh incessant wars, had steadily impoverished her treasury. The Treaty of Carlowitz had deprived her of her richest European provinces, and a succession of defeats and humiliating treaties had continued the process. In the early days of the decline the favourite method of coping with financial difficulties had been to debase the coinage. In the nineteenth century recourse was had to foreign loans, in exchange for which various items of State revenue were mortgaged. By 1881 the Ottoman Public Debt amounted to well over 100 million gold pounds, and foreign banks were drawing the revenues of the salt and tobacco monopolies, stamp duties, fisheries, customs, and fixed annual sums representing the tribute of Eastern Rumelia, Bulgaria and Cyprus. Then suddenly, when it seemed that the Sultan had nothing left to pawn, he found that Germany was ready and willing to grant him as much credit as he required. In 1898 the Kaiser paid a State visit to Istanbul, greeting Abdülhamid as a brother. From there he went on to Damascus, where in a widely-publicized speech he assured 'the Sultan and the 300 million Mohammedans scattered over the world who reverence him as their Caliph' of the undying friendship of the German Emperor.[1]

The first visible sign of the Kaiser's love for the Sultan was that a German syndicate financed the extension of the Istanbul–İzmit railway to Ankara and Konya, as a step towards the fulfilment of the Kaiser's pet scheme of a Berlin–Baghdad railway. Germany provided the equipment and the experts. All that the Turkish Government had to do was to guarantee the yearly payment of 14,000 marks for every completed kilometre of track, a condition

[1] The Kaiser's absurd claim to be the protector of Islam is well illustrated in an order given to the Turkish troops at Gallipoli. Written in Turkish, it includes the following words: 'We shall not retire one step. If we do, our religion . . . will perish.' It is signed, 'von Sodenstern'.

which explains some of those apparently purposeless meanderings whereby the passenger in the front coach of the Ankara train is afforded frequent glimpses of the guard's van.

Abdülhamid's extensive propaganda in favour of the Pan-Islamic ideal seemed to fall on particularly willing ears in India; it was no doubt consoling to the self-respect of Indian Muslims to think that they belonged to a great community beyond the frontiers of their own infidel-ridden country. Yet in the event, as the First World War showed, the Indian soldier's loyalty to the King-Emperor easily outweighed his devotion to the Sultan-Caliph.

But we are running ahead of our story. After the German financiers and railway engineers, came a German military mission. Abdülhamid, encouraged by the Kaiser's sympathy and the thought that the reverence of the Muslims outside his Empire could not fail to increase his prestige at home, showed no willingness at all to meet the new liberalism half-way. It is certain that his cruel despotism was the greatest single factor in the rapid growth of liberal ideas in Turkey.

In 1889 a group of students at the Army School of Medicine formed a secret organization which they called 'The Ottoman Society for Union and Progress'. Some of the leaders were driven into exile, some were executed for distributing pamphlets in which the Sultan's arbitrary rule was attacked, but the ardour of the survivors was unimpaired. From the safety of London, Paris, Naples and Cairo there flowed a stream of revolutionary publications, in which all Turkey's misfortunes were laid at the Sultan's door. His efforts to persuade the Governments concerned to suppress the exiles' publications met with little success.

A sharp reminder that his view of the Caliphate was one-sided came in a telegram addressed to him from Paris by one of the exiles, his own brother-in-law, Mahmud Pasha:

> Your Majesty's mode of government conforms to no law, nor does it resemble the behaviour of an upright Caliph, not even the methods of European sovereigns. You are empowered by the people to give effect to justice; you are bound to respect it.

The mainstay of the opposition consisted of young army officers, whose professional training brought them into contact with European ideas and technical development, and whose professional pride made them bitterly resentful of the debilitating influence of the Sultan's autocratic rule.

In the early years of the twentieth century revolutionary societies multiplied inside the Empire, not always through any great divergence in aims but because of the difficulties of maintaining communications in face of the omnipresent spies and *agents provocateurs* of the Sultan. By 1908, however, the underground stream of revolt was running so high that the Sultan could no longer rely on the repressive activity of his secret police. It is virtually certain that some of his chief agents had been deliberately betraying his confidence in them, on the orders of their German trainers. A man of Abdülhamid's suspicious nature could not have failed to realize that German penetration of the Ottoman Army was not entirely to his own advantage; the Kaiser may well have decided that the Sultan was not the complaisant simpleton he had at first appeared. At all events, when the blow fell, Germany did not lift a finger to maintain Abdülhamid in power.

On 22 July 1908, the Salonica branch of the Society for Union and Progress sent the Sultan a telegram, demanding that the Constitution be given effect and imposing a time-limit for convening the Chamber of Deputies, failing which it threatened action 'which will not meet with your Majesty's approval'. This ultimatum and the simultaneous revolt in Rumelia, the strength of which was greatly exaggerated in a telegram sent to the capital by the Governor of Monastir, terrified the Sultan into accepting the Society's demands. The next day he issued an *irade*, a decree, convening 'the Chamber of Deputies whose form of organization is set forth in the Constitution established by His Majesty'. For although the event is generally termed 'the proclamation of the Second Constitution', the Constitution of 1876 had never been repealed but was printed throughout the thirty years of absolutism in the *Salname*, the official almanac of the Empire.

On 24 July the Sultan's astonished subjects looked at their newspapers, to see words which had been proscribed for years: such words as 'freedom', 'nation', 'fatherland' and 'Chamber of Deputies', which formerly would have meant the ruin of any editor rash enough to print them.

Several European eye-witnesses have described the unprecedented demonstrations of popular joy which took place in the principal cities, once it was realized that the Sultan had been forced to yield. Bulgarian priests publicly shook hands with Turkish officers, Greeks embraced Armenians. In Macedonia, bands of revolutionaries, who had for years been waging war against the Government, came down into the towns and announced the end of hostilities.

Not everybody joined in the general rejoicing. In southern

Anatolia and in Tripolitania disorders broke out among the Muslim population, who looked on the restoration of the Constitution as a betrayal of Islam, involving as it did the granting of equal rights to non-Muslims. But apart from such diehards, the majority of people regarded that day in July 1908 as the beginning of a wonderful new era.

Chapter 5

The Constitutional Period, 1908–1918

All too soon it became apparent that the Turks and non-Turks, who had congratulated one another on the proclamation of the Constitution, had no more in common than joy at the downfall of Abdülhamid's tyranny. Their ideas about what was to succeed it were very different. Nor did the nations of Europe, who had for so many years been sadly shaking their heads over the condition of the Sick Man, rejoice with him now that he seemed to be on the road to recovery. Austria promptly annexed Bosnia and Herzegovina, the Bulgars proclaimed their independence. In 1910 there were revolts in the Yemen and in Albania. In 1911 Italy invaded Tripolitania, and in the following year Greece annexed Crete.

Nor must it be thought that there was any unity of purpose among the Turks themselves. Three distinct political creeds vied for supremacy amongst them: Ottomanism, Pan-Islamism and Pan-Turkism.

The first of these involved the vain hope that the various peoples of the Ottoman Empire could be integrated into a homogeneous modern State.

The Pan-Islamic ideal, which, as we have seen, enjoyed the Kaiser's blessing, remained in the running until the First World War revealed that the Arabs preferred to become independent rather than follow a Turkish caliph. Indeed, even before the war, numerous societies and parties were formed whose aim was Arab independence.

Pan-Turkism, which aspired to unite all the Turks of Asia into one State, was the latest of the three creeds to emerge, and this fact is hardly surprising, because the Turks were the least united of all the peoples of the Empire; the least self-conscious, the least advanced towards nationhood. Till quite recently 'Turk' had been almost a term of abuse in the Ottoman Empire, connoting something like 'yokel'. All the best people were *Osmanlı*. The policy which seemed natural, the policy which at first dominated the Society for Union and Progress, was Ottomanism, which envisaged a modernized Ottoman Empire, so well equipped with liberal institutions that all the conflicting religious and racial groups among the Sultan's subjects would be happy to belong to it. The hopes of the Ottomanists perished for ever in the Balkan Wars of 1912–1913, in which Turkey lost the Aegean Islands and all her European possessions, except part of Thrace.

Before the general election which followed the proclamation of the Constitution in 1908, the Society decided that those of its members who won seats in the Assembly should constitute the 'Party of Union and Progress', and this title was subsequently extended to the whole movement. The Party won a huge majority, not only because of its prestige as the vanquisher of Abdülhamid but also because it controlled the Army.

For some months the administration remained in the hands of politicians of the old school, but in February 1909 the Assembly dismissed the Grand Vizier Kâmil Pasha, on a vote of no confidence, and the Party formed a government. Two months later a mass revolt (known as the 'Thirty-first of March Incident') broke out in the capital, in which units of the Army joined, demanding the setting-up of an administration and government that would conform to the sacred law of Islam.

The newspaper *Volkan* ('Volcano') fanned the flames, inveighing against the 'Epoch of Devils', against the 'men of no honour who blindly imitate the West' and the 'ignoramuses who are so proud of their three days' education that they think they can look down on students of the sacred law'. The Sultan, overrating the strength of the insurrection, imprudently sent a decree to the Assembly, announcing that the State was a Muslim State, that henceforth more deference would be shown to the sacred law, and that the rebels were all pardoned.

The Commander of the Third Army, Mahmud Şevket Pasha, sent troops from Salonika 'to wipe out this stain on the honour of the Ottoman Army, with its six-century-long record of obedience' and 'to punish the secret agents of the Sultan and the base self-seekers who instigated the revolt'. The rising was speedily crushed and on 27 April 1909, Abdülhamid was deposed by the Assembly, with the approval of the *Şeyhü'l-İslâm*, and banished to Salonica. During the War he was brought back to Istanbul, where he died in 1918.

Abdülhamid having been deposed, his brother Mehmed was enthroned in his place, the fifth Sultan of the name. The pledge he gave on the day of his accession marked the opening of a new era in Turkish history. 'Since the nation (*millet*) wants me, I gratefully undertake this service. My chief hope is to carry on government in accordance with the sacred law and the Constitution. I shall not swerve by one iota from the will and aspirations of the nation.' The will of the nation! Never before had a sovereign of the House of Osman recognized the existence of such an entity.

But the Party of Union and Progress did not share the Sultan's liberal enthusiasm; the abortive revolt, which had provided ample justification for getting rid of Abdülhamid, also furnished them with a pretext to muzzle the opposition parties, whose strength grew as the ruling party abandoned its original Ottomanist policy and came out on the side of Turkish nationalism. Dissensions also abounded within the Party, however, and in July 1912 the Union and Progress Cabinet was forced to resign.

The succeeding Government put forward a programme which would seriously have limited the activities of Union and Progress: they proposed, *inter alia*, to look into allegations of official interference in elections, to forbid civil servants to belong to political parties, and to put an end to the Army's meddling in politics. The Party abandoned all pretence of loyalty to the Constitution: two of its most influential leaders, Enver and Talat, staged a *coup d'état*, as a result of which a new government took office, under Mahmud Şevket Pasha, who was sympathetic towards the Party. The new Cabinet had, in the words of the British Ambassador, 'a distinct German colouring'. In June 1913 Mahmud Şevket was assassinated and Union and Progress availed themselves of the opportunity to exile their principal opponents and to lay an iron hand on the administration.

Insofar as any one man can be held responsible for the Ottoman entry into the First World War, the ultimate disaster in the lamentable history of the declining Empire, that man was Enver. Born in 1881, he graduated from the Military College in 1903 with the rank of staff captain and was posted to the Third Army in Macedonia, where, like so many young officers, he joined the Society for Union and Progress. Courageous, intelligent and ambitious, he distinguished himself in the events leading up to the proclamation of the Constitution and, in 1909, was rewarded with the plum job of Military Attaché in Berlin. His stay there reinforced his belief in the measureless superiority of German military methods, a belief which was not shaken by the ignominious defeat of the German-trained Ottoman Army in the Balkan War. He went from success to success: leading the *coup d'état* of January 1913, stealing the limelight at the Turkish re-entry into Adrianople in the following July (it had been taken by Bulgaria four months previously), becoming Minister of War, with elevation to the rank of Pasha, and marrying into the Imperial family. This last step in his social climb convinced the sincere liberals that he had betrayed the cause of constitutionalism. When it became known that the hero of 1908 was to marry the Sultan's daughter, one of his former associates summed up the general feeling in these words: 'God damn Enver Pasha, for murdering our Enver!'

As soon as the 1914 War broke out, Enver proposed that Turkey throw in her lot with the Central Powers. Turkish public opinion was far from favouring the Allies; in 1907 Britain and Russia had blocked the Kaiser's ambitions in Persia by dividing the country into spheres of influence, and this British *rapprochement* with Turkey's ancient enemy had not been well received; nor, for that matter, had Britain's siding with Russia in July 1914. The fact that Germany was fighting against Russia was indeed one of the main arguments used by Enver. He nevertheless found himself in a minority; respect for British naval might was strong in Turkey and every responsible statesmen in the country knew that the Empire's only hope lay in neutrality. But the German web had been skilfully woven and the last word did not rest with the responsible statesmen. By a secret treaty signed on 2 August 1914, of which only three Turks beside himself had prior knowledge,[1] Enver irrevocably committed his country to war on the side of the Central Powers. When Germany's hopes of a speedy triumph had been dashed by defeats on the Marne and the Vistula, Turkish participartion, from being merely desirable, became essential. A *casus belli* was soon forthcoming.

On 2 August the British Government had commandeered two dreadnoughts which were being built in British yards for the Turkish Navy. This action had aroused great resentment in Turkey, the more so because the money for the ships had been raised by popular subscription. The German Government offered *Goeben* and *Breslau* in their place. To the dismay of those who had pointed to Allied naval supremacy as a reason for Turkey to keep out of hostilities, these two ships managed to dodge the Mediterranean blockade and make their way to Istanbul. There they were handed over to the Turkish Navy, in the person of its German

[1] They were the Grand Vizier Said Halim, Talat the Minister of the Interior and Halil the Chairman of the Chamber of Deputies.

commander, Admiral Souchon, who on 27 October sent them off to bombard the Russian Black Sea ports. The offer of an apology to Russia met with a demand by the Allies for the expulsion of all German naval and military officers from the Turkish forces; this demand was rejected by a majority vote of the Turkish ministers, and by 1 November 1914, the Ottoman Empire was engaged in its final war.

Of the course of the fighting it is unnecessary to speak. The position at the end of October 1918 is thus summarized by Hindenburg in his memoirs:

> In the East, the last resistance of the Turkish Empire had been broken. Mosul and Aleppo had fallen into enemy hands almost without a struggle. The armies of Iraq and Syria had practically ceased to exist.

Every Turkish commander in the field impressed on the Government the uselessness of further resistance.

On 30 October 1918, Turkish and British representatives signed an armistice agreement on board H.M.S. *Agamemnon*, at anchor off Mudros, in the island of Lemnos. All Ottoman possessions in Arabia, Syria, Iraq and Africa were placed under Allied military control, the Straits were to be opened and the Dardanelles and Black Sea fortifications to be occupied by the Allies, who were also given the right (by the notorious Article 7) to occupy any strategic point in the event of a threat to Allied security. These terms were made more palatable to the Ottoman representatives by a secret undertaking given by Admiral Calthorpe, the British delegate: he would recommend to his Government that no Greek troops should be sent to Istanbul or Smyrna (both cities having large indigenous Greek populations), and that Greek warships bound for the Black Sea should pass through the Straits only by night.

Although not a few Turkish writers have since described the 30th of October 1918, as a black day in Turkish history, news of the Mudros Armistice was greeted in Istanbul with relief. In the circumstances its terms were not unduly harsh. Recent criticisms are coloured by the memory of the unhappy events which followed because the Allies chose not only to ignore Admiral Calthorpe's recommendation but even to violate the letter of the agreement.

On 1 November 1918, Enver Pasha and other prominent members of the Party of Union and Progress fled to Berlin. Enver subsequently made his way to Moscow, where he engaged to further the Soviet cause among the Asiatic Turks. Once arrived in Turkestan, however, he set himself instead to carving out an independent kingdom there. This characteristically bold scheme was frustrated in August 1922, when Enver met his death fighting the Red Army near Bukhara.

Chapter 6

The Turkish Revolution, 1918–1920

IN JULY 1918 Sultan Mehmed V died and was succeeded by his brother Vahdettin, known as Mehmed VI. The new Sultan seems to have been characterized by the same egotism as his older brother Abdülhamid. He availed himself of the political bankruptcy of the Party of Union and Progress, and the flight of its leaders, to seize the reins in his own hands. The Party still commanded a majority in the Assembly; the Sultan therefore dissolved the Assembly (21 December 1918) and ruled through his brother-in-law, the Grand Vizier, Damad Ferid Pasha.

His policy was to maintain himself on the throne at any cost. To this end the Allies were to be conciliated and obeyed. No matter how much of his territories they might take from him, Vahdettin would raise no objection, so long as he could be Sultan of the remainder.

On 13 November 1918, an Allied fleet of sixty vessels, including the Greek ship *Averoff*, dropped anchor at Istanbul. Admiral Calthorpe explained to the Turks that no occupation of the capital was intended, that the purpose of the fleet was to fight the Bolsheviks in Russia. The following day Allied troops began to disembark, and buildings were commandeered for their use, but the Allies were careful to avoid using the word 'occupation'.

A Turkish writer has defined the Eastern Question as 'the problem of how to divide up the Ottoman Empire'. During the war, that problem had been solved to the satisfaction of the Allies by four secret agreements, whose main provisions were as follows.[1]

The 'Constantinople Agreement' (18 March 1915), between Britain, France and Russia, promised Russia Istanbul and the western coasts of the Bosphorus, Sea of Marmara and Dardanelles: Thrace, south of a line drawn between Midye and Enez; the north-western tip of Asia Minor; the islands of Imbros and Tenedos and those in the Sea of Marmara. Arabia was to become an independent Muslim State.

[1] See Volume VI of *A History of the Peace Conference of Paris*, edited for the British Institute of International Affairs by H. W. V. Temperley (Henry Frowde and Hodder & Stoughton, 1924).

By the Secret Treaty of London (26 April 1915), the same three Powers assigned to Italy, as her price for entering the war, 'a just share of the Mediterranean region adjacent to the province of Adalia' (now the vilayet of Antalya).

Under the Sykes–Picot Agreement (16 May 1916), between Britain and France, Russia was to be given the vilayets of Erzurum, Trabzon, Van and Bitlis. France would have Syria and the south-eastern quarter of Asia Minor. Britain's share would be the southern part of Mesopotamia with Baghdad, and the ports of Haifa and Acre. Between the French and British territories there would be an Arab State or confederation of States, divided into French and British zones of influence.[1]

The St Jean de Maurienne Agreement (17 April 1917), between Britain, France and Italy, was an attempt to reconcile the conflicting claims of France and Italy. France would have Adana, while Italy would be given the remainder of southern Asia Minor, including the city and vilayet of Smyrna.

The Russian Revolution had rendered void the promises given to the Tsar—indeed, the Bolsheviks formally renounced all claim to Turkish territory in 1917—but the other Allies were eager to enter upon their new acquisitions.

On 8 February 1919, French troops disembarked at Constantinople. Their commander, Franchet d'Esperey, rode a white horse, a gift from the local Greeks, in imitation of the way in which Mehmed II had entered the city on that day, long ago, when Byzantium fell. Wildly cheering crowds of non-Turks greeted the new conqueror, a bitter sight to Turkish eyes and one not soon forgotten.

Many Turks had been ready to face with equanimity the loss of the Arab provinces. A favourite theme of Turkish novelists has been the sorrows of Anatolia, with the flower of its young manhood sent to die in the service of an Empire from whose survival they had nothing to gain, wasting the best years of their lives amidst Arabs whose theoretical reverence for the Caliph of Islam did not inspire them with love for his tax-collectors and garrisons.

But this was something else. Here were foreigners lording it in the greatest of all Turkish cities, their path strewn with flowers by the Turks' ungrateful subjects. Spontaneously, all over the country,

[1] These terms were never put into effect, because President Wilson persuaded the Peace Conference to reject the principle of annexation of the Arab provinces and to establish mandates instead. Details will be found in Temperley, *op. cit.*, and in Sir Reader Bullard's *Britain and the Middle East* (Hutchinson's University Library, 1951).

were seen the first stirrings of a Turkish nationalist spirit, distinct from Pan-Turkism. The latter had never been much more than an impractical dream (though it had served a useful purpose in providing a mystique which kept Turkish hopes alive, at a time when the bases of Ottoman society were crumbling), and by now it was manifestly out-moded. The Turks of the former Russian Empire must dree their own weird; the Turks of Turkey would stand together.

In every part of Turkey patriotic societies sprang up. One of the earliest was the Ottoman Defence Committee of Thrace. Its avowed aim was local and regional: to keep Thrace in Turkish hands, but its real purpose went far beyond this, as was shown by the Committee's rejection of an offer of autonomy for the region, made by the Greek Prime Minister Venizelos. In Kars, a National Council actually ruled the province for half a year, latterly with the title of 'Provisional National Government of the South-western Caucasus', until it was dissolved by the British in April 1919. Weakened by years of war, despised by their former subjects, betrayed by their leaders, the Turks had suddenly begun to find themselves.

Early in February 1919 Venizelos presented to the Peace Conference at Paris a formal claim to possession of Smyrna. The St Jean de Maurienne Agreement, which assigned that region to Italy, had lapsed for want of Russian ratification, and Lloyd George and Clemenceau gave the Greek Prime Minister their backing. On 15 May a Greek division landed at Smyrna, with Allied naval support. This act was declared by the Allies to be in accordance with Article 7 of the Armistice agreement: without real justification, for, as was conclusively shown later, there was no threat to Allied security. The occupation troops were welcomed by delighted crowds of indigenous Greeks and were blessed by the Metropolitan of Smyrna. They then began a systematic massacre of Turks in the city and province. The civilized world was shocked, but could do little: Smyrna was the price the Allies had agreed to pay for Greece's entry into the war.

Enormous protest meetings took place in Istanbul. Speakers harangued vast crowds, while French Senegalese machine-gunners stood guard and Allied aircraft flew overhead. But there was no violence; only bitter speeches and tears of anger and frustration.

As soon as the Greek forces had established themselves in Smyrna, they began a drive into the interior, and a trail of hanged men and smoking rubble marked their advance. Turkish guerillas took up the struggle and a bloody war developed, in which no quarter was shown and atrocities were the norm.

The career of one guerilla leader may be taken as typical. Yörük Ali Efe was born in 1896 in a village of south-western Anatolia. He joined the Army during the First World War but deserted after being flogged by an N.C.O. For three years he lived by banditry in the hills and then gave himself up. Just at that time the Greeks occupied Smyrna, and Yörük Ali was enabled, by the connivance of the Turkish authorities, to reassemble his gang and resume his old way of life. In June 1920, with fifty followers, he crossed the river Menderes on rafts to wipe out a Greek detachment and take their weapons. This feat inspired a large-scale rising in the province of Aydın against the invader. With the extension of the Nationalists' authority, Yörük Ali's gang, considerably enlarged, was named 'The National Aydın Regiment', and he himself was given the rank of colonel of militia. At the end of the War of Independence he settled down to be a farmer, not far from his birthplace. His services are commemorated in the title of the 37th (Yörük Ali Efe's) Regiment of the 57th Division of the Republican Army.

But undirected, the Yörük Ali Efes of Turkey could have achieved little. The time has come to bring the hero into the story.

Already, a generation after the death of Mustafa Kemal, it is difficult for one who did not know him to ascertain what manner of man he really was. The adulation which was accorded him by his countrymen in his lifetime has not given place to a mature appreciation of his qualities. On the one hand there is a tacit assumption that he was something more than human, an attitude which leads to the dangerous conviction that any principle he ever enunciated is valid for all time. On the other hand, many of those who fawned on the living lion have now joined the ranks of the professional debunkers, who delight in exposing the weaknesses of the great.

Mustafa Kemal was born in Salonica in 1881. His father, Ali Rıza Efendi, a customs-official turned timber-merchant, died when the boy was seven. The widowed mother, Zübeyde, went to live on her brother's farm, with Mustafa and his young sister Makbule. He entered a school for prospective civil servants, but was taken away from it by his family after being flogged for starting a fight in class. His own ambition, which was strongly resisted by his mother, was to become a soldier. In 1893, without consulting her, he sat and passed the entrance examination for the Salonica Military School, and Zübeyde had the good sense to bow to the inevitable. After finishing at Salonica, he studied at the Monastir Military Academy, from which, in 1899, he went on to the War College in Istanbul. Like so many young soldiers, particularly in Salonica, he was an ardent opponent of the absolutism of Abdülhamid, and this characteristic developed with the passing years. Graduating from the War College at the beginning of 1905, with the rank of staff captain, he plunged still deeper into political intrigue, with the result that he was denounced to the Sultan. The consequences were not so grave as one might have expected, because if the Sultan had made away with every officer suspected of plotting against him he would have had no army left. Mustafa Kemal was posted to Damascus, where he joined the 'Fatherland' (*Vatan*), the local revolutionary group, which he helped to reorganize as the 'Fatherland and Freedom Society'. His talent for under-cover work is seen in the Society's constitution: each member was personally known only to the man who introduced him and to the man he introduced. Mustafa Kemal undertook the direction of propaganda and put the Society into contact with his old friends of the Salonica Headquarters of Union and Progress.

In September 1907, to his great joy, he was posted to the Third Army in Salonica. But there things did not go as well as he hoped. True, he played his part in the eventful days of 1908, but his opinions were never listened to with as much respect as he wished; he was never admitted to the forefront of the councils of Union and Progress. Advancement in the Society was for those willing to become tools of German policy, and Mustafa Kemal never made any secret of his contempt for those who did not put Turkey's interests first. His disappointment was canalized into dislike of Enver, whose star was then in the ascendant. To the successful and triumphant young officers who had secured the proclamation of the Constitution, Kemal propounded his view that as soldiers, their end having been gained, they should henceforth not meddle in politics: from this we may judge of his spiritual loneliness. He withdrew from the Society's activities, to the satisfaction of the innumerable men he had offended, and devoted himself to his profession, with conspicuous success. He served with distinction in the wars of 1911 and 1912. The outbreak of the First World War found him as Military Attaché in Sofia, with the rank of lieutenant-colonel. At the end of 1914 he was recalled and put in command of the 19th Division, which at that time scarcely existed except on paper. He threw all his energies into making of it a serviceable fighting force and was posted with it to Arıburnu, on the west side of Gallipoli. His leadership, more than any other single factor, frustrated the British landings and brought about the evacuation of the peninsula. This campaign, which had saved Istanbul, made him a national hero, much to Enver's displeasure. Mustafa Kemal, now a brigadier and a pasha, was consequently sent to the Caucasus, where the spectacle of his success could not affront the War Minister's vanity.

Enver had been to the eastern front himself, a year before, with a plan for driving the Russians back across the Caucasus. The plan had misfired disastrously and all but a tenth of the Turkish forces had met their death at Sarıkamış. Since then the eastern front had been left to take care of itself, and the Russians were in occupation of Bitlis and Muş. Luck was with Mustafa Kemal, for even his tireless endeavours could have done little with the dispirited remnant of the Eastern Army, had not the first stirrings of the Russian Revolution broken the back of the enemy's resistance.

The recapture of Bitlis and Muş in August 1916 was Kemal's last military achievement for many months, during which time he visited Germany with the Heir Apparent, Vahdettin. In August 1918 he was sent to the Syrian front, where Allenby's brilliant advance offered the Turks only a choice between rout and surrender. Kemal saved them from this; he organized a fighting retreat all the way to the mountains north of Aleppo, and was preparing to make a stand there, when news came of the Mudros Armistice. To the Turkish soldier in defeat, Mustafa Kemal Pasha was not just a hero, he was the only hero; the man who had hurled the British out of Gallipoli and cheated them of their prey in Syria.

For many months after the Armistice he remained inactive at Istanbul. He was there when the Allied warships anchored in the Bosphorus and when Franchet d'Esperey rode his white horse through the cheering crowds. There was nothing for him to do in the capital; it was too well policed by the victors. At General Allenby's suggestion he was offered the command of the Sixth Army at Nusaybin, away on the Syrian border, but he refused. His dream was to get into Anatolia, to organize the local nationalist groups into a force that the Allies would have to treat with more respect than they had yet shown to conquered Turkey. But this dream seemed wildly improbable, for he was under Allied surveillance, like other prominent Turks; he could not quietly slip away without arousing suspicion. And then the Government made the blunder of many a Turk before and since: they mistook Istanbul for Turkey.

It did not suit their purpose to have Mustafa Kemal in the capital; he was too popular and too ambitious, and his notorious outspokenness might offend the Allies. Once away from the capital he would be harmless. So in April 1919 the Minister of War sent for him and told him that the Allies were complaining of armed attacks by Turks on Greek-inhabited villages in the neighbourhood of Samsun. If the Ottoman Government could not maintain order there, Allied forces would do so. Mustafa Kemal had great influence with the Turkish soldiery; further, he was known as an inveterate opponent of Enver's pro-German policy and was therefore politically acceptable to the Allies. Would he be willing to put down the disorders, first in the north and then in the rest of Anatolia? Hardly able to believe his ears, he accepted, and was appointed Inspector-General of the Third Army, based on Samsun, with command of the 3rd and 15th Army Corps. On 19 May, four days after the Greek occupation of Smyrna, he reached Samsun.

Immediately, he set about acquainting himself with conditions in the area and getting into touch with the local resistance groups. Three days after his arrival he wrote a report to the Grand Vizier, to this effect: the lawlessness in the region of Samsun was the fault of the local Greeks; if they would abandon their political aspirations and their attacks on the Turks, the Turkish bands would cease from their activities or, if they did not, it would be a simple military task to suppress them. Turks would never submit to foreign rule; the occupation of İzmir was a matter of vital national concern and was so regarded 'by the simplest peasant'. İzmir was as important for the Turks as Istanbul and they would not consent to its occupation by any foreign power, 'least of all by a visionary government like that of Greece'. On 22 June, while at Amasya, he addressed a circular letter to all military and civil authorities whom he considered trustworthy, of which the following is a summary:

> The territorial integrity of the Fatherland and our national independence are in danger. The central Government is incapable of carrying out its responsibilities. A national body must be set up, free from all outside interference, to bring to the ears of the world the nation's cry for its rights. It has been decided to hold a national congress at Sivas in the near future, to which every province is to send delegates, who must, wherever necessary, travel incognito.

It is well established that Mustafa Kemal had confided his plans to certain of the other generals. Some writers however have argued that the Sultan's Government as a whole were not the traitors and dupes that the consensus of Republican historians makes them out to be: that they knew perfectly well what Mustafa Kemal's intentions were and deliberately sent him to Samsun, so that he might give the nation the lead which they themselves dared not give. On 23 June the Ministry of the Interior issued a circular which is worth quoting at length, as it effectively disposes of this theory:

> Although Mustafa Kemal Pasha is a great soldier, his political sagacity is not of the same standard. . . . He has added to his political mistakes the administrative error of sending telegrams on behalf of certain illegal bodies whose only function is to extort money from the people. To bring him back to Istanbul is the duty of the Ministry of War. The Ministry of the Interior, however, orders you to recognize that this man has been dismissed, to enter into no official dealings with him whatsoever and to see that no request of his relative to governmental affairs is complied with . . . In these critical moments, while our destinies are being decided on by the Peace Conference and an account is being taken of the acts of madness we have committed over the past five years, it is surely the duty of every Ottoman official and citizen to show that we have at last come to our senses, to act in a reasonable and prudent manner, and to protect the life, property and honour of every individual, without distinction of party, creed or race, and thus to avoid any further staining of this country in the eyes of civilization.

The Ministry of War did indeed try to recall Mustafa Kemal to Istanbul, but without effect. On 8 July 1919, as the climax to a spirited exchange of telegrams, the Ministry indicated that the Pasha was relieved of his post, and the Pasha instantly countered by resigning his commission. From that time on, until he received a new commission from the National Congress, he wore civilian clothes. Yet the military authorities of Anatolia, with very few exceptions, continued to regard him as their lawful superior. Reports and requests for instructions did not cease to come for him, addressed to 'The 3rd Army Corps Command at Sivas'.

With politicians he had more difficulty. To them he was a man who could be useful in unseating the Government but would then have served his purpose. For the moment, however, they were compelled to support him, because he was the only man the Army and the common people were prepared to follow.

A congress was held at Erzurum between 23 July and 6 August, of delegates from all the eastern provinces. It was not summoned by Kemal but by the 'Eastern Provinces Society for the Defence of National Rights'. Mustafa Kemal attended, however, and was elected chairman. The decisions reached by the Erzurum Congress were reaffirmed by that held at Sivas in early September.

The Sivas Congress was dominated by the personality of Mustafa Kemal, who was chosen by secret ballot to preside over it, with only three dissentient votes. He succeeded in obtaining the rejection of a proposal for seeking an American mandate over 'all the Ottoman dominions . . . since a mandate that will assure our territorial integrity is preferable to an independence that will be confined to two or three provinces'. Mustafa Kemal wondered what the boundaries were of 'all the Ottoman dominions'. 'Our pre-war boundaries? Including Syria and Iraq? If so, have the people of Anatolia the right and the authority to ask for a mandate in the name of the Arab world?' Supporters of the 'Friends of England Association' fared no better. Mustafa Kemal would settle for nothing less than the absolute independence of Turkey, a Turkey freed from the profitless burden of the Arab provinces.

The main conclusions of the Sivas Congress were these: resistance would be offered to any occupation of any part of Turkey. No minority within the country would be given any privileges which would 'upset our political and social equilibrium'. A national assembly should meet at once to settle the nation's destiny.

A message was then sent to the capital in the name of the Congress, demanding the resignation of the Cabinet of Damad Ferid Pasha and the immediate convening of the Chamber of Deputies. This demand was rejected but not ignored; the Congress was clearly a force to be reckoned with. An attempt was made, with the help of British agents, to rouse the Kurdish tribes against Kemal and his followers, but it was frustrated through efficient intelligence-work and a timely show of force. Repeated protests to the Sultan, against this 'treacherous and suicidal action against the fatherland and the nation', elicited no reply.

On 11 September, professing to regard this silence as due to the malevolence of the ministers rather than to the Sultan's own complicity, Mustafa Kemal telegraphed the following ultimatum to the Grand Vizier:

> Your reckless attempts to tread the nation's rights underfoot and to compromise the honour of H.M. the Sultan are known. The nation has no confidence in any of you apart from the Sultan; hence it is obliged to present its petitions to H.M. alone. Your Cabinet, fearing the perilous consequences of its unconstitutional actions, is coming between nation and Sultan. If your obstinacy in this matter continues for one hour longer, the nation will consider itself entitled to take any action it thinks fit, and will cut off all communication between the

country and your unconstitutional Cabinet. This is our last warning.

On the expiry of the ultimatum, this threat was carried out; with very few exceptions all telegraph offices ceased to handle official messages to and from the capital.

On 1 October the Grand Vizier resigned, 'for reasons of health'. A new Cabinet was formed by Ali Rıza Pasha, who prepared for new elections and sent his Navy Minister, Salih Pasha, to Amasya to confer with Kemal. After three days of discussion, they agreed on five important principles: the territorial integrity of Turkey was to be preserved, no special privileges were to be given to minorities, the Government was to recognize the Nationalist organization, the Turkish delegates at the Peace Conference were to be approved by the committee of the National Congress, and the new Chamber of Deputies was not to meet in Istanbul.

The Cabinet proceeded with arrangements for the election, but took no notice of the Amasya Protocol. The prudent Kemal moved his headquarters to Ankara, the capital of a province, with the advantages of railway communication with Istanbul, a central position in the country and strong natural defences.

The election gave the Nationalists a large majority and the newly-elected deputies joyfully prepared to hurry off to Istanbul, disregarding Mustafa Kemal's warnings. He himself had been elected for Erzurum, but was too wily to enter the spider's parlour. Some thought him unduly pessimistic, but many thought he was disgruntled at seeing his brief hour of glory fade. Outlaws no longer, but deputies, at last they could go back to the flesh-pots of Istanbul and settle their country's future like gentlemen. Some promised to elect Mustafa Kemal President of the Chamber *in absentia*, but the promise was not kept.

So Kemal remained in Ankara, and had the grim satisfaction of seeing his prophecies come true. The Chamber was opened on 12 January 1920. A week later the Allied representatives procured the dismissal of the Minister of War and the Chief of the General Staff, whom they rightly suspected of complicity in the theft of arms from Allied depôts, the Nationalists' main source of supply. This piece of interference, justifiable though it was except in Nationalist eyes, emboldened the deputies to vote for the proclamation of the National Pact (28 January 1920), a document which had been drafted by the Erzurum Congress and which is still regarded as the basis of Turkish foreign policy. Its provisions were these:

1. The destinies of those portions of the Ottoman Empire which are inhabited exclusively by Arabs and which were under enemy occupation on 30 October 1918, must be settled by free vote of the population. The remaining portions, inhabited by an Ottoman–Muslim majority, united by religion and race, linked to each other by feelings of mutual respect and self-sacrifice, form a whole which does not admit of division for any reason.

2. We accept that in the matter of the Three Sanjaks, which attached themselves to the mother-country by a plebiscite, recourse should again be had if necessary to a plebiscite.[1]

3. The determination of the legal status of Western Thrace, which has been left to the Turkish peace treaty, must be in accordance with the vote which the local people shall freely give.

4. Provided that the city of Istanbul and the Sea of Marmara are kept immune from all harm, any decision that may be reached between us and all other interested Powers regarding the opening of the Dardanelles and Bosphorus to the commerce and traffic of the world, is accepted.

5. The rights of minorities are to be guaranteed; this applies equally to Muslim minorities.

6. We accept no restriction that will hamper our political, judicial and financial development. The settlement of our proved debts shall not be contrary to these principles.

Such bold words on the part of a defeated people did not please the Allied Powers. Still less did they like the continued thefts of arms from Allied dumps. On the night of 26 January, for example, a well-planned and well-executed raid on a French depôt at Akbaş secured 8,000 rifles, 40 machine-guns and 20,000 boxes of ammunition, which were dispatched to the Nationalist forces in the interior.

All the Allies had their own domestic post-war problems to contend with, and the demobilization of their armies was making it every day more difficult to deal with the Turkish question. They forced the resignation of Ali Rıza Pasha, and he was succeeded in the Grand Vizierate by Salih Pasha, who showed the same readiness to come to an understanding with the Nationalists as he had when Navy Minister. The Allies, without the forces necessary to suppress the Nationalist movement in Anatolia, thereupon decided on the unwise step of formally placing the capital under military occupation

[1] The three sub-provinces of Kars, Ardahan and Batum, formerly part of the Russian Empire. In accordance with Article 4 of the Treaty of Brest-Litovsk, a free vote of the inhabitants was taken in 1918 and decided on union with the Ottoman Empire.

and arresting and deporting to Malta such Nationalist deputies as were within their reach (16 March 1920). Hearing the news, Mustafa Kemal said, 'Today, by the forcible occupation of Istanbul, an end has been made of the seven hundred years' life and sovereignty of the Ottoman Empire.'

The Grand Vizier, who resisted an Allied demand that he disavow the Nationalist movement, was obliged to resign, and the Sultan once again appointed his brother-in-law, Ferid Pasha.

Hüseyin Kâzım, the courageous Deputy-Chairman of the Assembly, sought an audience with the Sultan and begged him to reconsider this decision, which could mean only disaster for the country. Enraged, the Sultan replied, 'If I wish, I can appoint the Greek Patriarch to the Grand Vizierate, or the Armenian Patriarch, or the Chief Rabbi.' 'You can, Sire,' replied Hüseyin Kâzım, 'but you will not be able to remain on your throne.'

Ferid Pasha then took a step which previous governments had avoided: he declared the Nationalists to be rebels against the Sultan, and the *Şeyhü'l-İslâm* issued a *fetva*[1] in support of this view, ending with the words, 'Is it permissible to kill these rebels?—Answer: It is a duty to do so.'

On the same day (11 April 1920), the Sultan dissolved the Chamber of Deputies.

[1] A *responsum* given by a mufti on a point of sacred law.

Chapter 7

The Grand National Assembly, 1920–1922

THE OLD JEALOUSIES were forgotten. Those deputies who had escaped arrest made their way to Ankara, and there, on 23 April 1920, the Grand National Assembly of Turkey[1] began its first session. Mustafa Kemal was elected President of the Assembly, and the following statement of faith was proclaimed to the world:

> Sovereignty belongs unconditionally to the nation. The Grand National Assembly is the true and sole representative of the nation. Legislative authority and executive power are manifested and concentrated in the Grand National Assembly.

'Once the Sultan-Caliph has been delivered from the constraint he now suffers,' said Mustafa Kemal, 'he will take his place within the constitution to be drawn up by the Assembly.'

Soon the new Government was fighting for its life. Copies of the *fetva* outlawing Kemal and his colleagues were dropped by Allied aircraft over inland towns, and anti-Nationalist riots broke out in a score of places, despite a counter-*fetva* given by the mufti of Ankara and other Ulema who were friendly to the Nationalist cause: 'Are the *fetvas* issued by a government under foreign duress binding, according to the sacred law, upon Muslims?—Answer: No.'

A court-martial held in Istanbul tried the rebel leaders *in absentia* and condemned them to death. All over Anatolia the irregular forces glorified by the title of 'The Army of the Caliphate' fought the Nationalists. The battle came close to Ankara itself and more than once the vital telegraph lines were cut. At the same time, the Nationalists were waging unrelenting war against the Greeks in the west, the Armenian Republic in the north-east and, in the south-east, against the French troops who had occupied Adana.

To say that Mustafa Kemal alone kept the Nationalists fighting would be unjust to the thousands of nameless Turks who fought, often with home-made weapons, to rid their country of foreign

[1] *Türkiye Büyük Millet Meclisi.* Its English name may conveniently be abbreviated to 'G.N.A.'.

invaders and native dupes. But certainly it was his indomitable will and untiring energy which maintained the tenuous links of the Nationalist organization and saved it from piecemeal extermination.

The details of the military operations which confounded the pessimists are not essential to our story, though they constitute an epic of heroism and endurance. The town of Antep, besieged by 12,000 French troops, held out for over ten months. The inhabitants made rockets with crude gunpowder, they used unexploded enemy shells as grenades. They turned against the French an ancient muzzle-loading cannon which for many years had been used only to signal the end of the Fast of Ramadan. Hunger compelled them to surrender, in February 1921. The G.N.A. conferred on the town the title of 'Warrior for the Faith' and it is known as Gaziantep to this day.[1]

So hopeless did the Nationalist cause seem at first that even the London *Times* perpetrated what must ever remain a warning to all political prophets and Middle East experts. In its issue of 22 May 1920, a leading article stated authoritatively: 'Mustapha Kemal is no Hotspur, and his rabble lacks cohesion.' A month later its correspondent reported that the Nationalists controlled the greater part of Anatolia, with fully two-thirds of the literate and governing class behind them, including many thousands of officers who, with little to hope for from civilian life, had everything to gain from continuing the fight.

> But the attitude of the majority of the literate class, lawyers, politicians, journalists, above all officials, is less comprehensible. This class seems unconscious of the risk it is running.

'Heedless' would have been nearer the mark: the literate class supported the Kemalist movement because the alternative was national extinction; because there was no other way open to them if they wished to survive as Turks.

On 16 July 1920, a Greek communiqué announced that operations in Asia Minor had been concluded. East of the line occupied by the Greek troops (which ran southward from a point on the Sea of Marmara, nine miles east of Bursa, to the Menderes, seven miles east of Nazilli), 'the Nationalists have lost all prestige and have been everywhere repudiated by the Moslem population'. The Turks were 'expressing absolute confidence and sincere gratitude towards the Greeks, whom they consider as their friends and protectors'.

[1] The award of the George Cross to the island of Malta is a parallel from our own recent history.

In the summer of 1920, cushioned against the hardness of reality by their own cheerful communiqués, the Allied Powers decided to conclude a peace with the Sultan's Government. The terms proposed were such that even Damad Ferid Pasha jibbed and it was only the personal insistence of Vahdettin that compelled the Ottoman delegates to sign (10 August 1920). The Treaty of Sèvres has been described as the death-warrant of the Ottoman Empire. More; it would, if implemented, have meant the end of Turkey itself.

The Straits were to be neutralized and administered by a permanent Allied commission sitting at Istanbul. The city itself was to be a hostage for the good behaviour of the Turks towards the minorities; it would be taken away from Turkish administration if the rights of minorities were infringed. The eastern provinces were to be divided between an autonomous Kurdistan and an independent Armenia. Greece was to have Smyrna and its hinterland, and Thrace. Italy's share would be the southern half of western and central Anatolia, while France took the south-east. Rarely in history can so unrealistic a treaty have been signed. But its signing served only to inflame the Turks. From then on, although there were disagreements about who was to lead the Nationalist revolt, there was practically no dispute about its necessity.

Still the Allies continued to misjudge the situation. At the end of September, the Sultan's Government was reported to be seeking Allied financial help to pacify Anatolia.

> Nationalism is waning as a military force, but even so the Central Government must be enabled, after detaching the majority of the Angora Government's supporters by offers of amnesty, to deal with the minority of adventurers, criminals and fanatics whose crimes and follies exclude them from hope of pardon.[1]

Fortunately for the morale of the Nationalists, *The Times* was not generally read round their camp-fires.

The considerable Greek victories of 1919 and 1920 had been in part due to dissensions among the Nationalist leaders. Mustafa Kemal saw the futility of hoping to defeat a well-equipped modern army solely by guerilla action. This conviction brought him into conflict with Çerkez Ethem, Ethem the Circassian, the outstanding guerilla leader, who when instructed to place himself under the orders of İsmet, Kemal's Chief of Staff, refused, thus precipitating open war between his own 'Mobile Forces' and Mustafa Kemal's

[1] *The Times*, 27 September 1920.

'Regular Forces'. Defeated, Ethem went over to the Greeks, who took advantage of the apparent disunity among the Turks to advance eastward from Bursa, towards Eskişehir.

Their hopes were frustrated. The Turkish army on the western front, under İsmet, had been strengthened by reinforcements released by the cessation of hostilities in the east, where the Nationalist army commanded by Kâzım Karabekir had, with Russian help, taken Kars, Ardahan and Artvin from the Armenians. On 10 January 1921, İsmet drove the Greeks back to Bursa, after a fierce engagement at İnönü.

For this success, İsmet was promoted to brigadier by the Grand National Assembly and was thereafter known as İsmet Pasha (though it is a moot point whether the latter title could be conferred by anyone but the Sultan).

Alarmed by the Greek reverse at İnönü, the Allies made an effort to end hostilities before the Turks could gain the initiative. A conference was called in London, to which representatives of both Istanbul and Ankara were invited. Some modification of the terms of Sèvres was offered, but neither Turkish delegation would accept them. Britain, France and Italy then announced their neutrality in the struggle on the western front, which thus became a straight fight between Greeks and Turks. To safeguard Allied communications, a neutral zone was designated on either side of the Dardanelles, on which neither belligerent was to trespass.

Meanwhile the Grand National Assembly had passed the Provisional Law of Fundamental Organization (20 January 1921), whose terms may be summarized as follows:

1. Sovereignty belongs unconditionally to the nation.

2. Executive power and legislative authority are manifested and concentrated in the G.N.A., which is the sole rightful representative of the nation.

3. The Turkish State is administered by the G.N.A. and its Government is entitled 'Government of the Grand National Assembly of Turkey'.

4. The G.N.A. is composed of members elected by the people.

5. Elections are to be held once every two years. If the holding of new elections is impossible, the session may be prolonged for one year only. Every member of the G.N.A. is a deputy not of the particular province (*vilâyet*) electing him, but of the whole nation.

6. To the G.N.A. belong such fundamental rights as: putting into execution the ordinances of the sacred law; the laying-down, amending and abrogation of all laws; the concluding of treaties and peace; the proclaiming of the defence of the fatherland (i.e., the

declaring of war). For executive matters, the G.N.A. appoints and, if necessary, changes Ministers.

7. The President elected by the Assembly is authorized to sign in the name of the G.N.A. The Committee of Executive Ministers shall elect one of their number as President of the Committee.

The words 'ordinances of the sacred law' (*Ahkâm-ı şer'iye*), in the sixth section, call for some comment. They occur also in Article 26 of the 1924 Constitution, where however they were amended to *kavanin*, 'laws', in 1928. Although Mustafa Kemal subsequently declared that the words were redundant, meaning no more than 'legal ordinances', and that he had argued against their insertion as liable to mislead, there is no possible ambiguity about them. Whoever drafted this clause was arrogating to the G.N.A. the powers of the Caliphate. Mustafa Kemal tried to explain this fact away because he had no intention of letting the G.N.A. be used to perpetuate the reign of the *Şeriat*.

On 1 April, İsmet Pasha inflicted another defeat on the Greeks in a second battle at İnönü. For the next three months the Greeks prepared and regrouped, and on 10 July began a general advance. The Turkish forces were inferior numerically and in equipment, particularly in transport. They gave ground before the Greek onslaught and the enemy swept eastward. With his army in danger of encirclement at Eskişehir, İsmet telegraphed for Kemal, who came at once from Ankara and gave his orders. The army was to fall back beyond the Sakarya River and thus lengthen the enemy's lines of communication. This abandonment of 100 miles of Turkish territory to the invader would involve a terrific shock to public opinion; Mustafa Kemal would deal with that while İsmet was withdrawing his troops.

Back in Ankara, Kemal found that he had not overestimated the consternation that greeted the news of his decision. He faced an angry Assembly. The cry was raised that the man responsible for the imminent disaster ought to be at the head of the doomed army. With superb insolence, Mustafa Kemal agreed and formally accepted the 'invitation to become Commander-in-Chief', on condition that all the authority vested in the G.N.A. be transferred to him personally. A storm of protest arose: supreme command belonged to the Assembly alone; at most he could be appointed Deputy Commander-in-Chief. He stood his ground; he would not accept this antiquated title so often conferred by the Sultans; he would hold the supreme command in name as well as in fact. The following day, the Assembly voted him the powers he wished. Henceforth his orders had the force of law (5 August 1921).

At once he decreed the confiscation (against payment 'at some future date') of 40 per cent of all food, clothing, bedding, petrol, oil and motor-spares. A register was to be compiled of all mechanics, metal-workers and men in other trades of military importance. 'Independence Tribunals' were set up to ensure that the Commander-in-Chief's orders were obeyed.

There were to be no more retreats. Mustafa Kemal enunciated this principle in an Order of the Day:

> There is no defence-line. There is a defence-area, which is the whole country. Not one inch of it is to be given up until it is wet with Turkish blood. Any unit, large or small, may be thrown out of its position. But it will face the enemy and continue to fight at the first point where a stand is possible. Units which see a neighbouring unit obliged to retreat cannot follow. They must stay where they are and resist to the end.

To regard these words as so much rhetoric is to mistake the nature of Mustafa Kemal and of those he was addressing, who were, and are, probably the most disciplined people on earth. It is an old saying that if Satan were to order a Turkish soldier to bayonet his grandmother he would immediately do so, provided that Satan had taken the precaution of dressing in the uniform of a Turkish corporal. That Order of the Day was an order, and was obeyed.

For three weeks the battle raged over a sixty-mile front. On 13 September 1921, the Greeks fell back across the Sakarya and withdrew, burning and devastating, to their old positions round Eskişehir.

The news of the victory was greeted with wild rejoicing. The Grand National Assembly promoted Mustafa Kemal to Marshal and gave him the title of Ghazi. Five weeks later, an agreement was signed between Nationalist Turkey and France.[1] Hostilities in the south-east were to end, thus releasing many thousands of Turkish troops for the western front. But more important than the actual terms of the agreement was the fact that, by signing it, France had recognized the G.N.A. as the sovereign power in Turkey. Britain, who still recognized the Sultan's Government, protested strongly, but to no avail.

For many long months the Greek army dug itself in north and west of Afyonkarahisar, not daring to risk an offensive, while Kemal drove his weary people to ever greater efforts. His position was by no means easy. Towards the end of 1921 the deputies who

[1] This was the Franklin-Bouillon Agreement of 20 October 1921.

had been interned in Malta were released and made their way to Ankara, expecting a hero's welcome. But Mustafa Kemal made no secret of his feelings about them: they should have taken his advice not to go to Istanbul in the first place. Having gone, they should have had the sense to come back to Ankara as others had done, before the trap closed.

Some of them formed an opposition group, which tried to obstruct Kemal at every turn. His days were spent in talking down criticism of his conduct of affairs and where necessary he did not shrink from using force. When objections were raised to a motion renewing his tenure of the supreme command, he replied simply that no one but himself was fit for the job and that he did not intend to leave the nation without a leader.

For false modesty was not one of his failings. Here is his own appraisal of his services, from a speech he made in reply to a proposal that membership of the Assembly should be restricted to people born within the post-war frontiers of Turkey or who had lived in their constituencies for at least five years:

> Unfortunately my birth-place lies outside our present frontiers. That is not my fault. . . . And if I have not lived for five years in any one constituency, that is because of the services I have been rendering to this country. Had I tried to comply with the conditions this clause lays down, I should have been unable to conduct our defence at Arıburnu and Anafartalar, which would have meant the loss of Istanbul. If I had been obliged to spend five years in any one spot, I should not have been able to go out to meet the enemy when he fanned out towards Diyarbakır after taking Bitlis and Muş; I could not have done my duty, which was to recover Bitlis and Muş. If I had wanted to fulfill the conditions these gentlemen impose, I should not have been able to form a front at Aleppo and defend it against the enemy, and establish the line which now we call our national frontier. I think my subsequent efforts are known to you all. I've been working too hard to stay five years in any one place. I think that I have won the affection and regard of my nation—perhaps of the whole Muslim world—for these services of mine. So it never occurred to me that anyone might try to deprive me of my rights as a citizen.

In March 1922 representatives of the Allied Powers, meeting in Paris, made proposals for an armistice between Turkey and Greece. These were rejected out of hand; Mustafa Kemal would not accept any armistice unless the Greeks began immediately to evacuate Turkish territory. As they would not do this of their own accord, they must be made to go.

At dawn on 26 August the Greek positions were pulverized under an intense artillery bombardment. Then the Turkish infantry, with fixed bayonets, poured forth from their trenches. The Greek army broke and fled. A portion of it made a stand at Dumlupınar, but by the evening of the 30th there was no Greek army left. Its battered remnants were rushing headlong for Smyrna and the waiting ships.

On 9 September, Mustafa Kemal rode into Smyrna. As more and more Turkish troops entered the city, terror spread among the Greek population. For day the streets were hideous with murder and pillage. Then fire broke out, a fire which destroyed half the city and whose marks are still visible today.

A Greek army still remained in Thrace. The Turks marched northward to deal with them. Entering the neutral zone at Çanakkale, they found the Allied Army of Occupation, under General Harington, barring their way. The situation was grave, containing the seeds of a new war, a war in which Turkey could probably count on Soviet help. On 19 September, Harington's French and Italian contingents discreetly withdrew. Slowly the Turks moved closer to the British positions, each side wondering when the other would open fire. Then dramatically, in the nick of time, word came that an armistice had been arranged.

The armistice that was signed at Mudanya on 11 October 1922, represented a complete Allied surrender to the demands of the Nationalists. The agreement made no mention at all of the Sultan. Istanbul, the Straits and Eastern Thrace as far as the Maritsa were to be handed over to the Government of the Grand National Assembly, though Allied forces would remain in Istanbul until the signing of a definitive peace treaty.

Lloyd George's policy of encouraging Greece's imperialist adventure in Asia Minor had borne strange fruit. A week after the Mudanya Armistice, he handed in his resignation.

Chapter 8

From Sultanate to Republic (I)

THE MUDANYA ARMISTICE had been the work of professional soldiers. Now the professional politicians took over. On 27 October 1922, invitations to a peace conference at Lausanne were sent both to the Grand National Assembly and to 'the Government of His Imperial Majesty the Sultan'. This ill-considered action precipitated the end of the Sultanate. On 1 November 1922, a long and heated debate took place in the Assembly. Few if any members had a good word to say for Vahdettin, and the obvious move was to depose him and appoint his successor as Sultan-Caliph. But Mustafa Kemal had a more radical proposal. Sovereignty belonged to the nation; the Sultanate should be abolished and the Caliphate alone should be conferred on Vahdettin's successor.

It was decided to refer the question whether the Sultanate could legally be separated from the Caliphate, to a joint meeting of the Assembly's Committee for the *Şeriat* and the Judicial and Constitution Committees.

For hours the *hocas*—the learned doctors—wrangled, while Mustafa Kemal sat in a corner, listening to them. Finally his patience gave way. He asked the Chairman's leave to speak, jumped on a bench and shouted:

> Sovereignty and sultanate are not given to anyone by anyone because scholarship says so; because of debate or discussion. They are taken by strength, by power, by force. By force the Ottoman dynasty seized the sovereignty and sultanate of the Turkish nation; they have maintained this usurpation for six hundred years. The Turkish nation has called a halt; it has rebelled and taken the sovereignty into its own hands. This is an accomplished fact. The question is not whether or not we are going to leave the sovereignty to the nation; the question is merely how to give expression to the accomplished reality. This is going to be, come what may. If those who are present and the Assembly and everybody see the problem in its natural light, I believe they will agree. If not, the truth will still be

> given proper expression. Only maybe some heads will be cut off.[1] As for the academic side of the matter, the learned gentlemen need be in no doubt or anxiety. Let me give you a scientific exposition of the facts.

This he did, at great length, and, when he had finished, one of the *hocas* rose to his feet and said, 'Your pardon, Sir. We had been examining the question from a different viewpoint. We have found your explanation enlightening.'

A resolution was hurriedly prepared and read at a second sitting of the Assembly that same day. There were dissenting voices, but they were shouted down. The resolution declared that the Turkish people regarded 'the form of government in Istanbul, which is based on the sovereignty of an individual, as having for ever passed into history as from 16 March 1920'. That was the date of the Allies' official occupation of Istanbul.

On 16 November 1922, Sultan Mehmed VI Vahdettin wrote to General Harington, Commander-in-Chief of the occupation armies:

> Considering my life in danger in Istanbul, I take refuge with the illustrious English State and request my transfer as soon as possible from Istanbul to somewhere else.

He signed the letter as 'Caliph of the Muslims'.

The next morning he stole out of his palace and boarded a British warship which took him to Malta. That he saved his life by so doing is indicated by a passage in Mustafa Kemal's great apologia, the six-day speech which he delivered to the G.N.A. in October 1927.

> A weak and mean creature, devoid of sensibility and perception, may enter the protection of any foreigner who will take him, but surely such a creature cannot be said to possess the qualities necessary for the Caliph of all the Muslims. . . . We Turks are a people who, throughout our history, have been a byword for freedom and independence. We have shown ourselves capable of removing from the stage the puppet-show of Caliphs who regard as permissible any humiliation which enables their worthless lives to drag on in dishonour for two and a half days longer.

[1] This was a piece of grim humour, not a literal threat. Kemal was perfectly capable of hanging his opponents when necessary, but decapitation was no longer in vogue. No doubt however these words weighed more heavily with his audience than did the 'scientific exposition' which followed.

On 18 November, Vahdettin's cousin Abdülmecid became Caliph, by a vote of the Grand National Assembly.

For a little while, Vahdettin toyed with the idea of going to the Hijaz and establishing himself there as Caliph. But the Arab world was too busy dividing itself up into nationalist States to bother with the living symbol of the unity of Islam. The thirty-sixth and last Sultan of the House of Osman died at San Remo, in 1929.

Chapter 9

The Treaty of Lausanne

At the Peace Conference which opened at Lausanne on 21 November 1922, Turkey's chief delegate was İsmet Pasha, who had been appointed Foreign Minister three weeks before. If anyone still thought that the Allies would be dictating terms to a conquered people, half an hour at the conference table must have sufficed to dispel the idea. İsmet fought at Lausanne as hard and as obstinately as he had fought on the field of battle. He was fortified by the knowledge that the Allies were far from united in their aims, despite the appearance of unity presented by the opening words of the draft treaty: 'The British Empire, France, Italy, Japan, Greece, Roumania and the Serb-Croat-Slovene State of the one part and Turkey of the other part . . .'.

İsmet argued every point, until everyone's patience but his own was at an end. Lord Curzon, the head of the British delegation, broke off the Conference on 4 February 1923, as İsmet refused to accept certain economic clauses which he regarded as limiting Turkish sovereignty. To the journalists who asked him what had happened, İsmet replied, 'Nothing. We have refused to accept servitude.'

For some weeks the Allies waited hopefully for İsmet to change his mind, and then, seeing they might wait for ever, they invited him to reopen discussions. The Conference resumed at Lausanne on 23 April. On 24 July, eloquence having beaten in vain against İsmet's imperturbability, the Treaty was signed, embodying virtually all of Turkey's demands. The major provisions of the Treaty and its accompanying Conventions were:

1. The frontier with Greece was to be the river Maritsa, but Turkey would be given an enclave west of the river opposite Adrianople, containing a section of the Adrianople–Istanbul railway, by way of reparations from Greece.

2. The frontier with Iraq would be settled by subsequent discussions with Britain.

3. The Greek and Turkish populations of Turkey and Greece respectively were to be exchanged, except for the Greeks of Istanbul and the Turks of Western Thrace.[1]

[1] This exchange of populations (arranged in a convention signed on 30 January

4. Gallipoli was to be restored to Turkish sovereignty, but the Straits were to be demilitarized. Conditions for the passage of foreign warships in peace and war to be settled later.

5. The Capitulations were to be totally abolished.[1]

Thus Turkey won the last campaign in the War of Independence. İsmet Pasha preferred a different metaphor: this time, when the journalists asked him for a statement, he said, 'We've finished the exams and now we're graduating.'

1923), though well meant, was responsible for a great deal of unhappiness, because the criterion of 'Greek' and 'Turkish' was religion: as a result of it, many Greek-speaking Muslims and Turkish-speaking Christians found themselves living in virtual exile among their co-religionists of alien speech.

[1] The Ottoman Government had declared them abolished from 1 October 1914, but this unilateral act was not recognized by the Allied Powers.

Chapter 10

From Sultanate to Republic (II)

THE FRAMEWORK of the Nationalist movement was the League for the Defence of Rights, founded by the Sivas Congress. The military victories of the War of Independence and the final triumph of Lausanne had left the League with no serious rival for the mastery of Turkey. Opposition to the growing personal power of Mustafa Kemal appeared as a splinter group within the League, known as the 'Second Group', in contradistinction to the original 'Group', 260 strong, of Kemal's closest adherents. The members of the Second Group, who numbered about forty, set themselves firmly against Kemal, objecting to each renewal of his supreme command and insisting that the absolutism of the Sultan must not be replaced by the absolutism of the Commander-in-Chief. None of this Group stood at the 1923 elections.

In April 1923 the League held a congress at which it decided to transform itself into a political party, to be known as *Halk Fırkası*, 'People's Party'.

Although there was only the one party in the new G.N.A., it was far from being a rubber-stamp assembly. There was a good deal of opposition to Mustafa Kemal's personal and patriotic ambitions, and if he succeeded almost invariably in carrying the Assembly with him it was due to the deputies' knowledge that most of the people and army had confidence in the Ghazi Pasha and were not prepared to follow anyone else. He was not a man to trifle with. He did not suffer fools gladly, if at all. Though not cruel by nature, he had no compunction whatever about putting out of the way those he regarded as obstacles to the achievement of his plans for Turkey: witness the remark he himself quoted from a conversation between Rauf, one of his major adversaries in the Assembly, and another deputy whom Rauf was urging to join the opposition: 'Emin Bey said to Rauf Bey, "This road you are setting us on leads straight to the gallows. Will you be with us there?" '

Feeling his way carefully, Kemal continued on his chosen course. On 13 October 1923, the Assembly voted that Ankara should be the permanent seat of the Government. This action had not been taken until the Treaty of Lausanne was safely signed. Although the

Nationalists would never have allowed the old capital to be wrested from them, there was clearly no sense in running into trouble if it could be avoided. To have shifted the centre of government from Istanbul would have weakened the Turkish position at the Conference, if the Allies chose to revive the old claim that Istanbul was a predominantly Greek city. As a matter of fact, İsmet Pasha had thought it necessary to mention at Lausanne that the Turks were in a majority at Istanbul and had no more fear of a plebiscite there than in any other part of their country. This contention was not disputed; and it is notable that Lord Curzon mentioned, as a factor in the Allied decision on the future of the Straits, 'the existence of the capital of Turkey and the seat of the Caliphate on the shores of this waterway'.

The decision to move the capital into Central Anatolia was in recognition of the fact that Anatolia now was Turkey, unencumbered by European, Arab or African provinces. The shift to Ankara symbolized a clean break with the Ottoman past.[1]

On 2 October the Occupation forces had left Istanbul. Four days later, Turkish troops entered the city, and with them went a delegation to represent the Grand National Assembly at the ensuing celebrations. The delegation had a hostile reception from the crowds. The probability is not that this fact influenced the Assembly to move the seat of government, but, on the contrary, that news of the proposed move had leaked out.

The transfer of the Turkish capital to Ankara is responsible for one of the oddest features of the present-day Turkish scene: the lemming-like rush of deputies and civil servants to the sea as soon as the summer comes, exchanging their smart modern flats in Ankara for the discomfort and dinginess of their ancestral homes in overcrowded Istanbul.

The decision to make Turkey into a Republic, though hotly contested, did not come as a surprise. The existing system clearly could not last. The ministers, being at that time appointed by and responsible to the G.N.A., were subjected to constant criticism, not only from members who genuinely disapproved of their decisions or actions, but also from members who thought it was time they had a turn at running a ministry themselves.

The announcement by an Ankara newspaper of 9 October 1923,

[1] A favourite Nationalist epithet for Istanbul is *kozmopolit,* which is far more offensive than the English 'cosmopolitan'. A recent Turkish dictionary defines it thus: '(A person) having no national and local colour but assuming the outward form that suits his purpose'. An example of the use of the word is then given: 'Cosmopolitans are people dangerous to the country'.

that a Republic would soon be proclaimed, aroused violent controversy in and out of the Assembly. In accordance with Mustafa Kemal's carefully laid plan, the Cabinet presided over by Fethi Bey resigned on 27 October, and the deputies tried to agree on a new Cabinet which might have a chance of general acceptance. Jealousies made this impossible; the opposition were hopelessly divided. Mustafa Kemal and his immediate circle were the only people who knew exactly what they wanted. Kemal drafted the alterations he desired to make in the Constitution ('The Law of Fundamental Organization') and waited his opportunity.

Though several members tried to pin Fethi down, he would not state the reason for his resignation. He could hardly have told the truth, which was that the Ghazi Pasha had instructed him to resign in order to precipitate a constitutional crisis. Eventually, when the deputies had talked themselves to a standstill, it was decided to seek guidance from Mustafa Kemal, who was in his house at Çankaya, where over dinner the previous evening he had told his guests, who included Fethi and İsmet, 'Tomorrow we're going to proclaim the Republic.' He came down to the Assembly and said, his tongue well in his cheek, 'Gentlemen, I understand there is some divergence of opinion about the election of a Cabinet. If you will excuse me for one hour, I shall find a solution and submit it to you.'

He used that hour to present his proposals to certain key men and, sure of their support, returned to the Assembly. Mounting the rostrum, he explained his conviction that the trouble lay in the Constitution, which he proposed to amend. Then he handed his draft proposal to a clerk, to read aloud, and left the rostrum.

> The form of government of the Turkish State is a Republic. The President of the Turkish Republic is elected by the whole Assembly from among its members . . . The President is the Head of the State. As such, he may, if he thinks fit, preside over the Assembly and the Council of Ministers. The Prime Minister is chosen by the President from among the members of the Assembly . . . The other Ministers are chosen by the Prime Minister from among the members of the Assembly and the whole Council of Ministers is then submitted to the Assembly by the President for approval.

Everybody tried to speak at once. After a great deal of quibbling, one member (evidently a Turk, not an *Osmanlı*) put the realist point of view. 'Once you've said, "Sovereignty belongs unconditionally to the nation", you can ask anyone you like; it's a Republic.

That is the name of the new-born baby. We're told some people don't like the name. Then they can lump it.'

The motion was put to the vote. There were many abstentions, but it was carried (29 October 1923). The Assembly was then asked to approve the nomination of Mustafa Kemal as President of the Republic. One hundred and fifty-eight members voted for him, out of a total of 287. The rest abstained, and he was declared elected. İsmet Pasha became Prime Minister and Fethi Bey President of the G.N.A. At last Mustafa Kemal had the power he wanted to set his seal on the new Turkey. Only one obstacle remained.

Chapter 11

The End of the Caliphate

MUSTAFA KEMAL's purpose was to make Turkey into a modern State on the Western pattern. In his view, the native virtues of the Turks had been strangled for centuries under the alien, parasitical influence of the religion of the Arabs. He took no account of the fact that Islam had been the unifying force which enabled the Ottomans to build their great empire; he knew that other Turks had built empires without the help of Islam. What needed to be done was not analogous to a simple disestablishment of the Church; Kemal meant to uproot the whole system of law and life which had given the Ottoman Turks their distinctive colouring.

Here is a description by a Turkish author[1] of the things that come into his head on hearing the word 'religion':

> The Friday prayers, the evening prayers, the Prophet's Birthday and the sweets we had on it, pilgrimages to holy places, kissing our elders' hands, the meat of sacrifice, private devotions, rosaries, alms-giving, presents, donations, clothing the orphan and comforting the fatherless, feeding the poor, the drinking-fountains built by the pious, and good works, the Koran and its recitation, circumcision, duties, prayers on special occasions, congregations, the Beard and the Cloak of the Prophet, Ramadan and its night-prayers, its meals before dawn and after sunset and the gifts we were given at them, and the holiday that ends the Month of Fasting; the Night of Power, the candles, the votive offerings, the cry of the muezzin, the mosques, the fountains, the tombs, the prostrations, the hymns, the sermons and homilies, the Amens, the invocation of the Name of God, the tears, the sobs, the seed-cakes and the lighted minarets of festal days, the sweets and the roundabouts.

Islam dictates not merely the time and place and manner of your praying, but also the way you decorate your house and treat your wife; what you say when you sneeze, how your butcher kills a sheep, how much of your property your son will inherit, how you

[1] Selâhattin Şenelt, *Bu da Bizim Şehir* (Istanbul, 1950), page 71.

6—T

trim your beard and seal your letters, and where you carry your handkerchief, and the colour of your shroud.

Such was the nature of the obstacle to Westernization, which Mustafa Kemal had decided to remove. The first step was to get rid of the Caliph.

It is not without significance that the decision to abolish the Caliphate was taken while Kemal was attending the Army manoeuvres at Smyrna, in January and February of 1924; he acted only when he was sure that the Army was solidly behind him.

Abdülmecid, who had been appointed Caliph after the deposition of Vahdettin, took his duties seriously. The conditions under which he was to hold office had been clearly laid down. He was to use the title 'Caliph of the Muslims' and no other. He should issue a declaration to the Muslim world, expressing his pleasure at being elected Caliph by the Grand National Assembly of Turkey and his disapproval of the conduct of Vahdettin. He was to quote the substance of the Law of Fundamental Organization and speak appreciatively of the achievements of the new Government of Turkey.

Never dreaming that the Caliphate itself was in danger, and confident in the knowledge that he had lent his support to the Nationalists during the War of Independence, Abdülmecid did not hesitate to defy Kemal. He signed himself 'Caliph of the Messenger of God' and 'Servitor of the Two Holy Places'. In his declaration to the Muslim world he did not mention Vahdettin, considering that to denigrate his predecessor 'would manifestly accord ill with my office and my disposition'. He proposed to attend the Friday prayer wearing a robe of honour and a turban of the type worn by Mehmed the Conqueror. Large crowds gathered to cheer his public appearances; he held court, receiving foreign diplomats and official visitors. Until the proclamation of the Republic took the wind out of their sails, many deputies had favoured making him titular Head of the State, thus preserving for Turkey the distinction of being the personal domain of the Caliph.

All of Mustafa Kemal's great rhetorical powers were brought to bear on the unfortunate authors of this last suggestion.

> For centuries our people have been compelled to act in accordance with this absurd point of view. And what happened? Millions of them died, in every land they went to. Do you know how many Anatolian boys perished in the

> sweltering heat of the deserts of Yemen? How many men died to keep Syria and Iraq, to stay in Egypt, to cling on to Africa; do you know that? And do you see what good it all did?

Yet a large body of opinion in the country was against him, and Kemal knew it. Many ordinary people who cared not a scrap whether they were ruled by a Sultan or a President, so long as he was a Turk, cared very much about the Caliph of Islam.

Unwittingly two distinguished Indian Muslims came to the Ghazi's aid. On 24 November 1923, the Agha Khan and Mr Ameer Ali, a Privy Councillor, wrote to İsmet Pasha, respectfully urging 'the imminent necessity for maintaining the religious and moral solidarity of Islam by placing the Caliph-Imamate on a basis which would command the confidence and esteem of the Muslim nations, and thus impart to the Turkish State unique strength and dignity'.[1] The letter was published in three Istanbul newspapers on 5 December. The journalists responsible were arraigned before an Independence Tribunal for high treason but were acquitted on 2 January 1924.

The fact that the Agha Khan had consistently supported the Nationalist cause was not generally known in Turkey. Since he was not an orthodox Muslim, but head of a branch of the Isma'ilis, whom orthodoxy regards as heretical, his right to a say in the matter of the Caliphate was, in Turkish eyes, non-existent. By his intervention at this stage, therefore, he frustrated his own purpose. The Kemalists spread the story that his prestige in India had been largely manufactured by the British, so that he could be set up as a native leader of Islam in opposition to Abdülhamid.

Their propaganda was effective. On 3 March 1924, the Grand National Assembly, accurately reflecting the feeling of the country, voted for the deposition of Abdülmecid, the abolition of the Caliphate and the banishment from Turkey of all members of the Imperial family.[2]

In the course of the debate, a deputy who had been travelling in India and Egypt on behalf of the Red Crescent organization (the Muslim counterpart of the Red Cross) declared that a number of representative Muslim bodies in both these countries had authorized him to offer the Caliphate to Mustafa Kemal. The

[1] For full text see A. J. Toynbee, *Survey of International Affairs*, 1925, page 571.

[2] In June 1952, this law was amended so as to allow members of the Ottoman house to return to Turkey if they wished.

Ghazi's head was not turned. Thanking those concerned for their goodwill towards him, he said:

> You know that the Caliph is a political leader. How can I accept? Those who made this offer are subjects of a King, an Emperor. If I accept, will their rulers consent? . . . Have those who wish to make me Caliph the power to execute my orders? Would it not therefore be ridiculous to assume an empty title with no reality behind it?

At the same sitting two more blows were struck at the supremacy of Islam. The Law of Unification of Instruction gave into the charge of the Ministry of Public Instruction all educational institutions within the boundaries of the Republic. Now the *medreses* were under the direct control of the Government, which shortly afterwards closed them, thus putting a drastic end to the old grievance of the Westernizers, that schools and *medreses* produced two different nations, one European, one Asiatic.

The other business before the Assembly on that eventful day was the Law which, *inter alia*, replaced the Ministry of *Şeriat* and *Evkaf*[1] by a new department of the Prime Minister's office, the Directorate of Religious Affairs.

The religious courts were abolished on 8 April. The changes so far made were embodied in a new Constitution, accepted by the G.N.A. on 20 April 1924. Its fundamental provisions were these:

1. The Turkish State is a Republic.
2. The religion of the Turkish State is Islam. Its official language is Turkish. Its capital is the city of Ankara.
3. Sovereignty belongs unconditionally to the nation.
4. The Grand National Assembly of Turkey is the sole rightful representative of the nation and exercises, in the name of the nation, its right of sovereignty.
5. Legislative authority and executive power are manifested and concentrated in the Grand National Assembly.
6. The Assembly exercises its legislative authority directly.

[1] *Evkaf* is the Turkish form of the Arabic *awqāf*, plural of *waqf* (Turkish *vakıf*), a pious endowment. The original purpose of the institution was to further some religious or charitable cause, e.g. the upkeep of a mosque or orphanage. But, from an early date, *evkaf* were created with the aim of safeguarding one's land against the confiscations practised by the Sultans: the founder of a *vakıf* might appoint himself or his heir as administrator of it. As the administrator practically had a free hand with the income of the *vakıf*, the system was open to scandalous abuse. Accordingly, at the death of a wealthy man, an investigation would be held into his *evkaf* and the profit reserved to his family would be confiscated, whereas the portion actually devoted to pious purposes would be left alone.

7. The Assembly exercises its executive power through the President of the Republic, elected by it, and a Cabinet ('Council of Executive Ministers') to be chosen by him. The Assembly has at all times the power to keep a check on or to overthrow the Government.

8. The judicial function is exercised in the name of the nation by independent courts in accordance with the law.

Chapter 12

The First Opposition Party and the Kurdish Revolt

MUCH AS THE constitutional lawyers might amuse themselves by analysing the structure of the new Turkish State, the plain truth is that it was a dictatorship. And, although one's liberal sentiments may revolt at the thought, this dictatorship was the best possible thing that could have happened to the Turks. Fully 80 per cent of them were peasants: patient, hard-working, disciplined, honest; the salt of the earth, it may be, but peasants, illiterate and living brutally primitive lives, as incapable of participating in the business of government as they were of regulating the rhythm of the spheres. Defeated in the First World War, their land overrun by foreign troops, their morale would inevitably have collapsed had there been no Mustafa Kemal to make a nation of them. This fact is all too frequently overlooked by the modern Turkish *laudator temporis acti* ('You know, my dear fellow, the Ottoman Empire wasn't half so black as the Kemalists painted it') and the modern Turkish intellectual ('Mustafa Kemal was so *uncouth*, you can have no *idea*!').

Kemal was the master, and few dared criticize him to his face. Instead, İsmet Pasha became the target; nor was this wholly unfair, because he had made himself responsible for financial matters, of which he knew nothing. Trade was well-nigh at a standstill, partly through world conditions, partly through the departure of many Greek businessmen,[1] but partly also because of the irritating bureaucratic restrictions which discouraged foreign shipping from using the port of Istanbul. Lausanne had barred foreign shipping from the coastal trade, and port services were also nationalized.

The membership of the People's Party in the Assembly was ill-assorted. Besides those who unswervingly followed Kemal, there were many sincere republicans who disapproved of dictatorship. Then there were the *Hocas*, who were bitterly antagonistic to the Government's laicist policy and had been ready even to have Mustafa Kemal as Caliph, rather than to see the total disappearance

[1] By the transfer of populations agreed on at Lausanne. See page 75.

of the Caliphate. These men began to beat the democratic drum and to wave the banner of liberalism as soon as the establishment of the Republic showed them that any other form of opposition was foredoomed. Lastly there were those former Ottoman officials and deputies who saw no hope of personal advancement under the new order.

Early in October 1924 a wave of resignations began from the People's Party, headed by Hüseyin Rauf, İsmail Canbulat and Dr Abdülhak Adnan. In November however İsmet won a vote of confidence from a Party meeting by a comfortable majority. It was subsequently decided to add the word 'Republican' to the name of the party (*Cumhuriyet Halk Fırkası*, 10 November 1924). Two distinguished soldiers—Kâzım Karabekir Pasha and Ali Fuad Pasha—resigned from their military inspectorates to return to their seats in the Assembly and to take over the leadership of the rebels, who on 17 November formed themselves into the Progressive Republican Party (*Terakkiperver Cumhuriyet Fırkası*).

Four days later İsmet's Cabinet resigned and, in an attempt at reconciliation, the premiership was given to Fethi, a highly intelligent, cultured, gentle and transparently honest liberal. The Istanbul Press began a concerted attack on the People's Party, regarding Fethi's appointment as a confession of weakness.

In February 1925 a great insurrection broke out among the Kurds of the eastern provinces.

The Kurds are a wild, pastoral, semi-nomadic Muslim people whose homelands are divided among Turkey, Syria, Persia and Iraq. Those in Turkey number about a million and a half.[1] The Kurds of modern Turkey have no separate official existence as a people, being distinguished when necessary as 'Mountain Turks'. A recent history textbook published by the Turkish Ministry of Education describes the Kurdish insurrection as 'the Eastern Revolt' and refers to the rebels as 'a gang of ignorant villagers . . . in the eastern provinces'.

The tribal organization of the Kurds is strong, but they have no articulate national voice and seem unlikely ever to gain their independence, which would entail a surrender of territory on the part of four different countries. The still-born Treaty of Sèvres had envisaged an autonomous Kurdistan, but although Lord Curzon expressed his support for this plan at Lausanne, nothing came of it. It is hard to see why the Nationalists insisted on retaining so many Kurds within the new Turkey. Presumably they wished to secure the largest possible area of Anatolia, and therefore chose

[1] See table on page 176.

to ignore the fact that the Kurds were non-Turks. The use of the term 'Ottoman–Muslim' instead of 'Turkish' in the first article of the National Pact (see page 62) is probably significant in this connection.

The revolt of 1925 was due partly to resentment at Turkish rule and a positive desire for Kurdish independence, partly to outraged religious feeling at the abolition of the Caliphate. In a desire to play down the element of Kurdish nationalism, the Republican Government stressed the religious-reactionary nature of the insurrection and used it as an excuse to muzzle the opposition Press and Party. Nor was this totally unjust, for although information is scanty, it seems clear that however loudly the Progressive Republican leaders proclaimed their loyalty to the Republic, some of them were in communication with the insurgents. It is not without significance that the first branch-office of the Party was opened in the east, at Urfa.

The leader of the insurrection was Sheikh Said of Palu, the head of the Nakşıbendî order of dervishes, who on 11 February 1925, announced that the time had come to put an end to the impious Republic and restore the Sultan-Caliph. The Kurdish tribesmen flocked to his banner and for some weeks the situation was critical indeed, with the insurgents in control of large areas of the vilayets of Bingöl, Elâzığ and Diyarbakır. Martial law was proclaimed in thirteen eastern vilayets, but things went so badly that the People's Party passed a vote of censure on Fethi's Cabinet, and, on 3 March, İsmet's strong hand resumed control. Within three days the back of the revolt was broken. In the wake of the troops came the Bloody Assize of the Independence Tribunals. The last flickers of organized rebellion were stamped out by the end of April.

Information that came to light during the trial of the ringleaders was declared by the Cabinet to be clear evidence of a connection between the insurgents and the Progressive Party, which was accordingly suppressed on 5 June, under the provisions of the hastily-passed Establishment of Order Act. On 29 June the Independence Tribunal at Diyarbakır condemned Sheikh Said and forty-six others to death, and ordered the *tekkes*—the dervish lodges—of the eastern provinces to be closed.

In spite of the ruthlessness of these measures, sporadic unrest continued in the east for many years. In June 1930 a number of Kurdish chieftains, who had fled into Persia after the 1925 rising, returned with several hundred horsemen and established themselves on Mount Ararat, whence they succeeded in defying the authorities for some months.

In 1936 the province of Tunceli was placed under martial law and 3,000 Kurdish families were deported to western Turkey. Ten years were to pass before the Government felt satisfied that there was no more danger of a Kurdish insurrection. On 30 December 1946, civil administration was restored in Tunceli and the deported families were permitted to return home.

Chapter 13

The Progress of the Reforms

ALTHOUGH the Kurdish revolt had a partly religious motive and a wholly religious colour, it had won no support from the Turks of the eastern provinces, among whom Islamic feeling was, and is, traditionally strong. They seem to have felt no sympathy with the racially and linguistically alien Kurds, brother-Muslims though they were. But this fact did not lull Mustafa Kemal into complacency. The power of religion over the minds of the Turks had to be broken, or at least weakened, if his plans were to succeed.

The body of Muslims, those who believe that there is no god but Allah and that Muhammad is His messenger, is divided into two great sections, Sunnite and Shi'ite. The schism began soon after the death of Muhammad (A.D. 632), over the succession to the leadership of the new Islamic community. The Sunnites believe that the office of Caliph belongs to the man most capable of fulfilling its duties. Theoretically it is conferred by the Ulema as representatives of the community. Although it usually passed from father to son, the formal approval of the Ulema had to be obtained at the beginning of each reign.

The Shi'ites are the partisans of Ali, the Prophet's son-in-law, and have always held that the Imamate (their term for Caliphate) belonged exclusively to his line. They consequently regard as usurpers all the Caliphs acknowledged by the Sunnis, except of course Ali himself, who held the office from 656 to 661. Whereas one of the theoretical bases of Sunnite Islam is the consensus of the community, Shi'ism is authoritarian, being based on blind obedience to the Imams, who are sinless and infallible.

Although Turkish official statistics pay no heed to this division, lumping all Muslims together, there is in Turkey a large Shi'ite (or *Alevî*, to use the Turkish term) minority. It is probably not far off the mark to set the proportion of *Alevîs* as high as 20 per cent of the population. It is commonly said that the religion of many *Alevîs* is Islamic only in name, while in reality they follow the shamanistic practices of their fore-fathers. In the absence of an up-to-date study of popular religion in Turkey, it is impossible to estimate the truth in this assertion, which is mainly made about certain of the nomadic and semi-nomadic tribes collectively known as *Yürüks*.

But the position is further complicated. Even among the nominally Sunnite majority, Islam in Turkey has always existed on two different planes. There was the Islam of the State, with its salaried hierarchy speaking with the voice of orthodoxy, and there was the heterodox Islam of the people (and not only of the common people), embodied in the great dervish orders (*tarikat*, literally 'Way'). The most flourishing of these were the popular Bektaşi and the more aristocratic Mevlevî orders. The former was firmly entrenched in the Corps of Janissaries, who were sometimes called 'Sons of Hacı Bektaş', after the semi-legendary founder of the order. Before the abolition of the *tarikats*, of which we shall presently speak, a network of Bektaşi lodges (*tekke*) covered the Ottoman Empire, each, it is said, no more than 15 miles from the next. The doctrines of the order were mystical and tinged with Shi'ism. One remarkable feature which attracted much hostile attention from the orthodox was that women attended Bektaşi ceremonies unveiled, on equal terms with men. Bektaşi apologists plausibly claim this to be a survival of Turkish pre-Islamic custom.

The comparative indifference and calm with which the abolition of the Caliphate had been greeted, contrasts strangely with the widespread disorders which followed Mustafa Kemal's next move. Although many Turks had revered the Caliphate and deplored its passing, it was too remote and exalted an institution to mean much to the average Anatolian peasant. But the clothes he wore, especially his head-dress, meant a great deal to him, distinguishing him as they did from the Christian. The Ulema wore turbans, members of the *tarikats* wore distinctive conical caps, officials and townsmen generally wore the fez. Worn in conjunction with a black frock-coat, the fez has been well described as giving the wearer the appearance of a wine-bottle with red sealing-wax on the cork. Villagers usually wore a fez with a cloth wrapped round it, turban-wise. The essential was that the head-dress should not prevent the wearer's forehead from touching the ground during prayer. During the War of Independence the Nationalists had worn the tall lambskin *kalpak* (decree of the G.N.A., 12 April 1921), and after the abolition of the Caliphate the Army exchanged their *kalpaks* for peaked caps.

During the month of August 1925, Mustafa Kemal paid an official visit to the Black Sea coastal region. He and the civilians who accompanied him wore Panama hats. Addressing an open-air meeting at Kastamonu, a town which still has a name for conservatism, he gently broached the subject of dress. He pointed out that the traditional Anatolian male attire of full gown and baggy trousers took far more material than a suit of European cut, while the fez, with its skull-cap beneath and its cloth wrapped round, was far more expensive than a European hat.

A few days later, at İnebolu, he developed the theme in more forceful terms: 'We are going to adopt the civilized international mode of dress . . . including a head-dress with a brim; this I wish to say openly. The name of this head-dress is "hat".' These words may strike the reader as slightly ridiculous. The courage it demanded to say them in a hidebound Anatolian town may be judged from the fact that, in the Turkish idiom of that time, *şapka giymek*, 'to put on a hat', meant 'to apostasize from Islam' or 'to enter the service of a foreign power'.

Mustafa Kemal then dealt with those who maintained that the hat, an alien form of head-dress, was unnatural for Turks.

> To these people let me say that they are very unobservant and very ignorant. I should like to ask them why it is permissible to wear the fez, which is a Greek head-dress, and not the hat. Further, when, why and how did they come to wear the gown, which is the garment peculiar to Byzantine priests and Jewish rabbis?

Still treading on dangerous ground, he went on:

> In the course of my trip, I have seen that our women comrades—not in the villages but particularly in towns and cities—are careful to muffle up their faces and their eyes. I should think this habit must cause them great discomfort, especially now, in the hot weather. Men, this is to some extent the result of our selfishness. . . . Let them show their faces to the world and let them have the chance to see the world for themselves. There's nothing to be afraid of in that.

On 30 September he returned to Kastamonu and, in an address to Party members there, was even more outspoken.

> The aim of the revolutionary measures we have been and are taking, is to bring the people of the Turkish Republic into a state of society which is entirely modern and civilized, in every sense and in every way. . . . It is essential that we bring about the utter rout of mentalities incapable of accepting this fact.

In this same memorable speech he lashed out at most of the old

Muslim modes of conduct, which the vast majority of Turks would have considered immutable and unassailable. He touched on the exaggerated veneration paid to the tombs (*türbe*) of holy men: 'It is disgraceful for a civilized society to seek help from the dead.' Then he passed on to give the first warning of what was in store for the *tarikats*.

> I take it that the aim of the orders can only be the well-being of their followers, in wordly and spiritual life. I cannot accept the existence, in the civilized Turkish community, of people so primitive as to seek their material and spiritual well-being through the guidance of any old sheikh, today, when they stand in the radiant presence of learning and science, of civilization and all that it means. Gentlemen, I want you and the whole nation to understand well that the Republic of Turkey can never be the land of sheikhs, dervishes, disciples and lay-brothers. The straightest, truest Way (*tarikat*) is the Way of civilization. To be a man, it is enough to do what civilization dictates and demands. The heads of the orders will grasp this truth I have stated and will at once close their *tekkes*, of their own accord. They will acknowledge that their disciples have at last attained right guidance.

He modified this hectoring tone when going on to speak of the position of women, well knowing the damage that might be done by over-precipitate action in this matter.

> A society or nation consists of two kinds of people, called men and women. Can we shut our eyes to one portion of a group, while advancing the other, and still bring progress to the whole group? Can half a community ascend to the skies, while the other half remains chained in the dust? The road of progress must be trodden by both sexes together, marching arm in arm as comrades . . .
>
> In some places I see women who throw a cloth or a towel or something of the sort over their heads, covering their faces and their eyes. When a man passes by, they turn away, or sit huddled on the ground. What is the sense of this behaviour? Gentlemen, do the mothers and daughters of a civilized nation assume this curious attitude, this barbarian posture? It makes the nation look ridiculous: it must be rectified immediately.

If the Ghazi had hoped for a positive response to his eloquence, he was disappointed. The majority of educated women had discarded the veil years before, particular impetus being given to this trend by the First World War, during which many women had entered the Civil Service. Mustafa Kemal's speech was a factor in the disappearance of the veil from the big country-towns, and the process was accelerated by increased knowledge of, and interest in, Western fashions. But, outside the big towns, the generality of women remained shut off from the equality which the Ghazi had invited them to enjoy. Nor did he ever feel strong enough to attack this last citadel of Islamic conservatism, so that even today the visitor to Anatolia may see women put their shawls over their faces as he passes, or cringe with their faces to the wall, just as Mustafa Kemal saw them, forty years ago.

But there was no other stronghold he dared not attack. Shortly after this Black Sea tour, all Government officials were ordered to replace their fezzes by hats, a special allowance being given them for this purpose. On 25 October 1925, a law was passed compelling all male citizens to wear hats with effect from 28 November. The wearing of the fez became and remains a punishable offence.

It is one of the ironies of history that although the Muslims of Turkey scarcely lifted a finger to preserve the Caliphate, an institution venerated by Muslims for 1,300 years, many of them fought like tigers to keep the head-dress whose introduction had outraged their ancestors' susceptibilities a century before. So grave were the disturbances in the north-east that a cruiser was ordered to Rize, on the Black Sea, and the Independence Tribunals went into action. Not a few *hocas* were hanged for preaching against the new law. The Government, feeling presumably that it would be as well to get all the rioting over at once, pushed through a law dissolving all the *tarikats* and closing their *tekkes* and the *türbes*—the tombs of holy men. The Independence Tribunals did their work with ruthless efficiency. The reforms continued.

Three separate systems of dating had been in use in the Ottoman Empire. For general purposes there was the Islamic calendar, the era of which begins with the Prophet's departure from Mecca in A.D. 622. It is lunar, with no intercalary months, so that when we hear of Muslim centenarians we must remember that they have lived for only ninety-seven of our years. The beginning and end of the month of Ramadan was fixed in each separate locality by observation of the new moon. The obvious disadvantages of this system for agricultural and fiscal purposes led to the introduction, in A.D. 1740, of a new official system—the *Malî* or Financial calendar, which was the Old Style or Julian year, but with an era reckoned from the Islamic year of its inception. Thus the 'Thirty-first of March Incident' of 1325 (see page 47) took place on 13 April

1909, corresponding to 22 Rabi' al-Awwal 1327, of the Islamic era. In addition, the Gregorian calendar was latterly in semi-official use for foreign correspondence.

All this tangle was swept away with effect from 2 January 1926, by the adoption of the Gregorian calendar for all purposes. On tombstones however and in obituary notices the Turks still have the disconcerting habit of giving the birth-year of the deceased in *Malî* reckoning if it occurred before 1926; thus one may read of a man born in 1305 and dying in 1964. The inscription on the statue of Mustafa Kemal at Seraglio Point includes the words 'Proclamation of the Republic 1339. This statue erected 1925'.

At the same time the old Oriental way of time-reckoning, starting from sunset, was replaced by the international method. The pained conservatives steeled themselves for the next blow.

It was plain that Mustafa Kemal, having done away with so many of the outward signs of Islam in Turkey, would not tolerate much longer the existence of Islamic law as the law of the land. Between 1870 and 1877, the doctrines of the *Şeriat* as presented in the canonical works of the great masters had been promulgated in a well-classified Turkish translation known as the *Mecelle*, 'The Code'. Before the committee which was preparing it could deal with family law and the law of inheritance, it was dissolved by Abdülhamid, in 1888, so that in these matters Jews and Christians were still governed by their own religious laws. The continuance of this state of affairs was guaranteed by Article 41 of the Treaty of Lausanne:

> The Turkish Government undertakes to take, as regards non-Muslim minorities in so far as concerns their family law or personal status, measures permitting the settlement of these questions in accordance with the customs of these minorities.

In October 1925 the leaders of the Jewish and Armenian communities formally renounced this privilege, 'in view of the forthcoming introduction of a Western civil code'.

On 5 November, Mustafa Kemal opened the new School of Law at Ankara. In his inaugural speech he spoke of the Government's intention of bringing into existence 'completely new laws' and eradicating the old ones.

In January 1926 the Greek community, reluctantly making a virtue of necessity, following the example of the Jews and Armenians. The radical nature of the reform, when it came, surprised most foreign observers: the Turkish legal experts did not waste time trying to tinker with the existing laws; instead, the Swiss Civil Code was adopted *en bloc* on 17 February, an adaptation of the Italian Penal Code on 1 March, and a Commercial Code based chiefly on those of Germany and Italy on 29 May. The new Penal Code came into effect on 1 July, the other two Codes on 4 October. Henceforth all Turkish citizens were subject to the same laws.

The opposition made one last effort. In June 1926, Mustafa Kemal was to visit Smyrna. A few days before, a conspiracy came to light, one of its members having turned informer. A bomb was to have been thrown into Kemal's car as it passed along a narrow street, and gunmen would be standing by to finish the work if necessary. The ringleader was Ziya Hürşid, a former deputy who had aroused Kemal's anger in the Assembly by voting against the abolition of the Sultanate.

Kemal made this conspiracy the excuse for hanging virtually every prominent man known to be irredeemably opposed to his policies. Evidence is lacking to show how many of those excuted had really been implicated.

Now that the opposition leaders were gone, Mustafa Kemal had no fear of what the rank and file might do. In 1927 he paid his first visit to Istanbul since 1919, taking up his residence at Dolmabahçe, the summer palace of the Sultans.

On 10 April 1928, Article 2 of the Constitution was rewritten (see page 84), omitting the reference to Islam.

Chapter 14

The Language Reform and the New History

THE STRONG didactic streak in Mustafa Kemal's temperament was never more clearly exhibited than in the next part of his campaign to change the face of Turkey.

The spread of Islam made the Arabic script known to many non-Semitic peoples, as being that of the language in which God revealed the Koran to His Prophet. Since one alphabet is as much as the majority of mankind have time to learn, the many peoples who adopted the religion of the Arabs adopted their alphabet too.[1]

These characters are ill-suited to the writing of Turkish, particularly because Turkish has eight short vowels, while Arabic distinguishes only three. Nor are their consonant-systems alike: the Arabic letter *kāf*, for example, was used by the Turks to represent *k*, *g*, *ng*, *y* and *v*. At no period was there a universally recognized rule about the spelling of Turkish words. Words borrowed from Arabic and Persian, on the other hand, retained their original spelling, although their pronunciation changed, sometimes beyond recognition, on Turkish lips.

Its unsuitability for Turkish apart, the Arabic alphabet is intrinsically difficult. Most of its twenty-eight letters change their form according to whether they are initial, medial, final or isolated, so that the beginner has to learn over one hundred characters and orthographic signs.

Schemes for improving and standardizing Turkish orthography had been suggested at various times, but all had foundered on the rock of religious conservatism. In 1924 a conference of representatives of the Turkish peoples of the Soviet Union decided to introduce Latin letters in place of Arabic.

In February of that same year, Şükrü Saracoğlu, a prominent member of the G.N.A., said during a debate on education:

[1] Compare the use of the Cyrillic characters, of Greek derivation, by Slavs of the Eastern Church (Russians, Serbs, Bulgars), as against the use of Latin characters by Slavs of the Western Church (Czechs, Poles, Croats).

> I am convinced that the heaviest responsibility for this lamentable situation rests with the alphabet . . . The Arabic letters are not suited to the writing of Turkish. In spite of so many years, indeed centuries, of self-sacrificing labour on the part of our learned men and officials, only two or three per cent of our people are literate.[1]

He went on to ask the Minister of Education what his views were, but was howled down and his question remained unanswered.

For the next few years there was sporadic discussion of the problem, with no tangible result, until Mustafa Kemal found time to devote himself to it. One of the earliest official intimations that the Arabic letters were going to be not modified but superseded came in the course of a statement by the Minister of Education in the Assembly on 20 May 1928.

> If we have been slow in this matter, it is because we are waiting for the findings of the special Commission we are appointing. The question of the alphabet will naturally be resolved in accordance with the principles accepted by the civilized world.

The obvious objection to this course, that it would cut off the younger generation from all the vast heritage of Ottoman literature, had no weight at all with Kemal; it was precisely his purpose to do this, and so to divert their attention from East to West. In fairness to him it must be remembered how very few of the Turks could read enough to share in that heritage.

The Commission did its work well. The new Turkish alphabet, though not perfectly phonetic, is a good deal more so than that of most European languages, and is immeasurably superior to any other form of writing that has been applied to Turkish.

Mustafa Kemal inaugurated the new era in person, demonstrating the new letters on a blackboard to a gathering of the great men of the State, held at Seraglio Point on 9 August 1928.[1] Then he went on tour, setting up his blackboard and easel in village streets, giving spelling lessons to the assembled crowds. Between

[1] The speaker was overstating his case. The true figure was something under 9 per cent: 1,111,496 literates out of a population of 13,648,270 (census of 1927). There has been a steady increase in literacy in the Republican period. The 1945 census showed that 35 per cent of the male population and 14 per cent of the female population were literate; figures giving no cause for complacency but indicative of a substantial improvement.

The latest official figures for the total percentage of literates in the population aged 7 and over are: 20·4 in 1935; 30·2 in 1945; 34·6 in 1950; 40 in 1960.

8 and 25 October, all civil servants had to pass a test in the use of the new letters. On 1 November, the G.N.A. passed a law introducing the new alphabet and forbidding the use of the Arabic letters in works published after the end of the year. Threats and promises made everyone hurry to acquire the new script. The deputies to the Grand National Assembly suddenly found that Article 12 of the Constitution had taken on a sinister importance for them; among those it excluded from membership of the Assembly were 'those who are unable to read and write Turkish'. They hastened to raise themselves out of the state of illiteracy into which they had so abruptly thrown themselves.

But the language reform did not rest there. Ottoman Turkish, the official and literary language of the Ottoman Empire, was manifestly unsuited to be the language of an avowedly populist Republic, because it was too difficult. Readers of Robert Burton's *Anatomy of Melancholy* will know how he adds to the difficulty of his already heavily Latinized English by dropping without warning into Latin. In the same way, Ottoman writers considered themselves free to draw on all the vast resources of the Arabic and Persian vocabularies, frequently producing sentences in which only the final auxiliary verb was Turkish, the remainder being Arabic and Persian words, strung together in accordance with the laws of Arabic and Persian syntax. Thus the Ottoman Chamber of Deputies was known as *Meclis-i Meb'usan: meclis* and *meb'us* are the Turkish forms of the Arabic words *majlis* and *mab'ūth*, meaning 'assembly' and 'deputy' respectively. The *-i* is the Persian for 'of', the *-an* is the Persian plural termination. For many years, Turks had protested against this fantastic hotch-potch, but with no great success. The Ottoman language, affected and obscurantist though it may seem to modern taste, developed naturally out of Ottoman culture, which was equally hybrid,[2] and it maintained its sway until the emergence of the Turkish nation, which preferred to speak and write Turkish.

The measures taken by the pioneers of this change, always with the active interest and encouragement of Mustafa Kemal, have come in for a good deal of criticism, not all of it justified. Their

[1] The replacement of the Arab numerals by the European numerals had already been decided upon, on 24 May 1928.

[2] A word may here be said in rebuttal of an ancient calumny against the Ottoman governing class. More than one English writer has accused them of being mentally lazy and has adduced as evidence the 'fact' that Ottoman Turkish has no way of expressing the concept of being interested. It would be as true to say that English has no way of expressing it: just as English borrowed the word 'interest' from Latin, so Ottoman borrowed the equivalent from Arabic.

first enthusiastic attempts to eradicate all Arabic and Persian words from the language confronted them with the need for 'genuine Turkish' words to put in their place. Where none could be found ready to hand, recourse was had to ancient Turkish vocabularies and to those of related languages. Thousands of words were deliberately coined from existing roots (just as in English the entirely artificial 'foreword' was manufactured in the nineteenth century to replace the Latin 'preface'). The Turkish Linguistic Society,[1] founded by Mustafa Kemal in July 1932, busily turned out glossary after glossary of 'genuine Turkish' terms. Some caught on, many did not. It is remarkable that many of the new words which have been forced into general currency by official pressure are used only in their official connotations; for example *tekel* (literally 'single-hand') was coined to replace the Arabic *inhisar*, for 'monopoly'. But it is used exclusively with reference to the State monopolies. *Bayan*, the new term for 'lady', 'Mrs' or 'Miss', is sometimes employed with a subtly offensive overtone to mean something like our 'a bit of a madam'.

To heal the damage done to their national pride by their failure to expel all the foreign words from Turkish, the reformers cooked up a new philosophy of language. The 'Sun-Language Theory' was propounded at the Third Turkish Linguistic Congress,[2] held in 1936. It taught that all the languages of mankind derived from Turkish, so that in using any Arabic or Persian word they needed, the Turks were only reclaiming their own.

This remarkable notion was of a piece with the thesis regularly advanced at that time by Turkish historians, that most of the great peoples of antiquity were either Turks themselves or had been elevated out of their natural anarchy and brutishness by the spread of Turkish civilization. Mustafa Kemal, who was a keen amateur of history, regrettably lent his support to some of the wilder manifestations of this belief. Survivals of it are to be seen in the names of two big Turkish banks, *Eti* (Hittite) and *Sümer* (Sumerian), as also in the vogue for calling children by such names as Attilâ in preference to Islamic names like İsmail.

The history taught in pre-Republican Turkey had been mainly that of the Islamic dynasties, including the Ottomans, so that Turkish history began in 1299, the legendary date of the Ottomans' attaining their independence from the Seljuks. Now the study of

[1] *Türk Dili Tetkik Cemiyeti.* In 1936 the name was de-Arabized into *Türk Dil Kurumu.*

[2] *Türk Dil Kurultayı.* A more accurate translation of its official title would be 'Turkish Tongue-Moot'.

Islamic history was dropped from school curricula, and the history of the Turks, from the time of the 'Hun-Turks', was taught instead.[1] This innovation was beneficial to the Turkish ego at a critical time and did no lasting damage.

In recent years there has been a more realistic approach to history, thanks largely to the scholarly tone set by the *Türk Tarih Kurumu*, the Turkish History Society. Some schoolteachers however, themselves products of the nineteen-thirties, continue to purvey the old mythology. Çetin Altan, one of the most penetrating observers of contemporary Turkey, gives an impression, in dialogue-form, of the sort of attitude found in their pupils:[2]

— Are you trying to learn a foreign language?
— No.
— Do you follow world intellectual movements?
— No.
— Have you a clue about economics?
— No.

And so on, till:

— Well in that case what sort of man *are* you?
— My ancestors shot an arrow from the Altai mountains which fell to earth past the Alps. Isn't that enough?

To revert to the language reform: one must remember that, although it was marred by many absurdities (as all Turks now agree), it did an inestimable service in making the written language accessible to any Turkish-speaker who takes the trouble to learn the alphabet. While we may smile at the zealot who says 'Tongue-Moot' for 'Linguistic Congress', we should at the same time appreciate the change for the better that has come over the written language generally. The Republican civil servant will now write, 'I have been thinking about your suggestion.' His Imperial predecessor would have written, 'Your slave has been engaged in the exercise of cogitation in respect of the proposals vouchsafed by your exalted person.'

For many years now the Turkish Ministry of Education and

[1] As a reaction to the general Arab disapproval of Turkey's pro-Western policy, a change occurred in this regard under the Menderes regime. On 15 March 1958, the Director-General of the Press, Broadcasting and Tourist Department told a Press conference that the Brussels International Exhibition was intended to display each nation's contribution to human civilization, and to give an idea of the past glories, traditions and future plans of these countries. Turkey, he said, would represent Islam at its peak of civilization.

[2] *Milliyet*, 17 February 1963.

private publishers have been producing popular editions, in the new letters, of Ottoman classics, and scholarly transliterated texts with modern Turkish glossaries. Consequently the treasures of the old poetry, history and *belles-lettres* are open to a higher proportion of Turks than ever before. If the younger generation, in Turkey as elsewhere, prefers to read tough detective stories and *Sélection du 'Reader's Digest'*, that is not the fault of the Turkish language-reformers.

The most depressing feature of the modern Turkish linguistic landscape is the vast mass of unnecessary borrowings from French and, to a lesser extent, English. Where no 'genuine Turkish' word was available, it was understandable (though not necessarily right) that the Westernizers should exchange Arabic for European words. Thus in 1935 the Republican People's Party changed its name from *Cumhuriyet Halk Fırkası* to *Cumhuriyet Halk Partisi*, preferring the French *parti* to the Arabic *firka*, though the other two words in the title are still of Arabic origin. But it is impossible to justify the sort of snobbery that can put up a notice reading *İzmir Enternasyonal Fuarı Enformasyon Bürosu* or can engage on a campaign for the *eradikasyon* of malaria. Although there are perfectly good Turkish words for 'horse-race' and 'winner', the Turkish punter will go to the *konkuripik* in the hope of becoming a *ganyan*. The appendix 'On Foreign Nonsense' to George Borrow's *The Romany Rye* is worth reading in this connection.

Chapter 15

The Liberal Republican Party

THE END OF 1928 found Turkey full of resentment against the Republican Government. The Republican People's Party could hardly be held responsible for the run of bad harvests which had brought great hardship to many parts of Anatolia, but hungry men are not disposed to be reasonable. And the Party was certainly to blame for some of the decline in trade, which was worsened by İsmet's illiberal financial policy.

There was much to be said for the State's undertaking the creation and exploitation of industry, at a time when domestic capital was scarce and foreign capital shy, but the Government, with the memory of the Capitulations fresh in its mind, positively discouraged foreign investors. Moreover, the Government had erred from the first in devoting so much time and money to building up Turkish industry at the expense of agriculture.

There were two strong motives at work to make the Republicans aim at industrial self-sufficiency; one economic, one emotional. Turkey simply could not afford to buy all the manufactured goods she needed; but more than that, the new Turks, whose constant cry was (and indeed still is), 'What will Europe think of us?'[1] did not wish to be considered a nation of peasants. 'Turkey is a Western country. Western countries are industrial. . . .' And out of the completion of this dubious syllogism there arose the great blast-furnaces of Karabük.

The programme of industrialization, economically unsound though it may have been, was justifiable on patriotic grounds. Not so the deliberate attack on the wealth and trade of Istanbul. From its inception the Republican Government had treated the former capital as a milch-cow. Discriminatory taxation and the creation of State monopolies in sugar, salt, petrol, alcohol, tobacco, matches and shipping had bankrupted many old-established Istanbul firms and raised the cost of living to fantastic heights. The prices of some

[1] It would be interesting if some unenterprising but industrious research-student could be induced to count how many times the phrase *geri kalmamak* ('not to remain backward', 'not to be left behind') occurs in the speeches of Mustafa Kemal and his lieutenants.

basic foodstuffs were said to have risen to 14,000 per cent above their pre-war level.

The widespread discontent at the secularist reforms was accentuated by a rumour spread by elements hostile to the Government, to the effect that Kemal intended to 'abolish Islam altogether'. In December 1928 numerous arrests were made in Bursa of members of an organization calling itself 'The Revolutionary Committee for the Protection of the Muslim Religion', five of the accused being condemned to death for plotting against the State.

In the first four months of the following year some forty Communists were arrested in Istanbul and İzmir, but the Government, soberly judging that they had no mass support, announced on 4 March that the validity of the Establishment of Order Act would not be prolonged.

But although Communism represented no immediate danger, trouble was coming to the boil. In addition to the disaffected elements referred to above, there was the small but influential class of well-intentioned liberals for whom Paris was the heart of the world. The rigorous State control of commerce and industry went against their principles, as did the single-party system and the adulation of Mustafa Kemal.[1] They had taken it for granted a Republic would be democratic, and were bitterly disappointed.

Early in 1930 a new journal called *Yarın* ('Tomorrow') began to appear in Istanbul. It rapidly gained a large circulation by its attacks on the Prime Minister, particularly for his economic policy. To everyone's surprise, the authorities did not immediately clamp down on it. On 6 April it was suspended, but for one issue only, and although its editor, Arif Oruç, was arrested for having published articles 'calculated to trouble public opinion', he received quite a mild sentence. The rumour ran that the Ghazi himself was not displeased at the attacks on İsmet, who was prodded by the episode into announcing that the Government was preparing a new economic programme.

In a letter to Mustafa Kemal, dated 9 August 1930, the former Prime Minister Fethi, who since 1925 had been Ambassador in Paris, complained that the Government's financial policy was imposing an excessive burden of taxation on the people. The failure to protect home industries and agriculture was leading to a drop in exports, while there was less and less real debate in the Assembly, owing to the reluctance of Party members to criticize the Cabinet, which had therefore become quite irresponsible. The

[1] A writer in the newspaper *Cumhuriyet* of 9 September 1930, referred to him as *ezelî ve ebedî Şefimiz*, 'our Chief, from all eternity to all eternity'.

remedy as he saw it was to create a new party. In his reply, two days later, Kemal assured Fethi that he would not stand in his way:

> I have always been whole-heartedly in favour of the system of free discussion of national affairs and the seeking of the nation's best interests by the efforts of all men and parties of goodwill . . . I am happy to see that you are with me on the essential principle of a secular republic.

Thereupon Fethi announced the formation of his Liberal Republican Party (*Serbest Cumhuriyet Fırkası*). He made known his programme in a letter to the newspaper *Yarın*. Among the ends he promised to work for were: freedom of thought and the Press, reduction of taxes, a lessening of State control, speed in dealing with business in Goverment departments, and a merciless war again corruption.

During August, Fethi conferred with Kemal, repeatedly and at great length. The Ghazi's sister Makbule was the first woman to join the new Party, a fact which was seized on as confirming the gossip of a rift between him and İsmet. But this conclusion was not justified by the evidence. The Ghazi wanted Fethi's creation to prosper *qua* opposition party; whether or not it succeeded in wresting power from the Republican People's Party was of minor importance. The schoolmasterly spirit in which he approached the experiment is shown by his words to Fethi at dinner on 10 August:

> I am sure you'll argue a great deal with the leaders of the People's Party. But these arguments will ensure the strengthening of the foundations of the Republic and I shall be happy to watch them. I can tell you now that when you're quarrelling most I shall bring you together round my dinner-table and then I'll ask each one of you individually, 'What did you say? Why did you say it? What was your answer? What was it based on?' I confess that this is going to give me enormous pleasure.

It is uncertain whether İsmet was in agreement with this scheme to convert Turkey into a parliamentary democracy, but he was too good a soldier to do otherwise than conform to Kemal's wishes, so he and Fethi ostentatiously remained on the best of terms, to the mystification of the general public, unacquainted with the niceties of parliamentary behaviour.

But the Ghazi soon realized that his experiment was premature. In September, Fethi went to İzmir to begin his election campaign.

He was given a tumultuous welcome. Cabbies and wagon-drivers provided free transport into town for those wishing to attend his meetings. Pictures of İsmet were ceremonially torn up by the crowds, and the office windows of the local Republican newspaper were stoned.

Here at last was a situation the local authorities could understand. The talk of an Official Opposition seemed irrational to them; the sight of the Prime Minister walking arm in arm with Fethi, who spent all his time finding fault with him, passed their comprehension. But crowds breaking windows were within their competence. The police opened fire, killing one or two people and wounding several. Pleased with themselves for having done their job expeditiously, they were staggered when the Governor of the province passed on to them an urgent order from İsmet: Fethi and his supporters were to be given every facility and courtesy.

The gentle Fethi himself was probably appalled by the violent passions of the crowds who turned out to cheer him. At Akhisar he was hailed as the man who was going to save Islam from the godless Republic; the crowd bore banners inscribed in Arabic with the Profession of Faith.

Municipal elections were held in October; they were to have been Fethi's first test, but he failed utterly. The local authorities everywhere may have been uncertain whether the Government had gone raving mad or was merely playing a deep game, but they did their duty as they saw it: to save the Government from itself. In a vigorous speech to the G.N.A., Fethi protested against the conduct of the elections; there had been intimidation of voters and bare-faced trickery. He attacked the ruling Party for branding all his followers as 'reactionaries and Communists'.

> If reactionary movements are so widespread in our principal towns and cities, how is it that the local officials did not detect any such movement before the municipal elections and warn the Government? If a one-party Government uses State officials and the forces of law and order to strengthen its own position . . . the ethical foundations on which the Government is based are shaken and, by preventing demonstrations of national sovereignty, the political foundation is uprooted.

It is true that the elections had been rigged from start to finish, but Fethi was wrong to play down the strength of the reactionary elements which had eagerly joined his Party. This he soon realized for himself and, when he saw that he was in danger of becoming a figurehead for the opponents of the Ghazi, he wrote to the Minister of the Interior on 17 November 1930, announcing that he had decided to dissolve the Liberal Republican Party. Turkey was not yet ready for democracy.

Another new party had been formed in September by an Adana lawyer, Abdülkadir Kemalî. His 'Popular Republican Party' (*Ahali Cumhuriyet Fırkası*) announced that its chief aim was to bring prosperity to the people. This it proposed to do by restricting Government expenditure and permitting the property of the State to be sequestered 'to pay its debt to the people'. The organizer had no time to develop this interesting theme before the Party was dissolved by order of the Council of Ministers.

Any lingering regrets, on the part of the liberals, at the speedy finish to the experiment in parliamentary democracy were dispelled in December 1930, when a hideous manifestation of religious reaction occurred at Menemen, north of Smyrna. A large crowd was demonstrating against the 'impious Republic' when a young Reserve officer, Mustafa Fehmi Kubilây, courageously ordered them to disperse. The ringleader, Mehmed the Dervish, having brought him down with a bullet, unhurriedly decapitated him. Two municipal watchmen who tried to intervene were also murdered while the crowd looked on, some approving, some indifferent. A mob then ran wild through the streets with Kubilây's severed head. The local authorities could do nothing; troops had to be sent to restore order. Mehmed the Dervish and many others were killed.

Mustafa Kemal decided to give the common people a token representation in the Assembly by nominating some hand-picked labouring men and small shopkeepers as candidates of the Republican People's Party at the forthcoming general election. That was the maximum measure of democracy for which Turkey was ready; for the next fifteen years there was no organized opposition to the rule of the Party.

Chapter 16

The Later Reforms and the Death of Atatürk

WITH THE promulgation of the new Turkish Civil Code in 1926, the disabilities imposed on women by Islamic law were swept away. Polygamy, admittedly infrequent even before the Revolution, was now illegal. A wife now had the same rights as her husband in the matter of divorce; he could no longer repudiate her by pronouncing a brief formula. Henceforth only civil divorce and civil marriage were recognized.

The Municipalities Act of 16 April 1930, gave women the right to vote at municipal elections. Their political emancipation was completed on 5 December 1934, by a law entitling them to vote in the election of deputies and to stand for election themselves. In a notable speech, İsmet Pasha urged the Grand National Assembly not to regard this measure as a favour generously conferred, but as rectification of an ancient injustice. 'In a country whose women strove side by side with the men, under the invaders' fire, labouring to bring food from the earth to sustain and defend that portion of the land which remained free—surely these people have a right to their say.'

The right was first exercised in the general election of February 1935, as a result of which seventeen women were elected to the G.N.A. out of a total membership of 399.

A minor innovation of some interest was the request made in 1930 by the Turkish Government to the world at large, that only the Turkish names of cities should be used in addressing letters to Turkey: thus Ankara, İstanbul, İzmir, Edirne; not Angora, Constantinople, Smyrna, Adrianople. Two years later it was announced that letters addressed to the old names would not in future be delivered. It is noteworthy that in this matter the Turks' nationalistic pride outweighed their strong desire to be Western in all things.[1]

[1] *İstanbul*, the name by which the former capital has always been referred to in spoken Turkish, is generally explained as deriving from the Greek εἰς τὴν πόλιν ('in the City'). There is reason to believe that this is a too-clever etymology, of

At the 1931 Congress of the Republican People's Party, the principles which had been implicit in the Turkish Revolution from its beginning were formulated for the first time. They are these: Republicanism, Nationalism, Populism, Étatism, Laicism and Reformism. The last, *İnkılâpçılık*, may also be translated 'Revolutionism'. These six principles, which were written into the Turkish Constitution in 1937, are symbolized in the badge of the Party, a fan composed of six arrows.

A feature of the 1931 Congress was the determination shown to make the Revolution reach the people, to inculcate patriotism and to eradicate the sort of ignorance which had given rise to the Menemen incident. It was decided to set up a 'People's House' (*Halkevi*) in every city and town of any size. The activities of these *Halkevis* were to be organized in nine different sections: (*a*) Language, Literature and History, (*b*) Fine Arts, (*c*) Dramatics, (*d*) Sports, (*e*) Social Assistance, (*f*) People's Classrooms and Foreign Language Courses, (*g*) Library and Publications, (*h*) Rural Activities, (*i*) Museum and Exhibitions. Any Turk, whether a Party member or not, would be entitled to use facilities provided by the *Halkevis*, though the chairman of each *Halkevi* would be chosen from the local committee of the Party.

It was emphasized that internationally-minded people and reactionaries would be equally out of place in the *Halkevis*, which were to function 'in a sincere spirit of brotherhood, embracing all citizens of a nationalist outlook and loyal to the Revolution'.

The first fourteen People's Houses were opened in February and twenty more in June of the same year. In 1949, the last full year of their existence, there were 478. The quality of their contribution to Turkish cultural life naturally varied from place to place; so much depended on the local organizers. But, broadly speaking, they proved a blessing to Turkey, serving as true Community Centres. They arranged lectures, excursions, athletics-meetings, film-shows and concerts. Many of them published books and reviews descriptive of local dialects, customs and folklore.

From 1940 onward their work was supplemented by 'People's Rooms' (*Halkodaları*) in small towns and villages, performing the

---

the sort which would derive 'beef-eater' from *buffetier* or 'Welsh rabbit' from 'Welsh rarebit'. The probability is that *İstanbul* is simply a corruption of *Constantinopolis;* this will not seem so far-fetched if it is remembered that *Nicomedia* has been corrupted to *İzmit*. On Ottoman coins it is variously called *İstanbul*, *İslâmbol* ('Islam abounding', a punning variant) or by the Arabic name *Qostantiniyya*, the choice of name for official purposes depending on the Sultan's taste.

same kind of function but with a more limited range of activities. By 1950 there were 4,322 *Halkodaları* in Turkey.

The 'Village Institutes' (*Köy Enstitüleri*) may be conveniently mentioned here, although the first of them was not opened till 1939 and they were all closed in 1954. What prompted their inauguration was a realization of the impossibility of providing qualified teachers for all of Turkey's 40,000 villages. Nor was it only a question of numbers. It had been found that town-bred teachers, when posted to village schools, tended to panic at the sight of their future homes.

At the Village Institutes, children of either sex who had completed their course at a village primary school were trained as teachers. The period of instruction was five years. The boys were also taught a craft such as building or carpentry; the girls learned such things as midwifery and the care of children. All had to join in the work of the Institute farm. Those who failed to show promise as teachers were allowed to specialize in a craft or trade that would enable them to serve their community.

The work of these Institutes was of inestimable value; in many cases the buildings were put up by the students themselves, whose enthusiasm and faith were unbounded. The best of them went back to their villages qualified not only to teach reading, writing and civics, but also as pioneers of scientific farming. They were pledged to serve as teachers for at least twenty years after graduation.

The use of the metric system of weights and measures was made compulsory in Turkey from the end of 1932. The coinage remained anomalous, with 40 *para* to the *kuruş* and 100 *kuruş* to the *lira,* until the increase in world prices drove the *para* out of circulation.

Another radical change which affected all Turks was brought about by the law making the use of surnames compulsory from 1 January 1935. Previously the Arab system of nomenclature had been in force: Ahmed, son of Mehmed, might be distinguished from other Ahmeds whose fathers were also called Mehmed by the addition of a word indicating his birthplace or a physical peculiarity: Sivaslı Ahmed or Köse ('Bald') Ahmed. Men of ancient lineage might have a family-name, but the majority of people did not. Henceforth every family had to choose a surname. Many chose patronymics, ending in *-oğlu* ('-son'). At least one dairyman called himself *Özsüt*, 'Pure-milk'. İsmet decided on *İnönü*, after the scene of his two great victories in the War of Independence. Mustafa Kemal himself became Kemal Atatürk ('Father-Turk'). The titles Pasha, Efendi, Bey and Hanim ('Lady') were declared obsolete, being replaced by the ill-conceived terms Bay and Bayan, for men and women respectively. But old customs are not so easily altered by decree. Although Hasan the baker receives letters addressed to Bay Hasan Ekmekçi, his customers still call him Hasan Bey; while his wife, officially Bayan Ekmekçi, is still Fatma Hanım for social purposes. Indeed the Istanbul telephone-directory was classified by alphabetical order of first names until 1950.

On 3 December 1934, a new law forbade the wearing of distinctive dress by clerics of any religion outside their places of worship.

In May 1935 it was decreed that all official establishments should have a weekly holiday from 1 p.m. on Saturday till Monday morning. Since 1924, Friday had been the official weekly holiday: Friday is the Muslim day of obligatory congregational prayer but is not a day of rest. Muslims find shocking the implication of the Judaeo-Christian Sabbath, that God needed to rest after His labours. The feelings of the pietists at having the infidel Sabbath thrust on them may be imagined, but the innovation was well received by the working population. Nowadays all official departments and many private establishments hang out the Turkish flag at week-ends, a pleasing custom which adds to the brightness of city streets.

. . . . .

Ever since the inauguration of the Grand National Assembly in 1920, the opening speech of each new session had been delivered by Mustafa Kemal. When the Assembly met on 1 November 1938, the speech he had written for the occasion was read by the Prime Minister, Celâl Bayar. The President himself was confined to his bed by an illness from which he did not recover. He died on 10 November, in his fifty-seventh year. His body was laid to rest in a temporary tomb at the Ethnographical Museum in Ankara. In 1953 it was moved to an imposing new mausoleum on the outskirts of the city.

It would be idle to pretend he was a plaster saint, when it is common knowledge that he loved drink and gambling and women. His vices were a part of him, a manifestation of his tremendous vitality. But they are irrelevant to a consideration of his achievement, the nature and magnitude of which have been outlined in the preceding pages and need not be recapitulated at length. He forced the Turks to emerge from the crumbling ruins of the Ottoman Empire and to become a nation, at a time when many European and Asiatic peoples were lapsing into demoralization and despair amidst the wreckage of ancient empires. With an unconquerable faith in the potentialities of his people, he drove them along the road to Western civilization, which, as we read his speeches, we see that he came close to deifying.

> Resistance to the flood-tide of civilization is in vain; she is pitiless towards those who ignore or disobey her. Civilization pierces the hills, soars in the skies, sees and illuminates and studies all things, from the invisible atoms to the stars. Nations which try to function with medieval minds, with primitive superstitions, in the presence of her might and her sublime majesty, are doomed to annihilation or, at best, to servitude or ignominy.

And again:

> We have got to be men, from every point of view. We have suffered; and the reason has been that we did not understand the way the world was going. Our thoughts, our mentality, are going to be civilized. We're not going to pay any attention to what this one or that one says; we're going to be civilized and proud of it. Look at the state of the rest of the Turks and Muslims! What catastrophes and disasters have come upon them, because their minds could not adjust themselves to the all-encompassing and sublime dictates of civilization! This is why we too remained backward for so long, and why we finally plunged into the last morass. If, in the last few years, we have been able to save ourselves, it has been because of the change in our mentality. We can never stop again. We're going on, whatever happens; we can't go back. We must go on; we have no choice. The nation must understand this clearly. Civilization is a blazing fire that burns and obliterates those who will not acknowledge her.

His personal equipment for his task consisted of a fanatical belief in the Turks' high destiny, an over-riding strength of will, a quick wit, great powers of leadership and oratory, and the patience to bide his time. His achievement was made possible by a combination of various factors: the manifest political bankruptcy of the Sultanate, the disunity of the Allied powers; and, above all, the fact that his faith in his people was not misplaced.

. . . . .

On 11 November 1938, the day after Atatürk's death, his old friend İsmet succeeded him as President of the Republic, by unanimous vote of the Grand National Assembly.

İsmet İnönü was born in İzmir on 24 September 1884. His

father, Haci Reşid Bey, was a judge; his mother came of a Turkish family that had long been settled in Bulgaria. His education was almost exclusively military. Graduating from the Staff College in 1906, he was posted to the 2nd Army at Adrianople, where he soon became a leading figure in the local branch of the Society for Union and Progress, but withdrew from active association with it after the proclamation of the Constitution, sharing Mustafa Kemal's belief that the Army should thenceforth not meddle in politics.

In 1910 he was sent to Yemen, and in 1912 was appointed Chief of Staff of the forces in that province, at the same time receiving his majority, a rank then rarely conferred on one so young. He served on the commission which drafted the peace terms with Bulgaria in 1913; a small rehearsal of the part he was to play ten years later at Lausanne. For some time during the First World War he was Mustafa Kemal's Chief of Staff, and in this period the foundations were laid of their lifelong friendship.

By the end of the war, İsmet was a colonel. He worked at the Ministry of War until the Allies occupied the capital, when he escaped to Ankara, where the Grand National Assembly made him Chief of Staff of the Nationalist forces. Of his great services during the War of Independence some account has already been given. True to his principles, he resigned from the Army once the Republic was on its feet.

His qualities tend to be under-rated. Opponents of the regime used to blackguard him on principle, while ardent Kemalists played down his abilities, to enhance the glory of Atatürk. He has often been criticized, in particular, for his blinkered vision; 'a good staff officer and nothing more' is one common verdict. But few staff officers, of whatever nationality, could have conducted the brilliant campaign which İsmet won at Lausanne, against the great European masters of diplomacy. The slogan 'Sèvres, death; Lausanne, life' is not yet forgotten in Turkey. Nor have any of his political opponents, in a land where politicians do not go about their business wearing kid gloves, ever questioned his devotion to his Chief or to the Republic.

Chapter 17

Turkish Foreign Policy till 1939

In the summer of 1940 a Turkish friend of the author's was staying in a small town in western Anatolia. One morning, as he was sitting outside a café, reading the paper, an elderly man stopped and asked him if there was any news. 'Indeed there is!' he answered. 'The Soviet Union has annexed Estonia, Latvia and Lithuania.' 'What are they?' asked the old man. 'Countries in northern Europe.' 'How strange!' was the reply. 'When I was a boy, there were only two countries. There was the Ottoman Empire and there was Moscow.'

Russian dreams of capturing Constantinople began over a thousand years ago, and a glance at the map will show why. It has always been vitally important for Russia to have her outlet to the Mediterranean unimpeded, independently of her neighbours' goodwill. During the Armenian riots of 1896, when the Russian Ambassador in Constantinople was told that British warships might be coming there to protect British interests, he is reported to have said, in great agitation, 'We shall never give up the key of our front door!' Catherine the Great, who had cast covetous eyes on the Sultan's Bulgarian and Serbian provinces and desired to be acknowledged as 'Protector' of his Orthodox Christian subjects, named a gate in Moscow 'The Way to Constantinople' in token of her ambitions. In the eighteenth and nineteenth centuries, Russia and Turkey were at war at least a dozen times.

The continuity of Russo-Turkish hostilities was broken by the revolutions that came in the train of the First World War. It was natural for the new Republics to be thrown together; the Soviet Union, with every man's hand against it, and Turkey, the defeated Power which refused to admit defeat. Moreover, the Soviets won a great deal of goodwill by returning to Turkish sovereignty the region of Kars and Ardahan, by the Russo-Turkish Treaty of Friendship and Brotherhood, signed in Moscow on 16 March 1921, in which the G.N.A. was recognized as the only legitimate ruler of Turkey.

For at least a year before this, Russia had been giving financial and military aid to the Nationalists. An Islamic Bolshevist Committee had been formed at Eskişehir, of which *The Times* wrote (6 July 1920): 'Nationalist leaders cynically avow the artificiality of the movement, created with the object of intimidating the Allies.' The truth of this view is confirmed by the curious episode of the two Communist Parties of Turkey.

The first of these was founded in May 1920, by a number of members of the Grand National Assembly, acting on orders from Mustafa Kemal. It had no connection with the Third International and engaged in no political activity; its sole purpose was to show the Russians how friendly the new Turkey was to the ideas of the new Russia. The second Communist Party of Turkey was founded two months later. It was affiliated to the Third International and aimed at establishing an orthodox dictatorship of the proletariat. Its leader Mustafa Suphi and fifteen other influential members were all 'accidentally' drowned at Trabzon on 28 January 1921. In July 1922, when the Nationalists were certain of victory over the Greeks, all Communist activity was proscribed. For Mustafa Kemal never swerved from his aim: Turkey was to become a Western State, a European State; France and Britain were his models, not Russia. But there was no change in Turkey's external policy, of which Kemal spoke in the following terms on 1 November 1924, in a speech to the G.N.A.:

> Our amicable relations with our old friend the Soviet Russian Republic are developing and progressing every day. As in the past, our Republican Government regards genuine and extensive good relations with Soviet Russia as the keynote of our foreign policy.

These words were loudly applauded.

The two countries were brought even closer together by the question of Mosul. At the Lausanne Conference, İsmet had fought hard and long for possession of this former Ottoman province, because its population was largely Kurdish, and the Ankara Government felt that the integration of the Anatolian Kurds within the Turkish Republic would be rendered more difficult by the proximity of close on half a million unintegrated Kurds outside. Curzon had insisted that Mosul belonged to Iraq, on historical, economic, racial and military grounds (giving Mosul to Turkey would have meant bringing the Turkish frontier to within sixty miles of the Iraqi capital, Baghdad), but the Mosul oil-fields were doubtless in the minds of both parties. Neither then nor now would the Allied Powers seriously consider the creation of an independent Kurdistan.

The Treaty of Lausanne left the destinies of Mosul to be settled by Turco-British discussions, within nine months of the Treaty's coming into effect. As no agreement had been reached within the time stipulated, the question was referred to the Council of the League of Nations, which decided (16 December 1925) to attach the disputed territory to Iraq.

The Turks refused to accept this ruling, and on the very next day signed a Pact of Non-Aggression and Security with the U.S.S.R. By a triumph of diplomacy, however, Turkey was persuaded to conclude a treaty with Great Britain and Iraq (5 June 1926), accepting the League's decision.

On 18 July 1932, Turkey was admitted to membership of the League of Nations. But this did not indicate a breach in her new-found friendship for her old enemy. Mustafa Kemal's watchword was 'Peace at home and peace abroad'; he was determined not to let Turkey be drawn into any risk of conflict with anybody.[1] On the tenth anniversary of the foundation of the Republic, 29 October 1933, the Government newspaper *Hâkimiyet-i Milliye* wrote thus: 'The Turkish friendship for the Russian Soviet Republic is rooted in Kemalism. This friendship was begun by Lenin and Mustafa Kemal and is now confirmed.'

The greatest worry of Turkish statesmen in the nineteen-thirties arose from the aggressive policies of Bulgaria, and of Italy, whose war-time designs on southern Anatolia had not been forgotten. Turkey therefore entered into a defensive alliance, the Balkan Entente, with Yugoslavia, Greece and Rumania, on 9 February 1934. The signatories undertook to preserve the Balkan frontiers and to consult together in the event of any threat to peace in their area.

The fear of Italian aggression is referred to in the Note which Turkey sent to Great Britain in 1936, asking for revision of the Dardanelles Convention of 1923, which forbade the fortification of the Straits: 'The situation in the Black Sea is reassuring in every respect, but uncertainty has gradually arisen in the Mediterranean.'

In response to this Note, the Lausanne Powers[2] held a conference at Montreux, which, by the Convention of 20 July 1936, restored

[1] During 1932, Turkey received from the U.S.S.R. a credit of 8 million gold dollars for industrial development. Great Britain loaned her £3 million in 1937 and £16 million in 1938.

[2] Italy did not accede to the Montreux Convention till 1938. Turco-Italiad relations had been broken off in 1935, after Italy had attacked Ethiopia ann fortified the Dodecanese. Turkey recognized the Italian conquest of Ethiopia in 1937.

full Turkish sovereignty over the Straits, subject to the following conditions:

In peace-time, merchant shipping of all nations may pass freely, as may warships of Black Sea Powers. The total tonnage of warships which other nations may send through the Straits is restricted, as is the length of time for which they may stay in the Black Sea.

If Turkey is at war, she may forbid the passage not only of enemy ships but also of neutral merchantmen carrying troops or material in support of the enemy.

In time of war, Turkey being neutral, no belligerent warships may pass the Straits, except under orders from the League of Nations or in fulfilment of a treaty of mutual assistance to which Turkey is a signatory. Neutral ships may pass, provided that they respect the laws of neutrality.

If Turkey considers that there is a threat of war, she may close the Straits to foreign warships and compel foreign merchantmen to pass during the hours of daylight.

. . . . .

On 8 July 1937, the Saadabad Pact was signed at Teheran, by representatives of Turkey, Iraq, Persia and Afghanistan. The signatories undertook to preserve their common frontiers, to consult together in all matters of common interest, and to commit no aggression against one another's territory. Some commentators interpreted Turkey's adherence to this Pact as a return to Pan-Islamism. They were wrong. Mustafa Kemal, who had set out to make Turkey a Western nation, had succeeded to a large extent in overcoming the facts of history. The facts of geography are less submissive. Turkey may not be oriental but she cannot help being eastern. It was because Kemal wished to cut her off from her oriental and Islamic past that the several Islamic Congresses held between 1926 and 1931 had received no support from Turkey. But this purely defensive Pact, which helped guard her eastern frontiers, did not constitute a threat to the principle of laicism.

. . . . .

Turkey's frontiers did not assume their present shape until 23 July 1939, when Turkish troops took possession of Hatay, the former sanjak (sub-province) of Alexandretta. This had been annexed to Syria after the collapse of the Ottoman Empire, and the Turks had accepted this situation in the Ankara Agreement with France in 1921. In 1937, Turkey took advantage of France's desire for friendship with her to press for the cession of the region, at least 40 per cent of the population being Turks.[1] France declared her willingness to grant autonomy to Alexandretta, but Turkey was not satisfied and fighting broke out in the summer of 1938. On 3 July, a Franco-Turkish condominium was agreed upon. Elections for a local Assembly were held in August, the Turks securing twenty-two out of forty seats. On the strength of this majority, they proclaimed an independent Republic of Hatay. France, being eager to win Turkey's support in the coming struggle, raised no objection when the inevitable next step was taken: on 29 June 1939, the Hatay Assembly voted for union with Turkey.

France saw the reward of her forbearance on 19 October 1939, when the Anglo-Franco-Turkish Treaty was signed at Ankara. It provided that Turkey would give Britain and France every aid and support in her power, in the event of an act of aggression by a European Power which led to a war in the Mediterranean area in which Britain and France were involved, or if they had to go to war in fulfilment of their guarantees given to Greece and Rumania in April 1939. Britain and France, for their part, would aid Turkey to the limit of their power if she were the victim of aggression by a European state, or if she were involved in a war in the Mediterranean area occasioned by any such aggression.

[1] Atatürk, still obsessed with the theories of the Nationalist historians, declared: 'The land which has been Turkish for four thousand years cannot remain captive in foreign hands.'

Chapter 18

Turkey and the Second World War

Within a year from the signing of the Treaty, an act of aggression by a European Power had brought war to the Mediterranean. One of Turkey's Allies had laid down her arms and the other was fighting alone against a monstrous enemy, while Turkey looked on.

Mustafa Kemal was dead and lesser men were in control. They had signed the Treaty because they overestimated the strength of France; they broke it because they overestimated the strength of Germany. The Nazi propaganda had been active and many Turks found its message plausible: Britain was doomed. Soon it would be Russia's turn. There was no longer any need to maintain the unnatural friendship with her which it had previously been expedient to profess.

It is only fair to say that the Turkish Press was, for the most part, in favour of the Allies from the start. Turkish policy was dictated by the desire to safeguard Turkish soil from becoming a battlefield, and by the confident expectation that the Germans would make short work of the Red Army: these two reasons led Turkey to remain neutral, despite her perfectly clear obligations toward France and Britain under the 1939 Treaty, until February 1945.

In June 1941 Turkey negotiated a Non-Aggression Pact with Germany (ratified 6 July) and continued to sit adroitly on the fence.[1]

The influence of Nazi ideas was certainly in some measure responsible for the shameful episode of the *Varlık Vergisi*, the 'Property Tax', which a Turkish writer[2] has called 'the last manifestation of the vampire-mentality of extortion'. It seems highly improbable that such a thing can occur again, but the facts deserve to be placed on record, because they largely explain why, despite

[1] For a detailed account of events in Turkey during the war, see *The Middle East in the War*, Royal Institute of International Affairs (Oxford, revised edition 1953).

[2] Faik Ökte, in his *Varlık Vergisi Faciası* ('The Tragedy of the Property Tax'; Istanbul, 1948). Faik Ökte was Director of Finance (*Defterdar*) of Istanbul at the time of the Tax and played a major part in its enforcement.

the removal of all legal disabilities, the non-Muslim subjects of Turkey still feel qualms about the security of their position and cannot yet regard themselves as integrated in the citizen-body.

At the time of the French collapse in the summer of 1940 the Turkish Army was mobilized, imposing that disproportionate burden on the national income which still cheats the Turks of the full reward of their labours. At the same time, the world-wide rise in prices was beginning to affect the Turkish economy. The index of wholesale prices rose from 100 in 1938 to 126·6 in 1940; 175·3 in 1941; 339·6 in 1942; reaching a maximum of 590·1 in 1943. The farmers benefited enormously by this, but Turkish farmers, however prosperous, paid no tax whatever on the income from their produce. Some forty per cent of the revenues of the Ottoman Empire had come from agricultural tithe, but tithes had been abolished by Fethi's Cabinet in February 1925.

The Government decided that the times called for extraordinary measures to increase State revenues. By a law passed on 11 November 1942, the Assembly ordained a capital levy on all property-owners, 'big farmers' and business-men, including 'those who, while not being merchants, commission-agents, brokers or middlemen by profession, have at any time since 1939, be it only on one occasion, received money or payment in kind as brokerage or commission, under any name whatsoever, through engaging in commercial transactions'. In the preamble to the law, the levy was declared to be 'aimed at those who have amassed inflated profits by exploiting the difficult economic situation but do not pay commensurate taxes. Its purpose is to compel them to participate in the sacrifice demanded by the extraordinary circumstances in which we find ourselves, to an extent commensurate with their profits and capacity.'

These stern but righteous sentiments were unfortunately vitiated by the manifest intention of the promoters of the law that it should weigh very much more heavily on non-Muslims than on Muslims. The amounts to be paid were fixed by local committees of Government officials, according to their own estimates of the individual's ability to pay. There was no appeal against their assessment; the property of those who could not pay was sold at public auction and, if the price obtained was insufficient, they were sent away to forced labour under the direction of the Ministry of Public Works. The names of those liable to pay in each locality were placed in one of two lists, the *M* list or the *G* list; *M* standing for *Müslüman*, 'Muslim', and *G* for *Gayrimüslim*, 'non-Muslim'. It being a principle of international law that a State may not tax foreign subjects more heavily than its own nationals, orders were given that foreign residents in Turkey were to be treated like the *M*s, except for Jewish subjects of the Axis Powers. In practice, not only these but many other foreigners were assessed as *G*s; citizens of Greece, in particular, tended to be lumped together with the indigenous Greeks of Turkey, because of the defective system of identification records then in operation. In general, the non-Muslim paid up to ten times the amount levied from a Muslim of the same estimated wealth. Later a *D* list was instituted, for *Dönmes*,[1] who paid twice as much as Muslims.

This disgraceful chapter in Turkish history was ended by a law of 15 March 1944, releasing the defaulters from their forced labour and writing off amounts still unpaid. The Treasury had benefited by some 221 million lira (at that time roughly equivalent to £20 million), but against this must be set the dislocation brought about in the commercial life of the country through the ruin of many old-established businesses. Worse still was the blackening of the good name which the Republic had been winning for itself abroad by its scrupulousness in the payment of its share of the Ottoman Public Debt and the yearly instalments of the purchase price due to former owners of State-owned enterprises, as also by its humane reception of so many refugees from Nazi Germany.

But if we reflect for how many centuries it had been not merely a custom but even a religious duty for Turks to discriminate against non-Muslims, we shall perhaps not judge them too harshly for this atavistic relapse.

The end of the *Varlık Vergisi* coincided with the general realization the Germany had lost the war. In April 1944, an Allied *démarche* brought about a suspension of supplies of chrome to Germany; after the U.S.S.R., Turkey was at that time the world's largest producer of this essential war material.

The following month the Government at last took action to suppress a Nazi-inspired racialist Pan-Turanian movement which had been winning converts amongst university students in Ankara.

. . . . .

Turkey's claim that her entry into the war on the Allied side

[1] Descendants of the Jewish followers of the false Messiah, Sabbatai Zevi (1632–1675), who ostensibly became converts to Islam with him when he was forced by the Sultan to renounce his pretensions. They long maintained their identity as a sect, secretly following certain Jewish practices as well as some peculiar to themselves, and not intermarrying with Jews or Muslims. In recent years they have reputedly done their best to be assimilated into the Muslim community, abandoning their non-Muslim practices.

would only have meant diverting large Allied forces to her assistance from other fronts may have been justified at first but lost its validity once the tide had turned. This point was clearly brought out in a speech made on 24 May 1944, by Winston Churchill. In it he spoke of 'the great disappointment which I had last October . . . after the Italian collapse we could have gained command of the Aegean with Turkish forces, but for an exaggerated attitude of caution on the side of Turkey . . . The Turks magnified their danger . . . their military men took the gloomiest view of Russian prospects in south Russia and the Crimea . . . and demanded huge supplies . . . so the Allies have ceased the arming of Turkey.'

The Turks' caution was to some extent understandable, in that they had had a first-rate army by 1939 standards, but had seen it growing obsolete as the war progressed. Despite the considerable Allied deliveries of equipment, they wanted more modern tanks, aircraft, self-propelled artillery and radar. The disappearance of Italy from the arena had done nothing to quiet their fears; the utter defeat of the *Wehrmacht* in the East served only to strengthen Turkish apprehensions about Russia's future actions.

On 14 June 1944, it was announced that Turkey had consented to ban the passage through the Straits of the thinly-disguised German naval auxiliaries which had long been going through to the Black Sea, in defiance of the Montreux Convention and the 1939 Treaty with Britain and France. The next day, Numan Menemencioğlu, who as Foreign Minister had been primarily responsible for Turkey's wartime policy, was replaced by Şükrü Saracoğlu.

The black-out regulations in Istanbul and the Black Sea towns were intensified when Bulgaria capitulated to the Red Army in September 1944. A joke that went the rounds in Istanbul at the time, though totally apocryphal, is worth recording as illustrative of the Turkish state of mind. The story was that the Russian Ambassador had called on the Turkish Foreign Minister, to say: 'I am instructed by my Government to assure you that there is no need for you to inconvenience your people by this black-out. When we attack, it will be in the day-time.'

The 1925 Treaty with the U.S.S.R. had been renewed for a further ten years in 1935, but in March 1945 the Soviet Government gave notice that they would not renew it again in the following November, when it was due to expire. In June the U.S.S.R. declared her willingness to negotiate a new Treaty of Friendship if Turkey would agree to hand over Kars and Ardahan to Armenia and Georgia respectively and to accept Russian participation in the defence of the Straits. This suggestion was immediately turned down.

On 22 February 1945, Turkey declared war on Germany and Japan with effect from 1 March, as the Yalta Conference had decided that only those nations which had declared war on the Axis by the latter date would be invited to take part in the inaugural Conference of the United Nations at San Francisco.

Chapter 19

Post-War Developments in Turkey

THE LACK OF success of the various attempts to break the Republican Party's monopoly of power had not discouraged those who, for one reason or another, were opposed to the existing order.

The repressive measures that had been taken during the war, in an effort to keep the Press in conformity with the Government's delicately ambidextrous policy, had intensified the liberals' desire for a loosening of the reins. The commercial class, enlarged and enriched by Turkey's wartime neutrality, wanted more outlets for their capital than State socialism allowed. Labouring men, suffering from inflated prices and forbidden by law to strike, were ready to support any party strong enough to challenge the Government. The minorities, still reeling under the savage and unexpected blow of the *Varlık Vergisi*, felt that any change could only be for the better. The fanatically religious were, as ever, watchful of a chance to undo the Kemalist reforms.

The first attempt at organizing the opposition came from the National Recovery Party (*Millî Kalkınma Partisi*), founded in September 1945 by Nuri Demirağ, an outspoken advocate of free enterprise on the American model. It attacked the étatism of the Republican People's Party and accused it, quite unjustly, of being pro-Russian. Whereas Turkey's face had been set resolutely westward by Mustafa Kemal and the Republican Party, the new party proposed to establish close ties with the Muslim States of the East. The absence of popular response to this programme may be attributed to two reasons. In the first place, national pride, born during the years of revolution, had swamped, in the majority of Turks, any feeling of kinship they may have had for the Muslim world. Secondly, many of those who might have been sympathetic hesitated to link themselves to the new party because of memories of the fate of previous attempts at opposition.

These same fears persisted until 1 November 1945, when İsmet İnönü, addressing the G.N.A. at the beginning of the new session, declared himself in favour of having an opposition party: the Republican Government, he said, had never yet been in a position to permit argument about what needed to be done, but now that the war was over there was more room for democracy in Turkey.

This speech had been prompted by a serious split within the Republican ranks, which began in the summer of 1945 and culminated in the expulsion from the Party of three prominent members—Adnan Menderes, Mehmed Fuad Köprülü and Refik Koraltan—and the resignation of a fourth—Celâl Bayar. On 7 January 1946, these four men founded the Democratic Party (*Demokrat Parti*).

Mahmud Celâl Bayar was born in 1884, near Gemlik, on the south-east corner of the Sea of Marmara. His father, Abdullah Fehmi, though a mufti by profession, was a man of enlightened views and gave his son a European education, partly at the school of the Alliance Israélite at Bursa. On leaving school, he entered the Bursa office of the Deutsche Orientbank, devoting his spare time to the local branch of the Society for Union and Progress, of which he became chairman at the age of twenty-four. After the proclamation of the Constitution, he left the service of the Bank and became full-time secretary of the Smyrna branch of Union and Progress. He played a pioneer part in the War of Independence, working against the foreign invader even before the occupation of Smyrna, and had an exciting career as a leader of the Nationalist forces. He was elected to the last Ottoman Parliament as deputy for Smyrna and made his way to Ankara when that body was suppressed in 1920. In the early days of the Grand National Assembly he held several Cabinet posts: Minister of Economic Affairs, Deputy Foreign Minister, then Minister for Resettlement, with responsibility for, *inter alia*, the exchange of populations with Greece that had been decided on at Lausanne. In 1924 he resigned this office to take charge of the newly-formed *İş Bankası* ('The Business Bank'). In 1932, having put this new enterprise on its feet, he returned to the Ministry of Economic Affairs, where he rendered notable service in the development of State-owned factories. In 1937 he became Deputy Prime Minister and then Prime Minister, a post which he held till January 1939.

Adnan Menderes, born in 1899, was educated at the American College in Smyrna and the Faculty of Law at Ankara, but devoted much of his time to farming his large estates, on which he introduced a number of modern improvements. His American education contributed much to his anti-étatist views. The Premiership which he held from 1950 to 1960 was his only public office.

Refik Koraltan, born at Divriği in 1891, was also trained as a lawyer. He held several senior appointments in the police and judicial services, presided over one of the Independence Tribunals and was vice-chairman of the Republican People's Party group in the G.N.A. He left the Assembly in 1936 and held several provincial governorships, returning to parliamentary life in 1942. He was known as a rather slow and unimaginative but competent administrator. A reasonably well-authenticated piece of malicious gossip ran as follows. While Menderes was speaking during the Assembly debate on the 1947 budget, Âkil Muhtar, a Republican deputy who was also a medical man, having watched him intently for some time, turned to his neighbour, the Prime Minister Recep Peker, and whispered, 'The man's a psychopath!'—*psikopat*. The Prime Minister rose and tactlessly informed the House of this diagnosis, whereupon Refik Koraltan jumped to his feet and shouted indignantly, 'Arkadaşımız piskopos değil!—Our colleague is not a bishop! He's a good Muslim!'

The fourth Democrat leader, Mehmed Fuad Köprülü (born 1890), was a descendant of the great Köprülü dynasty of Grand Viziers, whose stern efficiency staved off the collapse that threatened the Empire in the seventeenth century. Before entering public life, Mehmed Fuad was Turkey's most outstanding scholar. His work on the history and literature of the Turks had won him an international reputation; the Universities of Heidelberg, Athens and Paris had conferred honorary doctorates on him. The decision he made, in 1943, to devote himself exclusively to politics was a great loss to scholarship.

These then were the men who, in 1946, broke away from the Republican People's Party. They considered that the need for étatism was passing and that Turkey's economy could best be served in future by the encouragement of private enterprise. They claimed also that the traditional concentration of power in the hands of the executive, with all the restriction of personal freedom that it involved, was inconsistent with Turkey's claim to be a modern Western state and with her support of the Charter of the United Nations.

The correctness of the latter belief was immediately demonstrated by the repressive measures taken against the new party, especially in the eastern provinces, where Governors regarded opposition as synonymous with insurrection. It must be recorded to the everlasting credit of İsmet İnönü that he published an unequivocal statement of his desire that the opposition party be allowed to work without hindrance from over-zealous officials. He then made a tour of the eastern provinces to press home the point, accompanied by a representative of the Democratic Party.

Celâl Bayar referred to this matter in the course of a speech to the second congress of the Democratic Party in June 1949. The passage is worth quoting for the clear picture it paints of conditions in the east of the country.

> One of our colleagues has asked why we detailed Nuri Özsan to accompany the President of the Republic on his eastern tour. Our answer is simple. We regard the country as the homeland of a number of people, all possessed of equal rights. Easterners and Westerners and men from Central Anatolia all have the same political rights. There is to be no distinction between them, in fact or in law. This is one of the main planks in the Democratic platform. These eastern provinces have many a time valiantly shed their blood in defence of their fatherland; they have frequently known the disaster of invasion. For this reason it has not been possible for government to be established there in the same regular form as elsewhere; exceptional laws have been laid down for those parts. Life in the east has not been so tranquil as in the west.
>
> Reproaches have been showered on us from the east; they want to know why we don't visit them. We should like our organization to be established in Siirt and Muş as quickly as we hope to see it established in Istanbul and Ankara. But everything is dependent on practical considerations. In the early days, joining the Democratic Party meant taking a considerable risk. In the east too, the weapons put into the hands of the Government and the gendarmerie—and the gendarmes are also sons of this country—have been given them for the purpose of defending the citizens' rights and liberties. But, in the east, the number of people who comprehend the nature of their duty is smaller; the fear of joining the Party was greater. Our friends there wondered if our hesitation in coming to see them was because we regarded them as a colonial people. . . . The President of the Republic said to me: 'I am going to the east. There I intend to say that the country must have a multi-party administration. I shall insist on equal treatment for all citizens; I shall order the *Valis* (Provincial Governors) to act impartially. I should like to have a reliable member of your Party by my side when I do this, to be a witness.'

İnönü's sincerity in this matter can scarcely be questioned, but he failed to persuade the local authorities to follow his statesmanlike lead. Nor is this really surprising. The officials had, for twenty years and more, been enforcing the dictates of the Government, which was but a manifestation of the Party to which they all belonged. They could not be expected to facilitate a new party's efforts to unseat that Government.

Elections were held in July 1946, in which Democratic candidates stood for 273 of the 465 seats. Nobody nowadays will seriously deny that the 1946 elections were marred in many districts by intimidation of voters and skulduggery in the counting. Even in a fair election the Democrats would probably not have gained a majority; as it was, they won sixty-two seats.

The new Republican Cabinet, headed by Recep Peker, did not long enjoy the ill-gotten fruits of office. It was assailed by the Democrat opposition in the Assembly and by the popular ex-Chief of the General Staff, Marshal Fevzi Çakmak, who had been elected as an Independent. But it had also to face the attacks of a group of young Republicans, who accused it of impeding President İnönü's efforts to liberalize Party policy and so to steal the Democrats' thunder. The Government did yield on one important matter of principle: from 2 July 1947, Muslim religious schools were allowed to reopen, but attendance at public elementary schools remained obligatory.

In September of the same year Recep Peker resigned, although he had recently won a vote of confidence, because he felt that İnönü was on the side of the rebels, several of whom were given portfolios in the succeeding Cabinet of Hasan Saka.

The Democrat Party underwent an even more serious split than its rival. The result was the emergence of the National Party (*Millet Partisi*) in July 1948. Its founders regarded the Democrat leadership as wanting in vigour, and certainly the level-headedness of Celâl Bayar and Adnan Menderes, and their refusal to abandon the cardinal principles of Kemalism, were disappointing to many who had seen in the rise of the new party a chance to undo the work of the 'godless Republic'. Some Republicans too joined the National Party, of which Marshal Çakmak accepted the honorary presidency. The Government made another concession to public opinion by introducing lessons in the principles of Islam as an optional subject in the fourth and fifth classes of primary schools—i.e., for children aged ten to twelve.

At the 1949 Congress of the Democratic Party many speakers rose to advocate revolt in the event of a repetition, at the next election, of the malpractices of 1946. Celâl Bayar was far too prudent to listen to such hot-headed talk, but it may have helped persuade the Republicans of the vanity of hoping to cling to power by perpetually rigging elections; and certainly the Republican officials who had falsified the returns in 1946 knew better than anybody the strength of the opposition in the country.

In February 1950 the G.N.A. passed a new electoral law, which had been drafted with the approval of both major Parties. It provided for secret ballot and public counting of votes (a reversal of the procedure previously in force), equality of parties in the allocation of political broadcasts, and supervision of the elections by the judiciary. The National Party deputies voted against the new law, because it did not meet their demand for proportional representation.

Both Republicans and Democrats adopted the innovation of permitting the constituency parties to nominate the great majority of candidates. On 14 May, 1950, Turkey went to the polls.

The results were variously described in the next day's newspapers as a landslide and a bloodless revolution. The latter term was the more accurate. The Democrats had won 408 seats, the Republicans 69, National Party 1 and Independents 9. Details of the voting are given in the table on page 136.

The striking disproportion between the percentages of votes cast and the number of seats won by each party is due to a peculiarity of the Turkish electoral system. Every voter has a choice between the lists of candidates nominated by the various parties for all the seats allocated to the vilayet in which he lives.[1] The number of seats depends on the population of the vilayet.

In British elections it is a fairly safe assumption that Chelsea will return a Conservative and Walthamstow a Labour man. If we used the Turkish system, residents in Chelsea and Walthamstow and all the other London boroughs would have to choose between a Conservative and a Labour list of candidates, and a simple majority would decide whether the whole County of London was to be represented in Parliament by an all-Conservative or an all-Labour group of members. There is nothing to prevent anyone from being nominated in more than one constituency; thus Adnan Menderes was returned for both Istanbul and Aydın, Celâl Bayar for both Istanbul and Bursa.

The reasons for the Democrats' success are not hard to seek. Once İsmet İnönü had assured the electorate that there wasn't a

[1] More accurately, every voter must put into the box a list of all the candidates he wishes to see elected for the whole vilayet. But most voters are content to use one of the printed lists distributed by the political parties, and few bother to write out the names of the individuals they prefer. Thus in 1957 the Democrats won 44 vilayets outright, the Republicans 18. The Democrats won 2 out of 3 seats for Bingöl, 3 out of 4 for Muş, and 1 out of 7 for Niğde, the remaining seats for these vilayets going to the Republicans.

catch in it, all the elements desirous of change, by far the most numerous being the pietists, hastened to strike their blow against the Government which had ruled them for a quarter of a century. The Democrats, however, had not passively waited for this to happen; for many months before the elections their organization was hard at work, particularly in country districts, promising everyone everything. Farmers were assured that a Democrat victory would mean higher prices for their produce, the religiously-minded were promised a relaxation of the anti-Islamic ordinances, the minorities were told they could expect compensation for their losses under the *Varlık* law.

So the Republican People's Party went down, and with it went its leader, İsmet İnönü. By a majority vote of the new Assembly on 22 May 1950, Celâl Bayar was elected President of the Republic and Adnan Menderes became the first Democrat Prime Minister. The Democrats had previously suggested that İnönü should resign from the Party and retain the Presidency of the Republic, whatever the election results might be. But that stubbornness in his character which had served Turkey so well would not let him take out this easy insurance against the electoral defeat of which he well realized the likelihood.

Cynics may say that in permitting free elections the Republicans were only making a virtue of necessity. Yet it must be remembered that had they wished to cling to office they could have used the perennial fear of Russia's intentions as an excuse to prolong the state of emergency. Their refusal to adopt this course must stand to their credit; the dignified and orderly way in which they abdicated the power they had wielded for so long compels our admiration.

Suggestions that the Republican Party's decision to hold fair elections was due in part to American pressure are supported by no evidence, and it is hard to see what inducement could have been offered to make the Republicans commit political suicide. On the other hand, there is some justification for thinking that the State Department made a gentle attempt to influence the Turkish electorate. Before the 1950 elections the American Information Service distributed copies of a handsome brochure in Turkish, entitled *A Goverment Founded by the People*, describing the American political system. On the first page, in large type, was a translated passage from the Declaration of Independence, beginning 'We hold these truths to be self-evident . . .' and ending '. . . it is the Right of the People to alter or to abolish it, and to institute new Government, laying its foundation on such principle and organizing its powers in such form, as to them shall seem most likely to effect their Safety and Happiness.' The sentence following was omitted: 'Prudence, indeed, will dictate that Governments long established shall not be changed for light and transient causes.'

The new Turkish Government's attitude towards private enterprise certainly made it more acceptable to America than its predecessor had been, though this is not to be taken as belittling the enormous scale of American generosity to Turkey while the Republican People's Party was still in office: during the first two years of the European Recovery Programme (ending 31 March 1950) Turkey had received grants totalling 82½ million dollars (excluding grants for military purposes), in addition to vast loans.

Chapter 20

The Democrats in Power, 1950–1960

COMPARATIVELY few ordinary citizens had really envisaged the possibility that the Republican People's Party might be defeated. When the election results became known, there was, metaphorically speaking, an awed hush throughout Turkey, as the voters realized what they had done. A usually well-informed Turk, when asked whether the change of Government would involve the replacement of officials known to be Republican Party supporters, replied, 'How do *I* know? How can *anyone* know? There are no precedents for this. This is a revolution.'

As a matter of fact, one of the first acts of the new Government was to dismiss the chief of the Istanbul broadcasting station. This unfortunate had occasioned a riot outside the station doors, by refusing to cancel the programme of light entainment that had been arranged for 10 April, on which day Marshal Fevzi Çakmak died. But otherwise the Democrats behaved with great restraint; there were no large-scale dismissals of civil servants. Postage stamps bearing the head of İsmet İnönü were withdrawn from sale but were subsequently reissued, with a heavy black overprint hiding the features of the former President, for franking official mail.

The most remarkable immediate consequence of the change of Government was an outbreak of fez-wearing in the eastern provinces. This may sound trivial, but its significance must not be overlooked: it carries the clear implication that the Democrats were expected to be more tolerant of reversions to the old religious way of life, and it is not unreasonable to conclude that this expectation was based on the pre-election promises of Democrat canvassers.[1]

It cannot be too often stated that three-quarters of the Turkish population are *köylü* (villagers), attached as strongly to their ancestral religion as to the soil on which they live. Nor are the remaining quarter by any means wholly irreligious. Far too much high-flown nonsense has been talked and written about the inborn

[1] A small straw in the wind: during the summer of 1953 the author saw, in a railway-siding in northern Anatolia, a waggon with the words 'Long live Celâl Bayar! Long live Adnan Menderes!' chalked on the side in Arabic script.

love of democracy which inspired the Turkish electors in 1950: the most powerful single motive at work was a desire to see Islam restored to its former place in the life of Turkey.

One step was taken down this road on 17 June 1950. From that day, which was the beginning of Ramadan, the month of fasting, the call to prayer was permitted to be recited in Arabic instead of Turkish.

A further instalment of the Democrats' debt to Islam was paid in March 1952, when religious instruction was added to the curriculum of the Village Institutes.

The Democrat Government begin to implement another pre-election promise in August 1951, with the handing over of the State Maritime Administration to a new corporation known as the Maritime Bank (*Denizcilik Bankası*), 51 per cent of its capital being subscribed by the Government and the remainder by private investors. Private firms were allowed also to participate in the manufacture of alcoholic drinks, and in February 1952 a Bill to end the State monopoly of the match industry was given its first reading, becoming law in May 1952.

August 1951 also saw the passage through the Assembly of a Bill to encourage foreign investment, whereby foreign investors would be able to transfer their profits out of Turkey, and, in the event of liquidation, their capital too, in the original currency.

By the end of 1955 some 150 applications from foreign firms had been approved, but Turkey's worsening economic position discouraged all but thirty from actually putting their money into the country.

For this situation a combination of chance and human misjudgment was to blame. Where chance came in (though Democrat supporters saw it as a mark of divine approbation) was that for the first few years of Democrat rule weather conditions were exceptionally favourable. From 1951 to 1953, harvests were the best in living memory. Cereal production in 1953 was 14 million tons, an 85 per cent increase over 1950. From 1952 till 1954, Turkey was a major exporter of wheat. But in 1954 harvests reverted to normal, or worse; not until 1958 did Turkey have another wheat surplus. In October 1954 the government had to import some 600,000 tons of wheat (half for consumption and half for seed), the deficiency of the crop having been aggravated by hoarding in the hope of higher prices.

The misjudgment was on the part of Menderes, though it must be said that there is some evidence that Celâl Bayar was his evil genius. Adnan Menderes was a man of great personal magnetism and high intelligence, with a deep understanding of the mind of the peasant. But his understanding of the mind of the intellectual —a category which in Turkey includes the officer—was not so profound. He had two other defects, which brought his country to insolvency and himself to the gallows: his addiction to free enterprise blinded him to Turkey's need for a planned economy if she was ever to develop her potentiality to the full, while his pathological vanity made him deaf to argument and intolerant of criticism.

His domestic policy was to maintain himself in power by giving the peasants what they wanted: loans for farm equipment,[1] public works in country districts, a relaxation of the official antipathy towards the more obscurantist manifestations of Islamic religious feeling. His economic policy was simple, ingenious and, to the economist, horrifying. It was to build up Turkey's agriculture and industry to the limit by importing all the necessary capital equipment without worrying about how to pay for it, in the sure knowledge that Turkey's allies would foot the bill. By the end of 1952, her debt to the European Payments Union amounted to $147·5 million. Inflation grew; with the official rate of exchange standing at 7·84 liras to the pound sterling, the black market rate was 12 in 1953, 15 in 1954 and 30 in 1956.

Opposition criticism was loud against him, and this he would not endure. As early as 1951 the *Halkevis* had been closed and their assets confiscated to the Treasury. This meant a heavy loss to the Republican People's Party, both financially and in terms of its ability to influence the electorate. The cessation of the educational, cultural and social work of the *Halkevis* constituted an even heavier loss to the people at large.

In July 1953 action was taken against another organization regarded as subversive: the National Party, which was accused of working for a restoration of the Islamic State and a reversion to the use of the Arabic script and to the veiling of women. The Party was suspended from activity and its offices closed. Its leaders were brought to trial on 26 September 1953, and judgment was delivered on 27 January 1954: the Party was dissolved and the leaders sentenced to one day's imprisonment and a nominal fine. They were understandably not deterred by this remarkably lenient

[1] Figures given in 1950 by the International Bank for Reconstruction and Development indicated that 8,000 tractors were the economic optimum for Turkey, 'even allowing for cooperative use'. By 1960 there were over 42,000, many of which 'still represent unpaid debts to the Agricultural Bank' (Nuri Eren, *Turkey Today—and Tomorrow*, Pall Mall Press, 1963, p.113).

punishment for having tried to overthrow the Constitution and, on 10 February 1954, they founded a 'new' party, the Republican National Party (*Cumhuriyetçi Millet Partisi*), which ostensibly accepted the principle of the division between religion and State (as it had done in its previous avatar) but demanded the recognition of 'full religious liberty'.

The Republican People's Party had protested against the suspension of the National Party in July 1953, regarding this action as the thin end of the wedge, in view of the imminence of the general election. They held that, in attacking the National Party, the Democrats were concerned less with the danger to the secular Republic than to their own majority. This belief, they maintained, was justified by the nominal nature of the punishment meted out to the National Party leaders; the Government's real aim was to dissolve the Party, not to defend the laws.

The attack on the main opposition Party was renewed on 14 December 1953, with the passage of a Bill confiscating all the property of the Republican People's Party. The Democratic Party claimed that its rival had embezzled huge sums of money during its long monopoly of power. The Republicans argued, not unreasonably, that all the leading Democrats had been members of the Republican Party in their time and bore their share of any guilt there might be. That Party funds and Government funds had been mixed up is hardly surprising; the Republicans had not regarded themselves as temporarily exercising the powers of government. The Party *was* the Government and, until the end of the Second World War, had not seriously considered the possibility that things might some day be different.

On 16 December 1953, the premises and plant of the leading Republican newspaper, *Ulus* ('The Nation'), which Mustafa Kemal had founded in 1920 under the title of *Hâkimiyet-i Milliye* ('National Sovereignty'), were taken over by Government representatives. The Party's 200-odd branch headquarters throughout the country were also closed down. İsmet İnönü protested that this action was unconstitutional, and demanded the creation of a supreme court, with power to decide on the legality of measures passed by the Grand National Assembly. The Government's answer was a threat to treat this speech as treason against the sovereign Assembly.

On 9 March 1954, a new Press Law was passed by the G.N.A., increasing from one to three years' imprisonment the maximum penalty for libel or for spreading inaccurate information 'calculated to endanger the political and economic stability of the country'.

It was in a strained and unhappy atmosphere that Turkey went to the polls on 2 May 1954.

Besides the three Parties already discussed, there were two more contestants in the 1954 election. The Democratic Workers' Party (*Demokrat İşçi Partisi*) was founded in 1950 by a lawyer, two fitters and a mechanic. Its membership was numbered in the hundreds and was confined to Istanbul. It preached the necessity of 'delivering from the hands of the professional politicians those who cower in fear of the police and who dread privation' and of eliminating 'the working-class aristocrats who betray the interests of the workers' and 'the domination of pseudo-syndicalists'.

The Peasants' Party of Turkey (*Türkiye Köylü Partisi*) was founded in Ankara in May 1952, by four ex-Democrat members of the G.N.A. Its aim was 'to bring all citizens who work, and peasants above all, into a new life; new in culture, technique and prosperity'.

But the real fight was between the two big parties. The results, which are tabulated below, showed the success of Menderes's policy of improving the lot of the Turkish villager at the expense of the British, French, West German, Italian and American taxpayer. It will be noted that there were 541 members of the new Assembly, against 487 in the old. This was due to the rise in population since 1950, the principle being that there should be one deputy for every 40,000 people.

Name of party	Votes received		Percentage of votes cast		Seats won		Gain or loss in seats
	1950	1954	1950	1954	1950	1954	
Democratic	4,391,694	5,313,659	55·22	58·42	408	503	+95
Rep. People's	3,148,626	3,193,471	39·59	35·11	69	31	−38
National	368,537	480,249	4·63	5·28	1	5	+ 4
Peasants'	—	50,935	—	0·56	—	0	—
Workers'	—	910	—	0·01	—	0	—
Independents	44,537[1]	56,293	0·56	0·62	9	2	− 7

[1] Included in this figure are the 9,257 votes cast for the National Recovery Party, which won no seats in 1950 and did not contest the 1954 election.

There was a high poll, 9,095,617 people using their votes out of a total electorate of 10,262,063 (88·63 per cent against 89·3 per cent in 1950). Once again a clear majority of the country had decided against the Republican People's Party. It had increased its vote, but, on account of the peculiar list-system of voting described on page 129, the small drop in its percentage of the total votes cast had cost it over half its representation in the Assembly. The Republicans voiced a perfunctory complaint of irregularities in the conduct of the elections, but their heart was not in it; they admitted that they had been thoroughly beaten.

Certain local authorities were reported to have hampered the work of Republican canvassers, taking the old view that opposition to the party in power constitutes a revolt against Government. It will be remembered that this was a difficulty the Democrats had had to face before their coming to power. The extent of this phenomenon in the 1954 elections should not be exaggerated; it only throws into relief the scrupulous fairness of the election procedure over most of the country. As for the Republican complaints that Democrat leaders had used Turkish Air Force aeroplanes in their pre-election tours, they show, if true, that local authorities were not alone in identifying the ruling party with the State.

With his mandate renewed, Menderes continued his efforts to silence the opposition. It was not enough for him that he had a majority of the electorate behind him; he seemed to regard each vote cast against him as a personal blow. Shortly after the election, the Democrats introduced a Bill to change the provincial boundaries in such a way as to eliminate the vilayet of Kırşehir, which had returned the five National Party deputies.[1] The Government denied Opposition charges of gerrymandering and maintained that the change was justified on economic and administrative grounds. Even if this was true, the Democrats must be held guilty of a remarkably tactless piece of timing.

And the opposition had much to criticize. The country's trade-gap, 382·1 million liras in 1953, rose to 401·6 million in 1954. By the end of the latter year, British exporters alone were owed £15 million, not because Turkish businessmen wanted to cheat them but because the Central Bank simply had no sterling. According to the Istanbul Chamber of Commerce, the city's cost-of-living index, on the basis of 100 in 1950, was 129 in 1954. By August 1955 it was 143. Newspapers were forbidden to publish photographs of queues outside shops. Tradesmen were forbidden to use the word *zam*, 'price-increase'; instead they had to use *ayar*, 'adjustment'. Nor, when asked for goods which had vanished from the market, could they say *yok*, 'there isn't any'; the officially imposed substitute was *gelecek*, 'it'll be coming'. The current name for Turkey was *Yokistan*, 'the Land of Not', but journalists who used it in print felt the weight of the Press Law, as they did if they ventured to give details of corruption in ruling circles. In October 1955, thirteen Democrat deputies proposed to amend the Press Law so as to give anyone accused under it 'the right of proof';

[1] The vilayet of Kırşehir was restored to existence in June 1957, and again returned the National Party candidates in the next elections.

i.e., the right to justify his allegations. They subsequently announced that their purpose was to enable the Press to publicize 'the misdeeds and crimes of people in the public service'. They were soon joined by six of their colleagues. A Party congress, on 15 October, expelled nine of them, and the other ten resigned.

Among the misdeeds and crimes they wanted to publicize was a fresh one. On 29 August, tripartite talks on Cyprus had opened in London. As far as the story can be reconstructed, the Turkish Foreign Minister, Zorlu, was stung by the Greek delegation's remarking that there did not seem to be much popular feeling in Turkey about the Cyprus situation. He cabled home a request for a popular demonstration. On 5 September an explosion damaged the Turkish Consulate in Salonica and the adjoining house, in which Mustafa Kemal was born. The next night, riots occurred simultaneously in the three chief cities of Turkey. The rioters travelled in lorries and had lists of addresses to visit. But soon the amateurs took over, and what had begun as anti-Greek became first anti-minority, then anti-foreign, ending as anti-rich. Churches, houses and shops were sacked; there was much looting but more wanton destruction. İstiklâl Caddesi, the main shopping street of Istanbul, was littered with the wreckage of furniture, refrigerators and radios. The police were slow to realise that the planned demonstration had changed its nature; by the time they and the military intervened the damage was done. Three thousand people were arrested but subsequently released. The government paid compensation; but the minorities' faith in the Democrat Party was shaken. So too was that of many other Democrat supporters: there were many resignations from local Party organisations.

On 13 November municipal elections were held. The Republican People's and National Parties put up no official candidates, in protest against alleged malpractices in the 1954 general elections, but independent Opposition candidates won eight of the sixty-six vilayets, and two more went to the liberal-led Peasants' Party. The awareness of the Government's unpopularity was such that several Democrats resigned to fight the election as independents, then rejoined the Party when they had been elected. The nineteen rebels, led by a former Minister of the Interior, Fevzi Lûtfi Karaosmanoğlu, formed a new Freedom Party (*Hürriyet Partisi*). Most of the Cabinet resigned, and ten days passed before Menderes could form another, which won a vote of confidence on 16 December, 1955, from which at least fifty Democrats abstained. Apparently chastened, Menderes promised that the Press Law would be amended to permit 'the right of proof', but instead, at the beginning of June 1956, when he felt that the fuss had blown over, the Press Law was strengthened; a new amendment made it an offence to summarize or comment on any speech made in the Assembly, except according to the official record. On 28 June a new law was passed which virtually prohibited political meetings except for the forty-five days before an election.

The previous month, sixteen judges, three of them members of the Supreme Court, had been placed on the retired list before reaching the retiring age of sixty. The opposition alleged that some of these judges had incurred the Government's displeasure by acquitting journalists accused under the Press Law.

In August, leaders of the three Opposition parties decided to unite their efforts at the next general election, due in May 1958. It came however on 27 October 1957, and a month before that date the hopes of the Opposition had been frustrated by an ingenious piece of *ad hoc* legislation. It ordained that every party must present a list of candidates in every vilayet in which it had a party organization. No one could be a candidate for two parties. Nor could anyone be included in any party's list who had resigned from another party less than six months before a normal election, or two months before an early election. As might have been expected, the election campaign was heated. In Ankara and Istanbul the police used tear-gas to break up demonstrations. Strict security measures were taken on polling day.

There is little doubt that honest elections would have given Menderes the victory; his hold on the peasants was still strong. But he took no chances and the elections were rigged. In Istanbul, for example, the results were announced before counting was complete. Detailed official returns were never issued; the following figures were published by the Republican People's Party.

Name of party	Votes	Percentage of poll	Seats won	Percentage of seats
Democrat .	4,394,893	47·91	424	69·50
Rep. People's	3,763,866	41·03	178	29·18
National	659,970	7·19	4	0·66
Freedom	346,881	3·78	4	0·66
Independents	5,972	0·06	2	0·33

Eight seats remained vacant, as three Democrats and five Republicans were elected in two vilayets each, and had to stand down from one. Ankara was among the eighteen vilayets won by the Republicans. The Freedom Party's four seats were won in Burdur, the National Party's in Kırşehir.

To say that Menderes was heading for destruction is not mere hindsight. Confident that he had the backing of the peasants, he underestimated the hatred he had roused in the intellectuals.

The only class-distinction which matters in Turkey is that between intellectuals and peasants, which fundamentally means that between literates and illiterates. All intellectuals in theory, and many in practice, are idealistically eager to educate their underprivileged brothers into equality with themselves. But Menderes courted the peasants for the sake of their votes; he let them believe that they were all right as they were and that they did not need improvement. Above all, although he never dared say openly that he thought Atatürk had gone too far and too fast in his reforms, he let it be known that reversions to the old ways would be winked at. He did not try to repeal the Hat Law, but under Menderes one could wear a turban and get away with it. Polygamy was condoned. Restaurateurs who did not voluntarily close their premises during the daylight hours of Ramadan were intimidated into doing so, and the police took no action. In Kemalist eyes, Menderes had betrayed Atatürk's revolution and his own class.

Chapter 21

Yirmi Yedi Mayıs

THE ROOTS OF the movement[1] which led to the *coup d'état* of the twenty-seventh of May, *yirmi yedi Mayıs*, 1960, go back to late 1946, when ten Staff colonels and majors decided that it was their duty to overthrow the government which had so shamelessly rigged the elections that year. They approached General Fahri Belen, then commanding an Army Corps at Gallipoli, and asked him to join them, but he advised against the violent remedy they had in mind; they should wait and see what the next elections brought. The honest elections of 1950 caused the officers to relax and, like so many of their countrymen, they prepared to enjoy the new era of liberal democracy. General Belen was appointed Minister of Works in the new Democrat administration. It was not long however before he found that the time he and the staff of his Ministry spent in weighing the pros and cons of the various projects presented to him was entirely wasted; as often as they decided that a particular project was unjustifiable, orders would come down from above to proceed with it. In March 1951 he therefore resigned.

As time passed, more and more officers became discontented with the regime. For this there were special reasons. Like their forebears under Abdülhamid, they knew Western languages and were in contact with Western colleagues. Many had served abroad, in Korea and with NATO. They knew that there was more to democracy than the mere name. They had a tradition, deriving from the days when the Army was Prussian-trained, that it was the business of the Army to keep an eye on the government. This did not conflict in their minds with Atatürk's injunction against interfering in politics; this injunction they interpreted as applicable only so long as the civilians were following the lines laid down by Atatürk. To a distortion of this fact was due the cocktail-party joke one heard after 27 May: that the Menderes government fell

[1] The fullest source for the history of the movement is a series of articles by Ömer Sâmi Coşar and Abdi İpekçi which appeared in the newspaper *Milliyet* from 27 May to 14 July 1962, under the title *İhtilâlin içyüzü*, 'The inside story of the Revolution'.

because, with all its faults, it was the only civilian government the Turks had ever had and the Army couldn't tolerate this anomaly any longer. Like other people on fixed incomes the officers were suffering from inflation and rising prices. Their duties took them to every corner of the land and they saw how far short the poor peasants were of the civilised Western standard of living which was the Kemalist goal. At the same time they were of a social position to see how well the rich were doing under Menderes. The Democrat Party neglected to woo the officers who, under the electoral laws of 1946 and 1950, did not have the vote. A minority of officers, notably Alpaslan Türkeş, believed sincerely that military discipline was the best instrument for governing a country. Lastly, there was a strong undirected desire to do something, no matter what, so that the splendid weapon of which they were part should not rust from lack of use; Korea had whetted their appetite for action and for glory.

In November 1954, Orhan Kabibay and Dündar Seyhan, two captains at the Anti-aircraft School in Ankara, agreed to work to form an organization among their brother-officers. Seyhan was posted in October 1955 to the Istanbul War College as a Staff candidate, and there he continued what he had begun in Ankara. He created an organization called *Atatürkçüler Cemiyeti*, the Society of Atatürkists, of which he became Secretary. At that stage the purpose did not go beyond a reform in the Army so that the power in it should not lie with senior officers prepared to kowtow to Menderes. Doubtless there were other such secret organizations all over the country; it is known that one was founded in Ankara at the beginning of 1956. One of its members was an artillery officer called Talât Aydemir. Posted to the War College in Istanbul, he put Seyhan and his group in touch with his friends in Ankara. By this time Seyhan had decided that a reform in the Army would not mend the nation's ills and that a revolt was necessary. In the autumn the courses finished and the conspirators were posted to units all over the country. Aydemir was all for a revolution before the 1957 elections. An approach was made to İsmet İnönü but he refused to see the officers, knowing how vigilant the secret police were.

On 20 December 1957, nine officers were denounced by an informer but were acquitted for lack of evidence, The result however was to introduce an element of caution into the movement's activities, and for a while recruiting was slow.

In February 1959, General Cemal Gürsel, recently appointed Commander of Land Forces, consented to head the movement but insisted that revolution must be a last resort. All agreed that there would be no alternative to revolution if the next elections were not conducted honestly. Some of the officers must have felt they were experiencing a *déjà vu*. And after the revolution, what then? A minority led by Türkeş wanted a military government. Some were for handing power over to the Republican People's Party, but this course was rejected by the majority, who saw their duty as the protection of the Constitution and not the furtherance of one party's interests. The eventual decision was that a provisional government should be set up to hold free elections as soon as possible.

On the twenty-seventh of the same month, Menderes flew to England to take part in the London conference on Cyprus. The aircraft crashed at Gatwick, killing fifteen of the twenty-five people on board. Menderes escaped with bruises. When radio interviewers came with their recording apparatus to see him and the other survivors in hospital, he told them 'No voice but mine is to go out to Turkey.' His escape was presented as a miracle by the Democrat Press and the Turkish State Radio; the other nine survivors were pushed into the remote background.

Since the 1957 elections there had been a change in the nature of the Democrat membership of the Assembly. The Party's constitution laid down that candidates should be chosen in local primaries but that the Leader of the Party could set aside these choices if he saw fit and nominate whom he wished. Menderes had exercised this power to such effect that the government benches were occupied almost exclusively by yes-men. One of these exclaimed, on the Prime Minister's return to Ankara, 'We are grateful to England! We sent her a Prime Minister; she has sent us back a prophet!' This view was enthusiastically shared by the rank and file of the Party. When President Bayar returned from a visit to the United States in March 1954, he had been welcomed home with showers of confetti and ticker-tape. Now, five years later, Menderes was welcomed with sacrifices of sheep and even camels. One loyal citizen won some notoriety by standing on the kerb with a knife pressed against his small son's throat, but Menderes indicated that this tribute, though appreciated, was unnecessary.[1]

Puffed up by all the adulation, Menderes became quite unable

[1] The author suggested to a Turkish journalist friend at the time that the incident might make the basis for a cartoon, showing the father with his knife at the son's throat, grandfather with his knife at father's throat, son with knife at teddy-bear's throat. The suggestion was declined with thanks, as being a bit too sick for contemporary Turkish taste.

to endure the sight of any support given to the opposition. İnönü visited Konya in February 1960 and the police used tear-gas and truncheons to disperse the Republicans who turned out to meet him. The next month he was to visit Kayseri and the government took it into their heads to prevent this. The Governor of Kayseri had his train stopped and ordered him to abandon his intention. İnönü took no notice and eventually the train took him on to his destination. The next day the Governor called on the troops to prevent him from going on to Yeşilhisar, half-way to Niğde. A colonel and two majors resigned their commissions in protest against being ordered to deprive a citizen of his constitutional right to travel where he pleased. They were at once arrested. General Gürsel tried to secure their release but failed; he thereupon asked to be relieved of his duties pending his retirement under the age-limit (65) in September.

It is probable that the government were planning to hold elections about this time but abandoned the idea when Ministers who had been touring the provinces made their reports about the state of feeling in the country. Menderes could still command his solid block of four million votes but the opposition was becoming militant. Most of the Press was against him and so were the universities, incensed by the legislation, some of it *ad hominem*, designed to prevent university teachers from commenting unfavourably on government policy.[1] The economic situation was farcical. In the 1960 Budget there was a deficit of 500 million liras, making a cumulative deficit for the ten years of Democrat rule of 2,141 million. The Treasury owed the Central Bank 1,350 million and civil servants were being paid with the soiled notes sent in by the banks to be destroyed. The total foreign indebtedness was 12,191 million liras, in spite of American gifts totalling $900 million and military aid totalling $1,650 million.

On 18 April the G.N.A. voted the establishment of a fifteen-man Commission 'to investigate the Opposition which, in co-operation with a section of the Press, is trying to set up illegal and secret columns and armed political gangs composed of ruffians and ex-convicts.' Only one Democrat, Sıtkı Yırcalı, voted against the motion. The Commission, 'to facilitate its investigations', at once banned all political activity and any published reference to the debates of the Assembly. On 27 April the Commission was voted dictatorial powers of search, arrest and detention. In spite of the ban, some newspapers printed this news the next day, with state-

[1] As far back as 1953, Nuri Esen, Professor of Constitutional Law at Ankara, had been suspended for six months for describing the government as a cacocracy.

ments by members of the Law faculties of the universities about the unconstitutionality of the measure. They also printed as their main news story the report from South Korea that Syngman Rhee had been forced to resign the presidency after large-scale rioting triggered off by student demonstrations.

Turkey's student demonstrations began after a Law professor at Istanbul had told his class that he did not propose to give his lecture on constitutional law that day (28 April) as there was no such thing in Turkey. Police riot-squads had been watching the universities for some days, as events in Korea had not escaped the notice of the Turkish authorities. The police invaded the university precincts and dragged away nine of the demonstrators. For the sake of the reader who has seen accounts *ad nauseam* of 'student riots' in one eastern country after another, it should be said that these demonstrators really were students and not schoolchildren and that such student activity was previously unknown in Turkey.

The Rector was manhandled when he protested to the police and, as the demonstrators grew more incensed, the police opened fire. One student was killed, though rumour put the figure at eleven or twelve. That afternoon martial law was proclaimed in Ankara and Istanbul. The martial law commander in Istanbul was Fahri Özdilek, a general sympathetic to the officers' movement. His counterpart in Ankara however was Namık Argüç, who was loyal to Menderes, and a demonstration the next day at the Faculty of Political Sciences in Ankara was fired on by the Army.

A group of Democrats called on Bayar and begged him to dissolve the Commission. His reply was, 'If we give them our hand they'll take our arm; if we give them our arm they'll take our head.'

In Istanbul, on the other hand, the students fraternized with the Army and hailed them as saviours; this points to the fact that the common soldier was neutral in the struggle but, as ever in Turkey, did what his superior officers told him to do. On 29 April all universities and institutions of higher education were closed. For the next few weeks Istanbul saw sporadic student demonstrations in which the general public took virtually no part at all; students arrested by the Army were taken off to barracks, fed on steak and beer until they could barely stagger to bed, and then sent home the next day. For a little while the undergraduate catchphrase was 'Where did you have dinner on Wednesday?'

The leave which General Gürsel had requested was granted on 2 May. He sent a farewell message to all units, which never reached them, urging them not to let the honour of the Army be sullied by involvement in the ambitions of politicians. To the

Minister of Defence he wrote a long memorandum deploring 'the unintelligent use of troops against the students'. It was essential that the President resign, 'because there is a general conviction in the country that all the evils originate from this gentleman'. The governors and police-chiefs of Ankara and Istanbul and the martial law commander of Ankara must be replaced; the Commission must be dissolved; the imprisoned journalists must be amnestied and the arrested students released. The exploitation of religion for political purposes must end. 'Whether acts of corruption are being committed I do not know, but there is a general conviction that they are and this is responsible for the nation's lack of confidence in the Government. Such evils must be forcibly eliminated'. The memorandum concluded with an urgent appeal for notice to be taken of it 'for the sake of the country and the safety of the nation and to save the Government and even your Party'. The appeal was ignored.

On 21 May, cadets of the War School in Ankara staged a silent protest-march. This caused a panic among the government as it was the first demonstration by members of the armed forces, however junior. Some ministers were reportedly ready to 'abolish' the military schools, by which they did not mean closing them but rather subjecting them to the sort of treatment the Janissaries had received in 1826.

After that, things moved very fast. At three o'clock in the morning of 27 May, officers and cadets took over every public building and communications centre in Istanbul and, half an hour later, in Ankara. The actions in the two cities were to have been simultaneous but there was a misunderstanding of a coded telephone message. This was the only slip; the *coup* was beautifully planned and executed. All the ministers were arrested, as were the Democrat members of the G.N.A. There was no bloodshed except for one Army lieutenant, shot dead by an auxiliary policeman during the take-over of a post office in Ankara.

Of the part played by the ordinary citizen, the street-sweeper outside the British Embassy is perhaps typical. He was busy with his broom when the tanks roared up the Çankaya hill to arrest Celâl Bayar. When they came down, bringing the President of the Republic in handcuffs, he was still sweeping the street and never raised his head.

Chapter 22

Turkey since Menderes

On the morning of 27 May, an Air Force jet brought General Gürsel from his home at İzmir to Ankara, where he was proclaimed President of the National Unity Committee,[1] a group of 38 officers who had played leading parts in the revolution and who now declared that the powers of the G.N.A. were vested in themselves. That same morning another Air Force machine brought to the capital five professors from Istanbul to help draw up a new Constitution. Now there was a new cocktail-party joke: that the first two clauses of the Constitution were to be amended to read, 'The Turkish State is a Republic. Its official language is Turkish. Its capital is the University of Istanbul.'

The next day, the General formed a provisional government, with himself as Head of State, Prime Minister and Minister of Defence, and two other generals as Ministers of the Interior and Communications. The remaining fifteen members were all civilians; professional men and civil servants, except for Ekrem Alican, a politician. A founder-member of the Democrat Party, he was one of those who left it in 1955 to found the Freedom Party and had not been re-elected to the Assembly in 1957. The General wanted a government of men above party, but he had not allowed for the enthusiasm with which the N.U.C. plunged into the task of putting the country to rights. The Minister of Agriculture complained that the officers who were planning a drastic land reform did not take him into their confidence; the Minister of Health was similarly ignored by those planning a national health service.

On 9 June, Gürsel made his position clear to a gathering of officers at the Ministry of Defence:

> The Army today has taken on a number of tasks all over the country. This is a matter of duty. But to continue it would be weakness . . . We must all be eager and anxious to slip away from this duty as soon as possible and return to our real jobs. Our highest ideal must be to go back to soldiering. Because our present duties involve a little less discipline, are a

[1] Hereafter referred to as 'N.U.C.'.

> bit more fancy than we're used to, people may be unwilling to leave them. That's human nature. But we aren't going to give in to it. . . . The world will see that the moment our task is done we shall return to our own honourable ranks, our own units, our own duties.

But not all the N.U.C. were of the same mind. A powerful group of them believed that İnönü had been premature in holding free elections in 1950 (a view, incidentally, which İnönü never held even in the darkest days). They resented the way in which Gürsel had let civilians into 'their' government and they did not propose to hold free elections and start the whole miserable process over again. They were great believers in purging. They began with the armed services. Of the 260 generals and admirals, 235 were placed on the retired list on 3 August and 5,000 colonels and majors followed them three days later.

Then came the universities' turn. On 27 October the N.U.C. decreed the dismissal of 147 university teachers on grounds of incompetence, absenteeism, homosexuality and communist sympathies. The 147 included two members of the Constitutional Commission and a large proportion of those Turkish scholars who have an international reputation. It is true that some of the reasons given for the dismissals could be held to apply to some of the 147. But they also applied to some university teachers who were not included. Analysis of the list suggested that one principle on which it had been compiled was to get rid of any teacher capable of influencing his pupils. The one factor common to all the 147 however was that they had clearly been denounced.

The judges and the civil service were to have been purged too, but Gürsel beat the purgers at their own game. They proposed a decree perpetuating their rule for four years. This was defeated by 19 votes to 18, Gürsel having used his casting vote (one member of the N.U.C., General İrfan Baştuğ, had been killed in a road accident on 12 September). On the Committee's agenda for 14 November was another decree, which Gürsel thought would be carried. It established a National Union of Ideals and Culture, into which the Ministry of Education would be absorbed, with a regional countrywide organization and an immovable head. Significantly, its various departments were to be called *masa*, the police term for 'desk' as in 'homicide desk'. The day before this was due to be voted on, Gürsel announced in a broadcast that he had dissolved the N.U.C. 'as its functioning was endangering the country's interests' and had created a new Committee consisting of twenty-three members of the old one. The explanation of this tortuous procedure was that the provisional Constitution, which had been promulgated on 12 June, made it impossible to dismiss a member of the N.U.C. unless a court found that he had broken his oath to hand over power as soon as possible to a freely elected Assembly. But no member could be put on trial except by vote of four-fifths of those present at a meeting attended by six-sevenths of the Committee, a majority which Gürsel knew he could not secure.

The most prominent of the fourteen thus dropped was Colonel Türkeş, who in his youth had been involved in the Pan-Turanian movement. Whether he still accepted this creed was impossible to establish with certainty; one well-informed and kind-hearted foreign correspondent argued that a man could be a nationalist and a socialist without being a National Socialist; this is true, but Türkeş was known to be in contact with people who indubitably were racialist Pan-Turanians. All fourteen were sent into a novel form of exile, being posted as 'attachés', with no specific duties, to widely-dispersed Turkish missions abroad. Gürsel's prompt action had saved the honour of the Army and possibly saved Turkey from a fascist dictatorship.

On 6 January, 1961 the Constituent Assembly met for the first time. It consisted of the N.U.C. as an upper house, with a House of Representatives of 272 members, including 74 representatives of the Republican (49) and National (25)[1] Parties; the Democrat Party had been liquidated by court order on 29 September 1960. There were also representatives of the professions, the universities, the trade unions, and the 67 provinces. Its task was to prepare a new Constitution and electoral law.

The ban on political activity, imposed immediately after the revolution, was lifted on 13 January. Eleven new parties were formed, the most noteworthy being the Justice Party of General Gümüşpala, whose avowed aim was to secure justice for the officers who, like himself, had been compulsorily retired the previous year. There is no reason to doubt his sincerity, but his vice-chairman, Mehmet Yorgancıoğlu, was arrested for declaring that the Party was a continuation of the outlawed Democrat Party, and thus it has proved to be. The New Turkey Party, under Ekrem Alican, sought the support of those who had left the Democrat Party before the end; it originally intended to call itself the Free Democrat Party but was forbidden to do so.

[1] To give it its full name, the Republican Peasants' National Party; it had amalgamated with the Peasants' Party after the 1957 elections.

A referendum on the new Constitution was held on 9 July. The results were:

Electorate	12,735,009
Votes cast	10,322,169
Abstentions	2,412,840
'Yes'	6,348,191
'No'	3,934,370
Invalid votes	39,608

Thus, in spite of the revolution, in spite of the trials of Menderes and his colleagues which had been dragging on since the previous October, there was hardly a dent in his four million votes. It is a mark of the provisional government's good faith that these results were announced immediately, depressing though they must have found them.

The trials of the former administration were held on Yassıada, the bleak 'Flat Island' in the Sea of Marmara, before a specially created High Court of Justice, consisting of nine regular judges. The charges were all brought under the existing penal code; there was no *ad hoc* legislation. The gravest charge was that of 'forcibly changing, modifying and abrogating the Constitution', with particular reference to the setting-up of the fifteen-man Commission, which was regarded by the prosecution as a violation of the fundamental provisions of the Constitution, in particular, of Articles 6, 7 and 8:

> Article 1.—The Turkish State is a Republic.
>
> Article 2.—The Turkish State is republican, nationalist, populist, étatist, secular and reformist. Its official language is Turkish. Its capital is the city of Ankara.
>
> Article 3.—Sovereignty belongs unconditionally to the nation.
>
> Article 4.—The Grand National Assembly of Turkey is the sole rightful representative of the nation and exercises the right of sovereignty in its name.
>
> Article 5.—Legislative authority and executive power are manifested and concentrated in the Grand National Assembly.
>
> Article 6.—The Grand National Assembly exercises its legislative authority directly.
>
> Article 7.—The Grand National Assembly exercises its executive authority through the person of the President of the Republic elected by it, and through a Council of Ministers chosen by the President.
>
> The Assembly may at any time scrutinize the acts of the Government and overthrow it.

Article 8.—Judicial authority is exercised by independent courts in the name of the nation, in accordance with the laws and regulations in force.

The defence argued that if the G.N.A. chose to vote its sovereign power over to a smaller body that was its own affair, but this view was held to be inconsistent with Articles 6 and 8. The argument that the Democrats had a sufficient majority in the Assembly to amend the Constitution under Article 102 ('Amendments can be adopted only by the vote of a majority numbering two-thirds of the total membership of the Assembly') was met by the short answer 'Well, why didn't they?' The argument that the N.U.C. and the provisional government were no less guilty, in that they had themselves first changed the Constitution[1] and then superseded it, was foredoomed; the N.U.C. and the provisional government were not on trial.

Other charges included organizing the riots of 6–7 September 1955, misuse of public funds, and various acts of corruption.

It may be wondered why there was not the slightest attempt by Menderes's supporters to save him from arrest or trial or execution. It is not unknown in Turkey for a rioting crowd to attack a gendarmerie post in order to rescue one of their number who has been arrested; true, it would have taken a foolhardy man to defy the extraordinary security precautions which surrounded Menderes and the other prisoners, but one might have expected there to be enough foolhardy men, among the millions who idolized him, to try a forlorn hope. The explanation lies in the deep-rooted reluctance of the peasantry to interfere in the affairs of *büyükler*, 'the great'. The efforts made by Mustafa Kemal, by İnönü and by Menderes himself, to arouse the electorate to an awareness of its political power and responsibilities had not been fruitless; people were certainly ready to vote for the party of their choice, but they were not prepared to stick their necks out in a quarrel among their 'betters'. During the trials, stories circulated of how Menderes flew from his prison every night on a winged white horse to pray in his favourite mosque at Eyüb; of how he had appeared in full view of this or that congregation. It was precisely this superstitious adoration of him which prevented—a psychologist might say 'excused'—even his most fanatical adherents from trying to rescue him; he was a saint, a prophet, *ergo* he was not one of them. If he could save himself, good luck to him; if not, what could human help achieve?

[1] By the 'Provisional Law on the Abolition and Amendment of Certain Articles of the Constitutional Law of 1924, No. 491', dated 12 June 1960. See page 208.

The proceedings were conducted scrupulously, the defence being given more latitude than usual. On 15 September 1961 the judges passed sentence. Fifteen of the accused were sentenced to death, 31 to life imprisonment, 418 to lesser terms and fines, while 123 were acquitted. The N.U.C. commuted the death sentences on eleven but confirmed those on Celâl Bayar, Adnan Menderes, the former Foreign Secretary Fatin Rüştü Zorlu and the former Minister of Finance, Hasan Polatkan. Celâl Bayar was reprieved on account of his age but the other death sentences were carried out. The feeling in the country had been that there would be no executions; there is reason to believe that the judges themselves, when they duly passed the sentences laid down by the penal code for the crimes they found proved, had expected the N.U.C. to exercise its prerogative of mercy.

At the time of the referendum on the new Constitution, Democrat canvassers had been telling the peasants, 'If you vote "yes" they will hang Adnan Menderes'. This was the reverse of the truth; it was the size of the vote against the Constitution which scared a group of officers outside the Committee into shocking action.[1] They gave the Committee the choice of executing Menderes, Zorlu and Polatkan or seeing Yassıada bombed with all the prisoners on it. Knowing that those who made this threat had the means and the ruthlessness to implement it, the Committee yielded. Zorlu and Polatkan were hanged on 16 September, Menderes the next day, in spite of appeals for clemency from İsmet İnönü, the British, French and American governments and the Pope. Such was the grim background to the general election of 15 October 1961.

Only four parties contested: Republican People's (R.P.P.), Justice (J.P.), Republican Peasants' National (R.P.N.P.) and New Turkey (N.T.P.), as the new electoral law debarred parties with a provincial organization in fewer than 15 of the 67 provinces. The new Constitution provided for a National Assembly of 450 elected members and a Senate of 150 elected members plus 15 appointed by the President and, as *ex officio* members, the N.U.C. The elections to the Senate were by majority vote, to the Assembly by proportional representation.[2] These were the results, in an 81 per cent poll:

These results were described by the foreign press as 'a shock to the military junta', a verdict which exaggerated the naïvety

[1] There is no documentary evidence for this but the story is fairly well substantiated.

[2] On 31 March 1964, the Assembly decided by 214 votes to 128 that future Senate elections should also be on the basis of proportional representation.

Party	Votes	Percentage	Seats	Percentage
		Assembly		
R.P.P.	3,724,752	36·7	173	38·4
J.P. .	3,527,435	34·7	158	35·1
R.P.N.P.	1,415,390	13·9	54	12·0
N.T.P.	1,391,934	13·7	65	14·4
		Senate		
R.P.P.	3,734,285	37·2	36	24·0
J.P. .	3,560,675	35·4	70	46·7
R.P.N.P.	1,350,892	13·4	16	10·7
N.T.P.	1,401,637	13·9	28	18·7

of the junta; they must have been relieved, if anything, that the whole of the old Democrat vote had not gone to the Justice Party.

A joint session of both Houses on 26 October elected General Gürsel as President of the Republic, by 434 votes to 173. The only other candidate was Professor Ali Fuad Başgil, leader of the extreme right wing of the J.P., who was opposed to Atatürkist secularism. The news of his candidature had prompted the Party Chairman, Gümüşpala, to disown him and had also occasioned protests from officers and cadets. Başgil was intimidated into leaving Ankara before the joint session and he telegraphed from Istanbul his resignation from the Senate, and therefore his candidature.

A fortnight later, after fruitless discussions among the party leaders about the possibility of a coalition, Gürsel appointed İnönü Prime Minister, an office he had last held in 1937. The J.P. were prepared to enter a coalition on their own terms, which included İnönü's resignation from the R.P.P. and an amnesty for the imprisoned Democrats. The Army lost patience; the *ex officio* Senators met in the Assembly building and there was much coming and going between there and the General Staff headquarters. Eventually, in what the newspapers realistically termed 'a triumph for Messrs Thompson and Sten', the J.P. were persuaded to agree to join a coalition with the R.P.P. A twenty-two-man cabinet was formed, half from each Party, which began work on 20 November.

For many months the coalition did nothing but quarrel about an amnesty and vote an increase in deputies' salaries. The Justice Party press poured forth abuse on the revolution and its makers. Though some of the J.P. had the sense to see that their first concern ought to be not to provoke a further Army intervention, most seemed to think that they had a mandate from the electors to take vengeance on the R.P.P. which had opposed Menderes and on the officers who had brought about his downfall and death. On 22 February, 1962, the Commandant of the Ankara War College, Talât Aydemir, led his cadets and some armoured units in an abortive *coup d'état*. The immediate cause was that he had learned that the government were about to transfer him, and the reason for that was that he was known to deplore the Army's quixotic honesty in handing back power to the politicians. The rising was put down, mainly by the Air Force, without bloodshed. İnönü broadcast to the nation on 26 February, saying that the officers responsible had lost confidence in democracy, under provocation. In a later statement he reminded the country how the Army had honoured its pledge to hand back power to the civilians and how infuriating it was for them to be exposed to insult and threats of vengeance. Aydemir and three other colonels were retired and a number of other officers transferred away from the capital. On 8 March a new law came into force, punishing with up to five years' hard labour anyone who claimed that his party was a continuation of the Democrat Party, or who impugned the legality and rightness of the revolution and the Yassıada trials. Sentences of up to two years awaited any who attacked the multi-party democratic order or suggested that a democratic regime could not be made to work in Turkey, or who provoked feelings of hatred and revenge. A writer in *Yön*, a new socialist weekly, commented:

> We were under the impression that the purpose of democracy and the revolution was to protect our rights. Now it seems they themselves need protection. And is a new law being contemplated, to protect *this* new law? You know the popular saying, 'If the meat smells you throw salt on it. But what do you do if the salt smells?'

The rest of the press too condemned the new law as undemocratic, but in fact it was not invoked. After all, everyone knew by now that the J.P. was the old D.P. writ small, so why risk gaol to say so? As for criticism of the multi-party order, that was likely to come only from the Army, and the government would not risk quarrelling with the Army so long as it confined itself to criticism. Far from scaring the J.P., the abortive rising only convinced them that the Army had shot its bolt.

The debate on the amnesty therefore continued to absorb most of the working time of the Assembly. In May 1962, in an attempt to heal the wound so that more vital matters could be discussed, İnönü agreed to a reduction in the sentences of the imprisoned members of the former government. The J.P. were not satisfied with his terms and he resigned. Gürsel told him to try again and in June a new coalition took office, composed of the R.P.P. and the two smaller parties, with the J.P. in opposition. The coalition agreed on an amnesty to be proclaimed in October, whereby those serving sentences of up to 6 years would be released and longer sentences would be reduced by 4 years.

On 22 March 1963, Celâl Bayar was released for six months on medical grounds. There were such scenes on his way to Ankara and such a triumphant welcome given to him there by the J.P. that the Army Council demanded action. There were demonstrations and counter-demonstrations, in which the J.P. headquarters was stoned and their newspaper buildings attacked. On 26 March troops intervened in Istanbul to keep 30,000 students away from 5,000 J.P. supporters. The same day, in Ankara, the J.P. headquarters was completely wrecked. After midnight, at the end of a seven-hour Cabinet meeting, Bayar's release was revoked and he was taken to a hospital under guard. Some J.P. members nervously proposed that the party dissolve itself; this did not happen, but on 12 March there were twelve resignations from the Party's central committee.

On the evening of 20 May, cadets of the Ankara War School again followed their brave but imprudent ex-Commandant, Talât Aydemir, in an abortive *coup d'état*. Twice during the night they gained control of Ankara Radio and broadcast announcements that the armed forces had taken over power. This claim was ridiculous, but there was nothing else amusing about that night's work, in which two cadets and five loyal soldiers were killed and twenty-six people wounded, of whom one died the next day. Aydemir was tried and sentenced to death; he was executed in July 1964. Colonel Türkeş and three others of the fourteen ex-members of the N.U.C., who had been permitted to return home in February, were tried on a charge of having been preparing an independent *coup*, but were acquitted. On 31 May, nine deputies and three senators resigned from the Justice Party to sit as Independents, apparently having found the pace too hot.

Meanwhile, some of the leaders of the two smaller parties in the coalition had been looking for an excuse to walk out. To help finance the Five-Year Development Plan, which came into operation on 1 January 1963, the coalition government had bravely taken the step no previous government had dared to take: on 10 February it introduced an agricultural income-tax. It was to be levied only on farms with a gross annual profit of over £1,600, i.e. one per cent of the country's two million farms; nevertheless, it did nothing to increase the government's popularity, as it was followed by increases in the prices of products of the State Monopolies, including cigarettes, spirits, beer and some wine, and of petrol. It was because of their unwillingness to share in the government's consequent unpopularity that the N.T.P. and R.P.N.P. were anxious to quit the coalition. They were on the verge of doing so in August but kept going on the insistence of President Gürsel. They found the excuse they were seeking when the results were declared of the local elections held on 10 November. These were to elect mayors and provincial, municipal and village councils. The more reputable commentators seemed to be agreed that the R.P.P. had a better set of candidates but that people do not vote for candidates but for parties; it had not taken the young Turkish democracy long to learn this sad truth.

The rising cost of living, principally due to higher taxation, had polarised political sympathies. Regularly one heard, 'We were better off under Menderes'. It was no good replying that their comparative prosperity in the old days was at the expense of their Western allies; this they considered no more than their just reward for standing between Russia and the West. Even people who detested Menderes, however, were saying, 'It wasn't worth hanging him for this.' The J.P. announced that it expected to win most of the votes which in the general election had gone to the two smaller parties, and this prognostication was correct. J.P. candidates were elected mayor in 42 provincial capitals, R.P.P. in 23, N.T.P. in one, an independent candidate in one. The J.P. candidate won in Istanbul, with 127,009 votes to the R.P.P.'s 99,437, but was disqualified on a technicality and the R.P.P. candidate took office instead.

In the following table, 'N.P.' stands for the Nation Party, formed as an offshoot from the R.P.N.P. on 1 June 1962, while 'T.W.P.' is the Turkish Workers' Party, founded in January 1961.

		Percentage
Electorate	12,860,191	
Votes cast	9,715,127	75·54
Valid votes	9,295,454	
J.P.	4,264,327	45·9
R.P.P.	3,437,149	37·0
N.T.P.	605,709	6·5
N.P.	289,023	3·1
R.P.N.P.	261,477	2·8
T.W.P.	35,507	0·4
Independents	402,272	4·3

By the time the results were known, İnönü had left for America to attend President Kennedy's funeral. In his absence, the R.P.N.P. and N.T.P. decided to leave the government. On 2 December, İnönü saw Gürsel and offered the Cabinet's resignation. As before, the President asked him to stay in office. Now in his eightieth year, İnönü had really had enough. When a journalist had asked him, a few months before, 'Pasha, what will happen after you leave politics?' the reply was, 'After me? After me the deluge.' The collapse of his coalition while he was abroad had been a heavy blow and he wanted to rest. But on 14 December it became known that Gümüşpala had failed to form a government—to no one's surprise, because sitting in opposition and sneering at the Five-Year Plan was one thing, whereas having to administer it or find an alternative was quite another—and on 25 December İnönü announced his new Cabinet, of twenty men of his own Party and three independents.

He got his vote of confidence on 4 January 1964: 177 R.P.P., 29 N.T.P. and 19 independents; 225 votes against 175. The next test came on 7 June, when one-third of the Senate places came up for election. The smallness of the poll suggested that the country was as weary of politics as was the Prime Minister.

		Percentage[1]	Seats Won
Electorate (26 provinces)	4,741,223		
Votes cast	2,868,594	60·5	
Valid votes	2,852,803		
J.P.	1,418,878	49·7	30
R.P.P.	1,175,778	41·2	20
N.T.P.	111,809	3·9	0
R.P.N.P.	85,362	3·1	0
Independents	60,976	2·1	1

The strength of the parties in the Senate was now: R.P.P. 35; J.P. 81; R.P.N.P., N.T.P. and Independents together 34.

As the Prime Minister was about to leave for Washington to discuss Cyprus with President Johnson, he decided to ask for another vote of confidence, not wishing to find himself again sitting on top of a non-existent tree. The constitutional requirement for defeating a vote of confidence was a majority of the votes of all 450 members of the Assembly, i.e. 226 votes. İnönü went further however and declared that he would resign unless he secured an absolute majority of all the votes cast, which he did. Fifteen of the J.P., 3 of the N.T.P. and 2 of the R.P.N.P. defied their Parties' decision to vote against the government; the three N.T.P. members voted for it and the others did not vote at all. Of the 396 members who voted, 200 were for, 194 against, the other two registering a *çekimser*, 'abstaining', vote.

So the Prime Minister left for Washington. One of the old Bosphorus paddle-steamers had recently been refitted and put

[1] The author having used logarithm tables, for the first time in 29 years, in order to work out these percentages, he would prefer them not to be quoted.

back into service. It was affectionately suggested that it ought to have been renamed *İsmet İnönü.*

The key question, obviously, is how long this situation can last. No foreseeable event could make the four million abandon their allegiance to Adnan Menderes, just as there are still, one gathers, Irishmen who vote against Oliver Cromwell. If the J.P. ever forms a government, however, it can only be in the sure knowledge that the Army will be watching for one false move. The one new factor in the situation is the as yet rather shapeless and unorganized labour movement. There have been many signs that thinking Turks, not only in the ranks of the intellectuals, disgusted by the squabbles of the politicians about the amnesty for the imprisoned Democrats to the exclusion of more urgent problems, are beginning to seek a political philosophy other than the two they have experience of: first, the étatism of the R.P.P. which till well after 1946 glorified the nation while bullying the citizen; second, the 'economic liberalism' of the Democrat Party which was the cover for a greedy and hypocritical exploitation.

Just before the end of 1961, notices appeared in Istanbul, signed by 'The Meetings Committee of the Istanbul Union of Workers' Syndicates' and reading: 'Worker Brother! For the human living conditions you want, come to Saraçhane at 11 a.m. on Sunday, 31 December.' A hundred thousand people turned up, some of whom, it may well be, had been paid to come, but this practice was of regular occurrence under the Democrats and does not detract from the importance of the occasion. There were banners with slogans such as have long been familiar in Western Europe but which were unprecedented in Turkey: 'You gave us your word, you got our votes, and now you've fallen asleep'; 'Cabbage for the worker, caviare for the boss'; 'We don't want favours, we want our rights'; 'A union without the right to strike is like an unarmed soldier'. For the new Constitution granted the right to strike but the relevant legislation was not passed till April 1963. Nevertheless there were strikes, towards which the authorities behaved in a sensible and restrained manner.

There are very few Communists in Turkey and probably all of them are known to the police, if not to the prison service. So the old device which has proved useful in other countries, of calling anyone who asks for social justice a Communist, is not likely to succeed. The Turkish working man is by birth and breeding wary of Russia and will not fall for this line; it is no use telling him he is a Communist because he knows perfectly well that he isn't. This point was well made some twenty years ago by one of the best of modern Turkish poets, Orhan Veli, in his sarcastic[1] *The Butcher's Cat Replies to the Alley-Cat:*

> You speak of hunger;
> That means you're a Communist.
> That means you're the chap who's been
> starting all the fires.
> All the ones in Istanbul,
> All the ones in Ankara.
> Ooh! What a *swine* you are!

It seems likely that in the next few years the labour movement, which is steadily growing in strength and maturity, will have an increasing influence in Turkish politics; that what the old-guard politicians ought most to fear is not a few impatient colonels but an exasperated people.

On 13 February 1965 the government resigned after a vote of 225 to 197 against its budget proposals. A cabinet of members of the four opposition parties took office a week later, under Suat Hayri Ürgüplü, an independent deputy and former ambassador. His successor was Süleyman Demirel, who in November 1964 had been elected chairman of the J.P. in succession to General Gümüşpala, who had died in June.

The general election of 10 October 1965 brought the J.P. under Demirel to power. The figures before the plus signs in the table below show the number of seats won directly; those after, the number allocated to the parties out of the 'national remainder', a feature of the system of proportional representation.

		Percentage	Seats won
Electorate	13,649,112		
Valid votes	9,308,019	68·2	
J.P.	4,908,125	52·73	204 + 36
R.P.P.	2,675,808	28·75	102 + 32
N.T.P.	346,476	3·72	3 + 16
N.P.	582,710	6·26	6 + 25
R.P.N.P.	208,694	2·24	0 + 11
T.W.P.	276,100	2·97	2 + 13
Independents	310,106	3·33	0 + 0

On 28 March 1966, President Gürsel having been pronounced unfit to resume his duties after a stroke, General Cevdet Sunay was elected President of the Republic. His place as Chief of the General Staff was taken by General Cemal Tural.

[1] The author asks indulgence for adding this apparently superfluous adjective, but one distinguished reviewer, in his notice of the first edition of this book in 1955, called these lines 'naïve'.

Chapter 23

Turkey's Post-War Foreign Policy

After the end of the war, Britain had resumed deliveries of equipment and material to reinforce Turkey's defences. Her gifts, up to the beginning of 1947, had amounted to 400 aircraft for the Turkish Air Force, as well as naval vessels and equipment to a value of over 2½ million pounds, including two destroyers and a submarine. Britain was also carrying the burden of the Greek economy, severely strained by the civil war. But her own post-war difficulties made these extraneous commitments intolerable, so, on 4 March 1947, Mr George Marshall, the American Secretary of State, asked Congress to undertake to continue the financial help to Greece and Turkey which Britain could no longer afford. On 22 April 1947, the Senate approved a Bill granting Turkey 100 million dollars for military aid, in the teeth of opposition from a group of isolationist senators. This was followed by a like gift under the Marshall Plan for the year beginning 1 April 1948. Turkey's share of American aid, both economic and military, from 1949 to 1953 inclusive, was 722 million lira, roughly 92½ million pounds.

The end of the war brought disappointment to those in Turkey who had expected a Russian defeat, and Russia was not slow to crack the whip at her neighbour. On 8 August 1946, a Russian Note declared that war-time events had revealed the inadequacy of the Montreux Convention to guarantee the security of the Black Sea Powers. It proposed a new régime for the Straits, to be confined to these Powers. Turkey and the U.S.S.R. should be jointly responsible for the defence of the Straits, which were to be always open to all merchant ships, but closed to warships other than those of the Black Sea Powers. The Turkish answer was equivocal: it insisted that there had not been 'one case of violation by German warships in which the security of the Soviet Government was at stake'. The Turks agreed, however, that the Montreux Convention should be amended, substituting the words 'United Nations' for 'League of Nations'.

This was followed by another Soviet Note refuting the Turkish claim to have adequately guarded the Straits, and indicating that the question of 'the security of the Soviet Government' was quite irrelevant; substantial Russian forces had had to be drawn from the battle-fronts to defend the Black Sea coast from the German naval vessels which Turkey had been allowing to come and go through the Straits until June 1944. The exchange of Notes was inconclusive.

On 1 August 1950, Turkey formally applied for admission to the North Atlantic Treaty Organization. At the N.A.T.O. Council meeting in September, Norway and Denmark strongly opposed the entry of Turkey and Greece. On 4 October, Turkey accepted an invitation 'to be associated with the planning work of the Organization, with regard to Mediterranean defence'—a consolation prize, tantamount to a rejection of her application for full membership. The British and French Governments, especially the latter, were opposed to the admission of Turkey, presumably because of their unwillingness to guarantee a country so much on Russia's doorstep, the justification being that Turkey is in no sense a North Atlantic Power.

Turkey's disappointment and chagrin were all the greater since she had loyally and promptly answered the United Nations' call for aid in the Korean War: over 5,000 Turkish troops disembarked at Pusan on 18 October 1950, and the total strength of the Turkish Brigade was subsequently raised to 7,000. It will hardly be necessary to remind the reader of the heroic and devoted service rendered by the 20,000 Turks who at various times formed part of the Turkish Brigade. Six hundred and seventeen were killed in action, 100 died from other causes, and 2,156 were wounded.

On 18 July 1951, however, Britain announced that she now favoured Turkey's admission to N.A.T.O., Turkey having undertaken to enter a Middle East defence pact. In September the Scandinavian countries also withdrew their objections. By 18 February 1952, the Parliaments of all the North Atlantic Powers had formally signified their acceptance, and on that date Turkey became a full member of N.A.T.O.

On 13 October 1951, Britain, France, the U.S.A. and Turkey invited Egypt to join in a proposed Middle East Command. This offer was immediately rejected, and indeed it is difficult to see how the Allies could have expected any other answer, as the Egyptian view was well known: no negotiations involving Britain were possible until after the evacuation of the Canal Zone. After this fiasco the scheme for a Middle East Command in that form was quietly dropped, although the idea behind it re-emerged in Turkey's Pact with Pakistan (see below). Instead, N.A.T.O.

announced the creation of a new South-East European Command on 16 July 1952. A month later İzmir was chosen to be the headquarters of the new Command, which includes Turkish and Greek forces and comes under the Southern European Command, whose headquarters are at Naples. This measure did something to assuage the hurt justifiably felt by the Turks at the shilly-shallying that had preceded their admission to N.A.T.O.

The incident of the still-born Middle East Command had exacerbated Turkey's relations with Egypt. The Egyptians regarded Turkey's siding with the 'Imperialists' as an act of treachery to Middle East and to Islam. An Egyptian periodical, *Roz al-Yusuf*, published a cartoon depicting a dog dressed in the Turkish national flag and having the features of Celâl Bayar, licking the boots of the three Western representatives. A vigorous Turkish protest elicited an 'apology' in the form of a second cartoon, in which the dog was seen now proudly erect, marching on a leash in front of the three Westerners.

A further display of bad feeling occurred in January 1954, when the Egyptian Government expelled the Turkish Ambassador, for some undiplomatic remarks he had made concerning the confiscation of property belonging to the former Egyptian royal house, of which his own wife was a member.

But Turkey's relations with Egypt had never been particularly cordial. Indeed, the common Turkish attitude towards the Arabs generally is one of thinly-veiled contempt.[1] Ask a Turk to explain this, and he will speak of the Arabs' poor showing as fighting men and their fatal inability to unite. The real reason is probably not unconnected with the jealousy all non-Arab Muslims feel, to a greater or lesser degree, towards the people amongst whom the Prophet arose, and who consequently tend to give themselves airs when dealing with lesser breeds within the Law. The achievements of Arab science and literature (many of which, though the work of non-Arabs, were recorded in Arabic) are another source of Arab pride and non-Arab resentment.

The Arab dislike for Turkey, on the other hand, is based partly on memories of long years of stern Turkish rule, partly on envy of Turkey's respected position in the modern world, and partly on Turkey's recognition of Israel (28 March 1949) and her continued friendly relations with that State. The nomination of Turkey, in 1949, to serve with France and the United States on the U.N.

[1] Witness the Turkish proverb: 'Neither the sweets of Damascus nor the Arab's face', used when refusing an attractive-seeming offer with unpleasant strings attached.

Palestine Conciliation Commission, though it further increased Arab resentment towards her, had a beneficial effect on her self-esteem and her prestige with the rest of the world. All in all, the lively, individualist Arab and the dour, disciplined Turk have little in common.

Trouble often flares up on Turkey's south-eastern frontier, where smuggling to and from Syria and Iraq is a regular profession. The outgoing commodities are livestock, tobacco, opium, carpets, guns and ammunition; the incoming commodities being synthetic fabrics, perfume, coffee, lighters and lighter-flints, cigarette-papers and playing-cards.

Turkey's state of war with Germany ended, so far as concerns the Bonn Government, on 24 July 1951. Western Germany has spared no effort to recapture the unique place Germany had long held in Turkish affections. Even Germany's defeat, in two successive wars of her own making, has done little to cure the Turks of their belief in German efficiency. The reasons for this phenomenon are difficult to pin down; when we have taken into account the obvious resemblances between the national characteristics of the two peoples, the fact that they fought side by side in the First World War, the traditional hostility between Germany and Russia, and the sustained and deliberate campaign to woo the Turks, begun by Prussia early in the nineteenth century and continued by German Governments ever since, we are still left with the feeling that there is more to it that that. Show a Turk a smart new British or American fountain-pen or lighter, and the odds are that he will say, 'Very nice! German?' Thirty-eight thousand Turks migrated to Germany in the three years 1961–1963.

Both Britain and France (the latter to a diminishing extent) have great prestige in Turkey, and the individual Englishman or Frenchman is sure of a welcome there. The author has been kept busy for more than one afternoon, striving to answer the complex genealogical and constitutional questions posed by Turkish undergraduates about our Royal Family. It is still true that most Turkish writers are steeped in French literature and that most educated Turks know French. But French is losing ground fast, while the study of English is making great strides, thanks largely to the increasing importance of America in world affairs.

At the Supreme Headquarters of the Allied Powers in Europe, at Saint-Germain near Versailles, a school is provided for children of officers and other ranks working there. The British members have claimed their rights under the regulation which lays down that where there are ten or more children of British servicemen, a qualified British teacher must be provided for them. So now the S.H.A.P.E. School is divided into two sections, one English, one International, the medium of instruction in the latter being French. The point which concerns us is that nearly all the Turkish members have chosen to send their children to the English side, on the grounds that 'most good Turkish schools nowadays specialize in English' and that 'everybody speaks English'.

Towards the U.S.A. the attitude is ambivalent. In this context it is customary to quote the Chinese saying, 'I have never helped you; why do you hate me?' But there is no question of hatred for Americans; there is the blend of admiration and envy found in other countries that have benefited from American aid. The one novelty Americans may find in the Turkish attitude is that some Turks resent the apparently inoffensive assumption that Turkey is a valuable ally of America in the present divided state of the world. The boot is on the other foot; hostility to Russia is a Turkish institution which is centuries older than the United States. The Turks are pleased to welcome America as an ally in their ancient struggle.

Turkey's participation in the Korean War, much though it raised her stock in Western eyes, did nothing to improve her relations with Russia, but as these were already confined to frozenly correct diplomatic exchanges, the fact was of no great consequence.

In August 1950, to punish the Turks for sending their contingent to Korea, the Bulgarian Government began to deport to Turkey a quarter-million Muslims of Turkish origin, many belonging to families that had been living in Bulgaria for generations. Most of these unhappy people were simply pushed across the frontier with only the clothes they stood up in. The Turkish Government could hardly refuse to admit them, as the Turkish Press had for some time been justly criticizing the Bulgars for ill-treating this minority. But the influx of refugees was not to the liking of the Turks, not only because of the difficulty of fitting these arrivals into the Turkish economy, but also because there was no way of ascertaining how many of them were Communist agents, availing themselves of the opportunity to infiltrate. In October the Turks closed the Bulgarian frontier, and did not reopen it till 2 December, the Bulgars having agreed to take back a number of non-Muslims who had been included amongst the deportees, and not to put across the border anybody who did not hold a Turkish entry-visa. The frontier was closed again on 8 November 1951, the Turks alleging that the Bulgars had sent across 1,000 gypsies 'camouflaged as Turkish emigrants'. On 21 February 1953, when Bulgaria agreed to take them back, the frontier was reopened.

One point in connection with Turkey's relations with Spain is worth a mention, for the light it throws on the guiding principles of Turkish policy. In 1946 United Nations recommended member-states to withdraw the heads of their diplomatic missions from Spain, and Turkey was one of the first nations to comply. On 5 November 1950, United Nations voted to annul this resolution. The former Turkish Minister to Spain arrived in Madrid the very same day. This is probably not to be taken as indicative of any special feeling for the present Spanish regime, but rather as a manifestation of the Turks' desire 'not to be left behind': to see what the other Western nations are going to do, and to do it first.

One of the few pleasant aspects of the immediate post-war scene was the growth of friendly relations between Turks and Greeks. It was made known in 1952 that Britain and America would welcome a defensive alliance of Greece, Turkey and Yugoslavia, to guard against a possible Russian drive through the Balkans. On 28 February 1953, representatives of the three Powers, meeting at Ankara, signed a Tripartite Treaty of Friendship and Co-operation, which was ratified by Greece and Yugoslavia on 23 March and by Turkey on 18 May. The new alliance had one great advantage over the short-lived Balkan Entente of the nineteen-thirties: it provided for a common defence organization, with a permanent secretariat, regular Staff conferences, and meetings of Foreign Ministers. On 5 June 1954, it was announced that the Treaty was to be converted into a formal military alliance, 'thus strengthening peace and collective security in the spirit of the U.N. Charter'. A joint consultative assembly of deputies of the three countries would be set up, to meet in the three capitals in rotation. Some delay in the signing of the instrument of alliance was expected, in view of the dispute which had arisen between Yugoslavia and Italy over Trieste: a peaceful settlement would clearly be hindered if the Italians thought that the Yugoslavs were strengthening their hand by a military alliance.

At the urgent request of the Greek Government, however, the Treaty 'of Alliance, Political Co-operation and Mutual Assistance' was signed at Bled on 9 August 1954. It provided that any aggression against one or more of the parties 'shall be considered as an aggression against all the parties'. In the event of aggression against any country towards which one or more of the parties have undertaken obligations of mutual assistance, 'the parties will consult each other on the measures to be taken, in conformity with the aims of the United Nations'.

The relations of the three Powers, however, soon deteriorated.

The outbreak of terrorism in Cyprus at the end of 1954, which differed from previous outbreaks in having the open support of the Greek Government and Athens Radio, was seen by the Turks as evidence that Greek protestations of friendship for her were false. Turkey's attitude was widely misinterpreted as due to concern for the Turkish-speaking fifth of the Colony's population. This concern, though real, was not paramount. Her chief anxiety was for her own security. Looking at the strength of the Communist element in Greece (where the pro-Communist E.D.A. won 24·3 per cent of the votes in the general election of May 1958), she found reason to doubt the country's internal stability, and feared that, if the demand for *enosis* were granted, a potentially Communist Cyprus, some 40 miles from Turkey, would menace the southern Turkish ports. The defence of Istanbul against a determined Russian attack could probably not be long maintained; İzmir and the whole Aegean coast is boxed in by the Greek-held offshore islands. To let Greece complete her encirclement by annexing Cyprus would be to prejudice the security of the entire population of Turkey, for the sake of the Greek 'pocket-majority' in the island.

On 15 September 1955, President Tito stated the official Yugoslav view, which, though expressed in friendly terms, was in favour of 'the right of self-determination of people in every country'. Since then, Greece has consistently pursued the support of Yugoslavia, leaving Turkey as odd man out, so that the new Balkan Entente can hardly be considered as a potent factor in the politics of the region.

When the Cyprus troubles started, late in 1954, the Turkish view was that so long as Britain retained the island Turkey would be content. The growing support for *enosis* shown by the leaders of the British Labour Party caused the Turks to worry about the likelihood of a Labour government's ceding Cyprus to Greece. They therefore seized on a suggestion (said to have been first made by Mr Walter Elliot, M.P., in a letter to *The Times* of 17 July 1956) that the island be partitioned. Their liking for this solution was increased by the outcome of the Suez landings, which seemed to indicate a diminution of Britain's power, as did the release of Archbishop Makarios from detention in March 1957. By mid-1957 the Turks were going all out for partition, and this was still their official policy on 19 June 1958, when Britain announced her 'Seven-Year Partnership Plan'. The Plan, after modification, was accepted by Turkey on 25 August. Representatives of the Greek and Turkish Governments would have a say in the administration, being given the right of direct access to the Governor. During the seven years for which British sovereignty would continue, separate Houses of Representatives would be established for the two communities. Pending elections to these Houses, separate Greek and Turkish municipal councils would be set up where the Governor thought fit. On 1 October 1958, the Turkish Consul-General in Cyprus officially assumed his duties as Turkish representative under the Plan.

The Greek government however refused to accept this decision and Archbishop Makarios proposed in September that the island should become independent. This was agreed after discussions in Zürich between the Greek and Turkish Prime Ministers and Foreign Ministers and subsequent discussions in London (February 1959). The Republic of Cyprus was inaugurated on 16 August 1960. Incorporated in its Constitution was the Treaty of Guarantee between the new Republic on the one hand and Britain, Greece and Turkey on the other. When trouble flared up again in December 1963, the Cyprus government denied the Turkish claim to the right to intervene; it may be of interest therefore to quote from the relevant documents so that the reader can judge for himself.

Article 181 of the Cyprus Constitution runs:

> The treaty guaranteeing the independence, territorial integrity and Constitution of the Republic concluded between the Republic, the Kingdom of Greece, the Republic of Turkey and the United Kingdom of Great Britain and Northern Ireland, and the Treaty of Military Alliance, concluded between the Republic, the Kingdom of Greece and the Republic of Turkey, copies of which are annexed to this Constitution as Annexes I and II, shall have constitutional force.

This Article is listed in Annex III as one of the 'basic articles' which, according to Article 182, 'cannot, in any way, be amended, whether by way of variation, addition or repeal.

Articles 2 and 3 of the Treaty of Guarantee:

> Article 2. Greece, the United Kingdom, and Turkey . . . recognize and guarantee the independence, territorial integrity, and security of the Republic of Cyprus, and also the provisions of the basic articles of its Constitution.
>
> They likewise undertake to prohibit, as far as lies within their power, all activity having the object of promoting directly or indirectly either the union of the Republic of Cyprus with any other State, or the partition of the Island.

> Article 3. In the event of any breach of the provisions of the Treaty, Greece, the United Kingdom, and Turkey undertake to consult together with a view to making representations or taking the necessary steps to ensure observance of these provisions.
>
> In so far as common or concerted action may prove impossible, each of the three guaranteeing Powers reserves the right to take action with the sole aim of re-establishing the state of affairs established by the Treaty.

A Treaty of Friendship with India was signed in Ankara on 14 December 1951.

In April 1954 Turkey concluded an 'Agreement for Friendly Co-operation' with Pakistan. An announcement was subsequently made that an exchange of missions would take place between the two countries to study the 'ways and extent of military assistance'.

Article 1 of the Agreement includes an undertaking that both countries will refrain from intervening in any way in each other's internal affairs. It would be interesting to know whether this is merely routine phraseology or whether it refers to the open secret that the Turkish National Party had received subsidies from Pakistani sources.

Article 6 begins thus:

> Any State, whose participation is considered by the contracting parties useful for achieving the purpose of the present agreement, may accede to the present agreement under the same conditions, and with the same obligations, as the contracting parties.

In this Article we see the second attempt to set up a Middle East defensive alliance. The agreement was a product of the new American policy of linking together in a system of alliances those Middle Eastern Powers which had not taken the neutralist line. The exclusion of Israel from the scope of this policy was intended to leave the door open for the eventual entry of the Arab States. The Turkish and Pakistani Prime Ministers decided in June 1954 that Staff talks should begin at once to prepared their common defence plans.

The Baghdad Pact grew out of the Treaty of Co-operation signed by Turkey and Iraq on 24 February, 1955, with the subsequent accession of Britain (4 April), Pakistan (23 September) and Persia (3 November). The idea behind it was to create a 'Northern Tier' of countries on the southern borders of the U.S.S.R. Militarily it added nothing to the strength of its stronger members; it is no discredit to the artistic and peace-loving people of Persia to say that they could not hold a Red Army attack for five minutes. Politically it was the cause of much trouble for Turkey, and of more than trouble for that well-intentioned and harmless young man, the late King Faisal II of Iraq. The Turks were ready to invade Iraq to suppress the revolution of 14 July 1958, which overthrew him, and they would have done so but for American pressure. After the revolution all Iraqis on the headquarters staff were given indefinite leave with pay 'pending a clarification of the present position'. The headquarters was transferred from Baghdad to Ankara in October 1958, and in August 1960 the organization changed its name to 'the Central Treaty Organization' (CENTO).

In common with the other Middle Eastern members of the Baghdad Pact, Turkey condemned the Israeli and Anglo-French attacks on Egypt in October–November 1956, but the feeling in the country, even amongst the officials, was far less critical than her official voice.

Aware that some Syrian politicians have not given up hope of regaining Hatay, the Turks regard the large-scale smuggling mentioned above as due to the connivance of the Syrian authorities through a desire to harm the Turkish economy. In the spring of 1955, Turkish armoured units were moved to the Syrian frontier, and there is some evidence that they were withdrawn only after a blunt warning from Moscow. In the autumn of 1957 came the 'artificial crisis', when Egyptian forces were landed in Syria to meet an alleged threat from Turkey. King Saud's offer of mediation was accepted by Turkey but rejected, after an initial acceptance, by Syria. On 30 October Syria asked the United Nations to set up a fact-finding commission; and dropped the request two days later. The crisis had fizzled out.

We cannot close this chapter without a word on Turkey's probable course of action in the event of war between the two world-blocs. To raise the subject at all may seem surprising, in face of all that we have said about Turkey's strong ties with the West and the long-standing enmity between her and Russia. But it must be remembered that the existence of the 1939 Treaty with France and Britain did not prevent Turkey from remaining neutral until two months before V.E. Day, although the Treaty was as binding as any Treaty can be. It would be imprudent, to say the least, to assume that Turkey would immediately go to war in the event of hostilities between the Communist Powers and the Western world. The Korean War showed once again that Turks can more than hold their own with any fighting-men in the world; a fact well known to the generation which fought in the First World War. It is beyond question that they would make any invader of their country pay a heavy price for his temerity. But if the potential aggressor has the sense to guarantee Turkey's territorial integrity, and if the Turks are not absolutely convinced of the certainty of Allied victory, the possibility must not be overlooked that they might find it politic to revive Atatürk's slogan of 'Peace at home and peace abroad', even though they are unlikely to return to his policy of positive friendship with the Soviets, notwithstanding occasional friendly nods towards Russia on the part of the Turks when they have felt neglected by their Western allies, notably in the matter of Cyprus.

In November 1964 the Turkish Foreign Minister visited Moscow and secured Russian support for the view that neither community in Cyprus should dominate the other. A cultural agreement was signed, but the Turks refused a proposal for an exchange of students (although the U.S.A. had accepted a similar Russian proposal in November 1959). The Western alliance means a great deal to the Turks and they will not lightly abandon it so long as the Cold War remains cold. But it would be unwise to assume that they would automatically take part in an armed conflict between Russia and the West.

Whether they would find it possible to remain neutral is quite another matter. On 14 October 1953, the Sixth Allied Tactical Air Force, staffed by Turks, Greeks and Americans, was established at İzmir. Commanded by an American officer, its function in the event of hostilities would be to provide air support for the Allied Land Forces, South-Eastern Europe. The following week, a new naval base, built at İskenderun at American expense, was formally handed over to the Turkish Government, to be placed at the disposal of the N.A.T.O. forces.

It is clear that, if war should break out, these new installations might be no less instrumental in forcing Turkey's hand than *Goeben* and *Breslau* were in 1914.

PART TWO

Chapter 24

Some Facts and Figures

(a) GEOGRAPHY

The territory of the Turkish Republic covers an area of 296,185 square miles, of which 9,256 form Thrace (*Trakya*) in the south-eastern tip of Europe, and the remainder Anatolia (*Anadolu*) in Asia Minor. The total length of her land-frontiers, is 1,637 miles, made up as follows:

Neighbour	Common Frontier in miles
Bulgaria	124
Greece	126
U.S.S.R.	366
Persia	294
Iraq	237
Syria	490

Turkey is a rugged land. The greater part of Anatolia is a treeless plateau, broken up by stretches of marshland and almost completely surrounded by mountains. This plateau rises steadily towards the eastern highlands. The highest peak, Mount Ararat (*Ağrı dağı*; 16,945 feet), on the frontier with Soviet Armenia, is the meeting-point of three great ranges, one skirting the Black Sea, the other two, Taurus and Anti-Taurus, running south-west towards the Mediterranean. South of the Anti-Taurus range lies a smaller plateau, which falls away into the great plain of Syria and Iraq and is watered by the Tigris and Euphrates.

North of the Gulf of İskenderun is the small but immensely fertile plain of Adana, rich in soil brought down from the Anti-Taurus by the Seyhan and Ceyhan rivers. Apart from this, the coastal plains are narrow, except on the Aegean and the Sea of Marmara.

In climate, Turkey presents a wide range of extremes, touching the warm temperate Mediterranean, the cold rainy Caucasus and the belt of desert and steppe which runs from the Sahara to Central Asia.

The Black Sea region has a generally mild climate, with a narrow range of winter and summer temperatures, though towards the east summers are hotter and rainfall greater, because the mountains shut off the cold dry north winds. In this warm damp climate the mountain-slopes are wooded, and lemons, oranges and hazel-nuts grow in abundance. Bafra, where the Kızıl Irmak ('Red River', the Halys of antiquity) meets the sea, is a particularly fertile region, and the whole coastal strip eastward from Sinop is famous for its tobacco. The west of the Black Sea area receives most of its rain in winter, the east in autumn. The highest mean annual rainfall of the whole country is at Rize, with over 70 inches.

The geological fault which runs parallel with the Black Sea coast, from the head of the Gulf of İzmit, through Bolu to Erzurum, is responsible for the not infrequent earthquakes which afflict this region, whose population is consequently smaller than one would otherwise expect in so fertile a zone.

The western and southern coastal plains enjoy a Mediterranean climate, with mild rainy winters and hot dry summers. The mean annual rainfall of the plains is about 25 inches and of the hills just over 30 inches. There is occasional snow, which does not stay long except on high ground. Rice grows well in these plains, especially round Antalya and Adana.

In the Marmara basin the Mediterranean and Black Sea climates overlap. Autumn and winter are rainy, and sudden rain-storms are frequent in spring. The north-west winds of winter bring snow from the Balkans. Istanbul, like England, has no climate, but only weather. Broadly speaking, winter there is colder but shorter than in England; spring and summer are warmer. But the temperature is governed by two winds—*Poyraz*, the north-easter, and *Lodos*, the soft south wind—and nobody knows which of the two will blow on any given day.

The climate of the central plateau is extreme, with temperatures ranging from —15°F. in winter to over 100°F. in summer. Violent rains are common in spring and autumn, the mean annual rainfall varying between 8 and 12 inches, except in the nighbourhood of the great Salt Lake (*Tuz gölü*), where it is considerably less.

Life is harsh in the eastern uplands. Summer comes late and soon passes, to be followed by a long hard winter. Round Kars and Erzurum the thermometer scarcely ever rises above freezing-point in winter, temperatures of —40°F. being not unknown.

(b) The People

The ethnological history of Asia Minor is of great complexity. For thousands of years it has been a seat of empires, and a highway and a battlefield for migrating peoples. Phrygians, Hittites, Lydians, Cimmerians, Thracians, Persians and Greeks had all set their seal on the land before the coming of the Romans. After the Roman Empire was divided, the Byzantines held sway over Asia Minor till the eleventh century of our era. But even in the comparatively settled conditions of the early Byzantine Empire, the ethnic picture did not remain static; whether as peaceful wanderers or reckless invaders, there was an endless stream of new-comers out of southern Russia and Central Asia. In the seventh century came the first Muslim armies, adding still more to the mixture of peoples. These new arrivals were not Arabs alone, for when the followers of the Prophet erupted from the Peninsula their numbers were swollen by non-Arab converts whom they picked up in their triumphant progress. Other converts came out of Asia, so that when the Seljuks arrived they found many bands of Turks settled in the land before them. Christianized Turks there were too, transplanted from the Balkans to meet some requirement of Byzantine imperial policy.

A striking symbol of the heterogeneity of the people of Asia Minor is to be seen at Ankara, where the Mosque of Hacı Bayram encroaches on the site of the Temple of Augustus. This was built on the foundations of a Phrygian sanctuary and was converted to a place of Christian worship under the Byzantines.

The consequence of all this is that the visitor to Turkey who expects to see a country full of slant-eyed Mongols is due for a surprise. The Turks are, broadly speaking, indistinguishable from their Balkan neighbours.

An anthropometric investigation, carried out in 1937 and 1938 on 64,000 Turks in all parts of the country, produced these results: the average height of Turkish men is 1·652 metres (5 feet 5 inches), of women 1·522 metres (5 feet), the tallest people being found in the east of the country. Roughly three-quarters of the population are brachycephalic, the average cranial index of men being 83·33, of women 83·78. The straight and 'leptorrhine' (narrow-nostrilled) type of nose predominates. Concave noses are rare. Only 14 per cent of men and 17 per cent of women have dark eyes, blue eyes being not uncommon. The slanting Mongoloid eyes were found in barely 5 per cent of all those examined. The most common hair-colouring is medium to light brown. Only 30 per cent of the samples had dark hair. The general conclusion was that most Turks are of Alpine type, with a sprinkling of Dinaric.

Although this investigation is the most comprehensive yet carried out in Turkey, the figures involved may not seem impressive to the layman. The results, however, square with one's subjective impressions. Certainly the amateur ethnographer will find his self-confidence shaken if he tries to identify the Turkish students among a crowd at the Sorbonne.

The first table, based on the 1945 census, shows the division of the population by language.

Abaza	8,602
Albanian	14,165
Armenian	56,179
Arabic	247,204
Bosnian	13,280
Bulgarian	8,750
Circassian	66,691
Coptic	4,463
English	1,773
French	5,233
Georgian	40,076
German	2,342
Greek	88,680
Italian	2,640
Jewish	51,019
Kurdish	1,476,562
Laz	46,987
Spanish	11,152
Tartar	10,047
Turkish	16,598,037
Other tongues	36,161
Unknown	131
TOTAL	18,790,174

Rough percentages of the main linguistic groups in 1960:[1]

	Percentage
Turkish	92·0
Kurdish	5·8
Arabic	1·0
Armenian	1·0
Greek	1·0
Others	1·2

In the first table, the figures against each language show the number of people (including infants) whose mother-tongue it is.

Abaza is spoken by the Abkhaz, a Georgian people, while Laz is the language of a maritime people of the Black Sea coast, east of Trabzon.

The quarter-million speakers of Arabic are to be found mainly in the south-east, along the Syrian border.[2]

[1] Figures of the 1960 census are drawn from 1960 *Population Census of Turkey: Estimated National Totals Based on 1% Sample* (Ankara, 1962).

[2] Ömer Asım Aksoy, in his brilliant study of the dialect of Gaziantep (*Gaziantep ağzı*, Istanbul, 1945–1946), insists that there are no Arabic-speakers there at all. This would suggest a high concentration of Arabic-speakers in the other frontier

The 4,000 claimants of 'Coptic' (*Kıptice*) which ceased to be a spoken language many centuries ago, might conceivably have been members of the Coptic and Uniate Coptic Churches, putting a liberal interpretation on the term 'mother-tongue' in order to assert their group identity (as will be seen in the next table, the census-takers did not list Copts separately). It is far more likely, however, that they were Gipsies (*Kıpti*).

The term 'Jewish' (*Yahudice*) can hardly mean Yiddish, because most of the Jews of Turkey are Sephardi. Probably the mother-tongue of the majority of people under this heading was Ladino. This is, basically, the Spanish of the fifteenth century, brought with them by Jewish refugees after the expulsion from Spain in 1492, with numerous borrowings from the languages of the eastern Mediterranean and, more recently, from French. It was formerly written in Hebrew characters, but nowadays in the Latin letters of the new Turkish alphabet. Most likely, some of the 11,000 people who gave their mother-tongue as Spanish also really meant Ladino.

To complete this brief linguistic note on the Turkish Jews, it should be pointed out that many of them, especially members of the wealthier families, speak French at home, because they received their education at the schools of the Alliance Israélite Universelle. This organization was founded by French Jews in 1860, to establish schools for Jewish communities in French North Africa and the Middle East, and so to bring about their emancipation by bridging the gulf between medievalism and modern civilization.

The next table shows the division of the population by religion (1945).

Muslims	18,497,801
Christians	
Orthodox	103,839
Gregorian	60,260
Roman Catholic	21,950
Protestant	5,213
Other denominations	10,782
Total of Christians	202,044
Jews	76,965
Other faiths	12,582
Atheists	561
Total of non-Muslims	292,152
Unknown	221
GRAND TOTAL	18,790,174

vilayets, but the assertion more probably represents a victory of patriotism over scholarship. It is conventional among Republican Turks to pretend that the population is homogeneous.

Rough percentages for 1960:

	Percentage
Muslims	99·0
Christians	
Orthodox	0·4
Gregorian	0·3
Roman Catholic	0·3
Protestant	0·2
Jewish	0·1
Others	0·2

The figure given for Muslims includes both Sunnites and Shi'ites (see page 90).

The head of the Orthodox Church is the Oecumenical Patriarch, whose seat is at Istanbul, as is that of the Gregorian (Armenian) Patriarch. The latter is under the authority of the Katholikos of Echmiadzin. There is an Apostolic Delegate in Istanbul and a Roman Catholic Archbishop of İzmir. The Roman Catholic dignitary known as the Patriarch of Istanbul does not reside in Turkey.

The 'other denominations' include the Nestorian Uniates (Chaldaeans), who have a Bishop at Mardin, and the Armenian Uniates, under the Patriarch of Cilicia.

The offices of the Chief Rabbinate are in Istanbul. The only figure in the table that has changed substantially since 1945 (apart from the general rise in population) is that for the Jews. In 1953 they numbered approximately 59,000; the difference is due to large-scale emigration to Israel. By the end of 1949 some 30,000 Jews were reported to have reached Israel from Turkey, but several thousands subsequently decided to return. The number of these is not as great as the figures given above would seem to indicate; some allowance must be made for statistical errors and for the fact that, as the majority of the emigrants were young people, the death-rate among those who stayed in Turkey would be above normal. Still, we can safely assume that 15,000 Jews have left Turkey for good.

The explanation which one of them (an engineer who had been educated in France) gave the author for his decision to leave Turkey, reflects the opinion of a good many members of the minorities. 'I am going because, although I have lived here most of my life, and my family has been here for nearly five hundred years, I don't feel at home here. It's not that we're ill-treated, it's just that I can't talk to a Turk on equal terms; it's his country, not mine, and he won't let me forget it.' The suggestion that he, too, was a Turk was greeted at first with incomprehension and then with wry amusement. 'I've met Jews in France who regard themselves as "Frenchmen of the Jewish faith". Such a thing isn't possible here. If you're a Jew, how can you be a Turk?' Then, revealingly, he added, 'After all, I don't even talk Turkish properly.' In this last remark is the key to much of the problem.

In the mid-19th century there were Greek and Armenians who wrote Turkish in their own alphabets. In 1841 the Imprimerie de Castro issued a broadsheet in Hebrew, Turkish and Ladino, by command of Sultan Abdülmecid, urging the Jews of Istanbul to learn to speak Turkish, and in 1867 the Ottoman Ministry of Education accepted the principle that non-Muslim children should be admitted to State secondary schools. But two years later new regulations for public instruction were put into force by the Ministry, and these included the following clauses:

> In every city-ward and village, or, if the circumstances warrant it, in every two wards or villages, there shall be at least one boys' school. In mixed wards or villages, there shall be separate Muslim and non-Muslim schools. The period of instruction shall be four years. The syllabus for the Muslim schools shall be as follows: the alphabet, Koran-recitation, elements of religion and ethics, with the rudiments of Ottoman history and geography, and useful knowledge. The three last subjects shall be taught to non-Muslims also, in their own languages.
>
> The syllabus for non-Muslim schools is as follows: religious instruction under the direction of their spiritual heads, writing, and outlines of arithmetic.
>
> In towns of mixed population, there shall be one grammar school for Muslims and one for Christians, if their community numbers more than 100 families. The same applies to other non-Muslim communities. . . .
>
> Lessons are to be given to every *millet* in its own language, from books written in that language. In the final year of the four, those who wish may learn French.

With minor modifications, these provisions remained in force till the proclamation of the Republic. In other words, non-Muslims born before, say, 1915 did not, as a general rule, speak Turkish at home or in school. In the special case of Jewish children whose parents spoke Ladino but who went to one of the schools of the Alliance Israélite, Turkish was learned, if at all, as a third language. So the impatient cry of the Nationalists, 'Citizen! Speak Turkish!', was not really fair, although the motives behind it were laudable.

But the Nationalists did not confine their efforts to nagging at the older generation; concerned as they were to make Turks out of all who dwelt within the boundaries of the Republic, they decreed that Turkish should be taught in all schools and should be the language of instruction in history and geography.

The consequence is that those Christians and Jews who have grown up under the Republic differ from their parents in speaking Turkish well. Their children will speak it perfectly.

Till well into the nineteenth century, a Christian or Jew was usually identifiable by his dress. The fact that this had ceased to be the case by 1922 was not generally known outside Turkey, which is why not a few Greeks were killed at Smyrna by the Greek Army of Occupation, who took to shooting anyone they saw wearing a fez. More recently the infallible criterion was accent. If a man told you he lived at Nisantas, instead of Nişantaş, you knew at once he was a Greek.[1] Now this criterion, too, is losing its value.

Not of course that the minorities problem is merely one of language, in Turkey or anywhere else. The following passages are quoted from an article[2] which appeared in the January–February 1950 number of the 'Journal of Administration' (*İdare Dergisi*), published by the Ministry of the Interior. The subject of the article was a proposal to give Istanbul a municipal police-force, independent of the national force.

> Istanbul is a cosmopolitan city. A quarter of its population are non-Turkish and non-Muslim. These elements either enjoyed the protection of the Capitulations themselves or have breathed the atmosphere of those who did so, and have assumed their mentality. In spite of the 25-odd years that have passed since the abolition of the Capitulations, they have not been erased from the minds of this class. With them, as with the Turkish element, the State police have great influence and prestige. If executive authority is transferred to a private police-force, such as a municipal force, the executive power cannot be effective. . . . Istanbul, which is difficult enough to administer as it is, would then be heading straight for anarchy . . . Today, when the executive power of the Municipality is in the hands of the Government police, things are done which the devil himself would not think of; we must agree that far more numerous and varied offences would be committed here-

[1] 'Then said they unto him, Say now Shibboleth: and he said Sibboleth: for he could not frame to pronounce it right' (Judges xii, 6).

[2] *İstanbul İdaresi,* by Ekrem Talat Avşaroğlu.

> after . . . For a long time, an anti-Turkish campaign has been going on in Europe, arising out of Christian sectarianism and imperialist notions. This campaign may have slackened in the Republic period, but it is still going on. Our own minorities are serving it as volunteers. It is a fact that they spread poison, in a scarcely credible fashion, amongst all our foreign visitors. They have been doing so for centuries. Henceforth we should cease to give this class any opportunity.

Turkey had changed since then, and probably no official or semi-official journal would print such stuff now. But it does represent a point of view that is not confined to the writer of the article. All one can say is that the Turkish Government's policy is one of complete liberality; officially there is no minorities problem because officially there are no minorities. It has always been theoretically possible for non-Muslims to hold commissions in the armed services of the Republic.[1] Now it really happens. Each successive generation of Turkish-born Christians and Jews will feel more at home in Turkey, though members of the Jewish community may grow tired of waiting and go to seek, in Israel, a land they can call their own. But most will stay.

The author was once dining in a restaurant at Antalya, at the next table to a large party of Greeks. His Turkish companion explained that they were not exactly local people; the older members of the party, whom he knew by sight, had lived in Antalya many years before but had thought it politic to move to Athens when the Greek Army withdrew from Anatolia. 'Now, for the last few years, they've been coming here for their holidays, every summer, with their children and grandchildren. Odd, isn't it?'

The point need not be laboured, but it may be noted that the principle works both ways. In his *Grey Wolf*,[2] Armstrong tells how Mustafa Kemal's mother, very old and quite blind, came to live with her son at Çankaya during the War of Independence: 'Her greatest pleasure was to be allowed to talk to the Greek prisoners, who could give her news of the village in southern Albania where she had been born.'

. . . . .

[1] Non-Muslims were occasionally commissioned in the Ottoman Army and Navy, but only in the medical branch.

[2] See Bibliography.

The increase in the population of Turkey is shown in the following table:

Year	
1927	13,648,270
1939	16,158,018
1940	17,820,950
1945	18,790,174
1950	20,947,188
1955	24,121,778
1960	27,829,000
1961	28,602,000
1962	29,418,000
1963	30,256,000

The rate of increase is 2·8 per cent per annum, the highest of any of the member states of O.E.C.D. The average rate for Western Europe is 1 per cent and for the U.S.A. 1·7.

The 1960 census showed the populations of the principal cities to be as follows:

Ankara	646,151
Istanbul	1,459,528
Izmir.	370,923
Adana	230,024
Bursa.	153,574
Eskişehir	153,190

. . . . .

On 21 February 1955, there took place in the Grand National Assembly a debate which helps to complete the picture of Islam in Turkey. The subject was the 1955 budget of the Directorate of Religious Affairs, which pays the stipends of muftis, preachers and urban imams (village imams are supported by their congregations). In 1950 it was allotted 4 million lira (just over £505,000). This figure had steadily risen until now it stood at 17 million lira.

This was not a large fraction of the total budget of about 3,000 million lira; on the other hand, it did not represent the whole of the expenditure from public funds on Sunnite Islam. Religious teaching in primary schools is paid for by the Ministry of Education, as is the Faculty of Divinity at Ankara University. Local authorities make grants for the building and repair of mosques.[1]

The debate was noisy and acrimonious. A Democrat member demanded higher stipends for the imams and preachers who 'represent the spiritual values which ensure the prosperity and

[1] Most of the great city mosques are maintained by the Directorate-General of *Evkaf*, out of the ancient endowments, which are now worth about £50 million.

well-being of the nation'. This speech was received with cheers, some ironical. A Republican tartly replied that however small an imam's stipend might be, he could always supplement it by writing amulets for the ignorant and superstitious.

The next Republican speaker declared that certain imams and preachers, one of whom he named, had spoken against the Kemalist reforms. Why did the Directorate of Religious Affairs take no action against them? At this point, the commotion in the usually decorous Assembly prevented the speaker from being heard. When silence had been restored, member after member arose to castigate him as a freemason and an atheist. 'We have left freemasonry alone', said one, 'why can't they leave our religion alone?' The Republican took the rostrum again. 'Why all the fuss?' he asked. 'All I did was say that religion should be kept apart from politics.' He added that some deputies did not know the difference between freemasonry and laicism.

The remarkable point about this answer is not what it said but what it did not say. After all, freemasonry and atheism do not receive subsidies from the State; one might have expected the speaker to ask why a country which has no official religion should spend millions of lira on one particular faith. But that is a question no Republican is likely to ask, because the Directorate of Religious Affairs was a creation of the Republican People's Party and has always been financed by the State.

The truth is that the men who made the Republic were not, as a body, opposed to Islamic worship, though Mustafa Kemal personally was not a religious man. What he and his supporters denied was the claim of Islam to regulate the whole lives of its adherents; their aim was to confine it to the mosque, to reduce it to a matter of belief and prayer. Once Islamic law had been replaced by western law, it would have been false and hypocritical to call Islam the State religion, although it was the ancestral faith of almost 97 per cent of citizens. And knowing that one cannot legislate the religion out of a man, Kemal saw that there would continue to be religious leaders, who would have to be under Governmental control. Hence the Directorate of Religious Affairs.

The attitude of the educated modern Turk was well expressed in an editorial in *Zafer*, the Democrat Party's newspaper (21 February 1955):

> We are all of us, thank God, Muslims, but this fact is between our souls and our consciences. In the State, religious and mundane affairs have been decisively separated. The howl of

the ignorant *medrese*-louts, 'We want the sacred law!', is buried in the dark of history, together with the tragedies of the Thirty-first of March, never to rise again. Great though our need and respect may be for the learned men of the Faith, we shall have no mercy on any word or deed of theirs that conflicts with the interests of the country, the citizen's conscience, or the Constitution.

In the last few years the impression has been growing in the Western world that the power of the 'black reaction' in Turkey was on the increase. This is not so much because there have been more signs of it, as because more Western writers have mentioned it. A heartening development came in June 1957. Three years before, an Imam had been sentenced to ten months' imprisonment for telling his congregation that those of them who failed to attend a forthcoming meeting of the Democrat Party should be regarded as infidels. For various reasons he had not yet served his sentence, and now an attempt was made to procure a pardon for him from the Grand National Assembly. The motion was heavily defeated, most of the Democrats voting against it with the Opposition.

The liberal element in the Assembly won another victory in March 1958, when a Bill providing for heavier penalties for insulting 'God, the prophets, and the sacred objects of any of the four religions recognized by Turkey (Islam, Christianity, Judaism and Buddhism)' was referred back to the Judicial Committee of the G.N.A., as being contrary to the Constitution, which did not officially recognize any religion.

Islam, in the sense of the letter and spirit of the faith preached by Muhammad, is not necessarily a bar to 'progress', certainly not to human happiness. But that was not what the '*medrese*-louts' wanted when they shouted for the sacred law. They did not mean the system erected by the wisdom and devotion of the great jurists, on the basis of the revealed Word; they meant the way of life of the decaying Ottoman Empire, they meant their own personal prejudices. Only so long as the dichotomy of religion and State is preserved can the Turkish Republic endure as its founders conceived it, and as the majority of its thinking men and women wish it to be.

(c) Agriculture

Agriculture provides 40 per cent of the national income.

In 1960, Turkey's total acreage was divided up as follows:

	Percentage
Arable	30·0
Meadows and pastures	36·9
Vineyards	1·0
Gardens and orchards	0·9
Olive groves	0·7
Forest	13·6
Wasteland, lakes, marshes	16·9

In ten years the area under cultivation had increased by half. Wheat accounts for more than half of the total cereal crop and barley for a quarter. The remaining cereals grown are maize, rye, oats, spelt, millet and rice.

Total cereal production in 1962 was 14·6 million tons. The yield of cereals, in kilogrammes per hectare, was 1,295 in 1953, 854 in 1954, 1,029 in 1955, 975 in 1956, 1,175 in 1960, 982 in 1961, 1,127 in 1962 and 1,337 in 1963. The wheat-growing region has always been western Anatolia, the Marmara basin and the slopes that edge the north and south of the central plateau. To this there has recently been added a large tract east of Urfa and south of Diyarbakır, and another in the southern half of the plateau.

Cotton, both for textile manufacture and for animal feeding-stuff, is grown mainly in Çukurova, the 'Sunken Plain' between the Seyhan and Ceyhan rivers, with a lesser area round Smyrna and Aydın. Production rose from 165,000 tons in 1952 to 246,000 tons in 1963.

Olives grow all round the coast, except in the extreme north-east. There are some 60 million olive-trees in the country, which produce over a quarter-million tons of olives and 50,000 tons of oil annually.

Opium, of which Turkey is the world's chief producer, comes mostly from the vilayets of Afyonkarahisar (the name means 'Opium-Black-Fortress'), Denizli, Isparta and other places on the west of the plateau. The 1962 crop yielded 300 tons of gum.

Tobacco is grown by almost a quarter of a million farmers all over Turkey, but the main areas are centred on Smyrna and Samsun. Annual production varies between 80,000 and 140,000 tons.

Turkish sultanas have always been famous, but recent years have seen a great increase in viticulture for the purpose of wine-making, notably in the Smyrna plain, and the results are eminently drinkable. Almost ten million litres of wine were produced in 1962, in addition to six million litres of *rakı*, the potent national drink, which is distilled from the juice of grapes and tastes of aniseed. It is taken in water, even by the strongest heads. Much of the wine goes to France, where it joins the Algerian wine in the carafes of *vin ordinaire*. Some Turkish cynics suggested that their country's support for the Algerian independence movement was based on the hope that an independent Muslim Algeria would end the production of wine, thus increasing the sales to France of the Turkish product. This is worth recording only as a reply to any who doubt whether the Turkish mind is capable of subtlety.

An idea of the importance of pastoralism in the Turkish economy is given by the following figures (in thousands) of domesticated animals existing in 1962:

Sheep	31,614
Goats	16,420
Angora goats	5,655
Cattle	12,662
Water-buffalo	1,160
Horses	1,239
Donkeys	1,880
Mules	208
Camels	53

As one would expect in a Muslim country, comparatively few pigs are kept; there are only 4,000 pigs among the 7·5 million animals slaughtered for meat in each year.

Deforestation is a grave problem, which is taken so seriously by the authorities that offenders against the Forestry Law are always excluded from general amnesties. Nevertheless, a great deal of unlicensed felling goes on; as the alternative fuel is dung, which the peasant is equally exhorted not to waste, he is in a cleft stick. In fact, over much of the eastern half of the country, dung is the usual fuel for cooking and for warming the house in winter.

The mechanization of agriculture and the growth of industry in the nineteen-fifties led to an influx of villagers to the big cities and to the Eastern Marmara region, which is rapidly developing as an industrial area. Well over half a million came to Istanbul alone, mostly from the provinces of Sivas and Kastamonu.

The following table[1] may help to keep in perspective reports of increased mechanization:

	1960	1961	1962
Number of tractors in use	42,505	42,183	43,747
Number of wooden ploughs in use	1,991,259	2,065,012	2,087,025

[1] Extracted from *Agricultural Structure and Production*, 1960–1962 (Ankara, 1964).

Rather than weary the reader with an account of the various attempts at land-reform which have been and are being made, it may be said simply that the size of the average land-holding in 1952 was 19 acres and that the much publicized distributions of the Menderes era did little more than increase the number of unworkably tiny holdings, so that in 1961, out of more than 2 million farms in private hands, there were only 3,358 exceeding 25 acres in area. The distributions had been mainly of uncultivated State land; the aghas (*ağa*), the big landowners, had not suffered. Over half the national income from agriculture still went to one-tenth of the farmers.

Not long after the 1960 revolution, the N.U.C. exiled 56 aghas of the east and south-east, but in August 1962 they were allowed to return, because in fact fifty of them had turned out to be not particularly big landowners; they had been chosen more or less at random, while many richer and more grasping aghas had escaped. But instead of setting about the job properly the government let the matter drop, because aghas control votes as effectively as any pre-Reform Bill English squire. Here is a not unprecedented news-item of 20 April 1963:

> An agha called İsa Rejo, who bought the village of Sirbe, in the Açkale department of Urfa province, sent his men to demolish the 41 houses of the village while the villagers were away in the summer-pasture and to plough over the site with a tractor, thus leaving 300 people homeless.

(d) Minerals

Turkey's great subterranean riches are only now beginning to be exploited to the full. The proclamation of the Republic found 90 per cent of the mining industry in foreign hands, but it is now largely owned by the State, through the Eti Bank (founded 1935).

Great deposits of high-grade bituminous coal lie along the Black Sea coast, between Ereğli and Cide, with Zonguldak as the chief mining centre. The Zonguldak coalfields were not nationalized until 1940, when wartime difficulties prevented the importation of the equipment needed for modernization. Average daily production is 18,500 tons.

Lignite is found all over Turkey, and for some years the Government has been trying to popularize its use for domestic purposes. The main workings are at Kütahya.

Iron is mined at Divriği, in the mountains south-east of Sivas, and smelted at Karabük near Zonguldak, 600 miles away. Criticism has been levelled at the Turks by foreign economists for their short-sightedness in putting their only blast furnaces so far from their only source of ore, which has to be carried all those miles by rail. But, this criticism is unfair; or rather it is on the wrong plane. In 1937 when it was decided to build an iron-works at Karabük, in proximity to the coal-workings, mining had not yet started at Divriği, although it has long been known that iron ore existed in the neighbourhood. The original intention was to import ore from abroad to feed the furnaces of Karabük, which had a major place in Mustafa Kemal's plan to industrialize Turkey. One feels that the same critics would have been no less scathing if the blast-furnaces had been erected near Divriği, when it would have been necessary to bring coal all the way from Zonguldak and to transport the smelted iron some 250 miles to the nearest port, Samsun. Mustafa Kemal would no doubt have pleased the economists better by not building an iron-works at all, but he did not base his actions solely on economic grounds.

Chrome is one of Turkey's principal dollar-earning exports. It is mined at Güleman, north-west of Diyarbakır, and, on a smaller scale, at Kütahya, Eskişehir, Denizli and Marmaris. The total production expanded from 422,532 tons in 1950 to 910,000 tons in 1957, but contracted to a yearly average of 480,276 tons in 1958–1963.

Copper is mined at Ergani, near Güleman, and at Hopa, in the extreme north-east of the country. Production rose from 11,700 tons in 1950 to 24,792 in 1963. Hopa is also the centre of manganese-mining; the total Turkish production for 1963 being 19,188 tons.

Wolfram, the ore of tungsten, is mined at Uludağ (the ancient Mysian Olympus), and a highly promising new deposit was found in late 1953 near Edremit.

At Akseki, in the Devil's Mountains, north of the Gulf of Antalya, are bauxite reserves estimated at 5 million tons.

Turkish oil has only lately come into the news, although its existence has been known for many years. Khanzadian's *Atlas de géographie économique de la Turquie*, published in 1924, marks two deposits immediately to the east of Lake Van and mentions another in the vilayet of Erzurum. Some desultory test-borings had been made before the First World War, round the Sea of Marmara and the Gulf of İskenderun, but the results were not encouraging. In the nineteen-thirties, however, a systematic exploration was begun, because the Republican Party's industrial programme was calling for more and more oil, which Turkey's shortage of foreign exchange made it difficult to buy abroad. The proximity of the Mosul oil-fields gave grounds for hoping that workable deposits might be found within Turkey's eastern borders.

The original exploration was entrusted to a Turkish Government agency, the Mineral Research and Exploration Institute (*Maden Tetkik ve Arama Enstitüsü*). Drilling began at Basbirin, some 25 miles north-west of Nusaybin, in 1934 and was continued in that region for several years. After the annexation of Hatay, drilling was also started at two sites there.

The first strike worth mentioning was made in 1940, at Ramandağ 60 miles due east of Diyarbakır. The oil was found at a depth of 1,060 metres and had to be pumped to the surface for want of natural gas-pressure; still, the results were sufficiently promising for work to continue. Development was understandably slow during the war-years, as at Zonguldak, but as the end of 1947 approached with little to show for so much labour and expense, the Turks wisely brought in expert American help. Within a matter of months several strikes of commercial importance were made, and by mid-1953 nineteen wells were operating there. In 1952 oil was also found at Garzan, 10 miles north-east of Ramandağ. The reserves of the Ramandağ area are estimated to be close on 12 million tons.

Between the towns of Adıyaman and Kâhta, in the south of the vilayet of Malatya, a new oil-field was discovered by chance in 1953, through an investigation into complaints that the water of a public fountain was tainted. The complaints proved to be justified; the foreign body was found to be crude oil.

In November 1952 the Council of Ministers, in accordance with the Democrat policy of denationalization, and profiting by recent experience, decided that the State should not attempt to compete with those better qualified to establish and run an oil industry. A contract was signed with an American firm to build a refinery and operate it for a year, after which time it would be handed over to the Turkish Government, who would entrust it to a corporation in which private capital would be encouraged to participate. The site chosen was at Batman, within a few miles of Ramandağ and Garzan, where a small experimental refinery had already been operating for several years. By the end of 1953 eight foreign oil companies were conducting geological surveys in south and south-east Turkey.

The production of crude oil rose from 178,596 tons in 1955 to 729,060 tons in 1963.

(e) Transport and Communications

The progressive-minded Pasha in Kinglake's *Eothen*, who was so preoccupied with wheels, would have been overjoyed to see the revolution which has come over Turkish transport since his day. The War of Independence showed up the disastrous paucity of roads and railways in Anatolia; when village women had walked over the mountains of the Black Sea coast, humping shells on their backs for the Nationalist guns in the interior.

The establishment of the Republic found the following railways in existence. Istanbul was linked to Europe by the Oriental Railway through Adrianople and Sofia. From Haydarpaşa, on the Asian side of the Bosphorus, a line ran south-east, forking at Eskişehir; one line straggling eastward across the plateau to Ankara, the other running through Alayunt (whence a short spur led to Kütahya), then Afyon, Konya and Adana to Fevzipaşa, throwing out short branches to the ports of Mersin and İskenderun. At Fevzipaşa it turned to cross the present Syrian border for Aleppo. At Muslimiya, between the border and Aleppo, was a junction from which a line came back to Mardin, Nusaybin and eventually Baghdad.

From Bandırma, on the southern shore of the Sea of Marmara, a railway ran to Smyrna, sending out a branch from Manisa to Afyon, where, however, it did not connect with the main Istanbul–Baghdad line. From Smyrna went the old British-built line to Aydın, Sarayköy and Eğridir, north-east of Isparta. The ancient capital at Bursa was linked by a short line (now disused) to the Marmara port of Mudanya. And that was all, except for a line from Erzurum into Armenia, built by the Russians during the First World War, of narrow gauge as far as Sarıkamış and Russian broad gauge thereafter.

One of the Republican Government's first concerns was to improve rail communications, an obvious prerequisite of any scheme for agrarian or industrial development. A further consideration was that the existing skeletal railway system radiated from Istanbul, whereas in the new Turkey all roads must lead to Ankara.

As early as March 1924 funds were voted to construct a line joining the new capital to Kayseri, Sivas and Samsun, and work began at once. A rail-link between Fevzipaşa and Diyarbakır was then decided on, with the avowed purpose of improving access to the copper-mines at Ergani, though the difficulties experienced in moving troops during the Kurdish Revolt may have been an additional incentive.

From Irmak, on the Kayseri line 30 miles east of Ankara, a branch was driven north to Karabük and Zonguldak (the mountains close the direct northward route from Ankara itself). This branch, of immense importance for mineral traffic, is called the Filyos line, after the stream in whose valley it runs from Karabük to the sea. A Government publication recording the achievements of the first ten years of the Republic was able to say with pride:

> By means of the railways, we are reaching the coal and the copper, we have joined the Mediterranean to the Black Sea, we have reached Balıkesir [by the line built westward from Kütahya], we have passed Sivas. Tomorrow we shall be in Erzurum.

The Government was determined not only to build new railways, but also to bring the existing ones under State ownership. At the beginning of the First World War, the German-owned stock in the Baghdad railway had been made over to a Swiss bank, and was therefore beyond the reach of the Reparations Commission. In 1922 a group of British banks came to an understanding with the Swiss and formed a new organization to resume control of the railway. It was when this organization made its purpose known that the Turks resolved to buy the foreigners out. In spite of all the difficulties confronting the young Republic, this aim was eventually achieved; the Istanbul–Konya section became Turkish on 1 January, 1928, and the portion from Konya to the Syrian frontier in 1937. Meanwhile, the French-owned Bandırma–Smyrna and Smyrna–Afyon lines had been purchased in 1934, and in the following year the British-owned Smyrna–Aydın–Eğridir line. By the end of 1947, the last few kilometres of foreign-owned railway had been brought under State control.

To find the money (some £15 million sterling) for these purchases, while continuing to build new lines, was no mean feat. But it was done, with Turkish capital and by Turkish engineers, and the Turkish State Railways are now a credit to the country. The railway has reached Erzurum and passed it. The old narrow and broad sections to the Soviet frontier have been replaced by normal gauge. From Diyarbakır the line has been driven east as far as Kurtalan; the extension from Elâzığ to Lake Van has reached Tatvan. The next step will probably be to introduce double-track working on some of the more important stretches of line, most of which are still single-track.

On 24 July 1958, the Economic Committee of the Baghdad Pact announced that work had begun on linking the Persian and Turkish road and railway systems. Britain had agreed to give each country £100,000 towards the construction of the rail link from Muş to Tabriz.

From the Ottoman Empire the Republic inherited some 17,500 kilometres of roads. Despite the Government's early preoccupation with railways, this figure had been raised to over 40,000 by the end of 1947, over 47,000 by the end of 1950 and over 61,000 by the end of 1960. Of this latest figure, just over a third represents roads negotiable by motor transport all the year round. Details are appended of the various types of road as they were in 1961.

Type of road	Length in kilometres
Paved	156
Concrete	22
Asphalt	6,880
Good macadam	2,286
Ruined macadam	1,782
Stabilized	30,922
Graded earth	9,168
Unmade tracks negotiable by motor transport	10,335

Since 1948 a team of experts supplied by the American Bureau of Public Roads had been actively helping the Turkish Ministry of Public Works to promote the busier highways to the higher categories of this table.

The improvement in the highways system and in Turkish standards of living is reflected in the increased number of vehicles:

	1949	1950	1951	1952	1953	1957	1961
Cars	8,001	10,071	13,465	16,457	23,879	33,377	45,767
Buses	2,622	3,185	3,755	4,469	5,494	7,414	10,981
Motor-lorries	11,470	13,201	15,404	18,356	24,596	35,070	57,460

To keep the picture in perspective, however, it should be noted that there are still over 600,000 ox-carts in the country, over half of them being of the solid-wheeled variety.

The *dolmuş*-system is one Turkish idea in the field of transport which other nations might usefully adopt. A *dolmuş* is a taxi, distinctively marked, which plies on a regular route and starts as soon as it has its complement of passengers (the name literally means 'filled'). At busy centres of traffic in the cities there are *dolmuş*-stands, with a sign showing the authorized fares for each run; *dolmuş*-drivers, unlike ordinary cabbies, never haggle about the fare and do not expect tips. During rush-hours there is never a delay of more than a few minutes before the *dolmuş* fills up and moves off.

This mode of travel is cheap and speedy; and even though no driver considers his car full, however small its seating capacity, until it has at least five passengers on board, the occasional discomfort is well worth while. In terms of English money, a journey which would cost 6*d.* by tram, 7*d.* by bus, or 4*s.* by taxi, costs 10*d.* by *dolmuş*. The system operates between towns too; for such long journeys one may book a place in advance.

At the proclamation of the Republic, Turkey's merchant navy consisted of 88 vessels, mostly decrepit, totalling some 30,000 gross tons. The coasting-trade, of vital importance to a country with over 4,400 miles of coast and with poor internal communications, was perforce left in foreign hands until 1926.

By that time the number of Turkish-owned ships had risen enough for them to be given a monopoly of the coasting-trade. The monopoly was at first vested in two corporations, one a Government agency, the other working with private capital, but within a short time the State Seaways Administration became the owner of all Turkish steamers, whose gross tonnage amounted, in 1932, to 110,170. By 1951 the Turkish mercantile marine comprised 890 vessels, of almost half a million gross tonnage. By mid-1952 the gross tonnage had reached 552,989. Of this figure, 325,000 tons represented shipping operated by private owners, while the remainder belonged to the Maritime Bank. The total gross tonnage in February 1958 was 668,000. Turkish shipping now carries 22 per cent of the country's foreign trade, as against 8 per cent in 1949.

The chief Turkish ports, in order of importance, are Istanbul, İzmir, Samsun, Trabzon, İskenderun and Mersin. Extensive programmes of modernization have been carried out at all of these. A new suspension bridge has been planned, to cross the Bosphorus, but has so far proved financially impossible. It would doubtless be more economical than the ferry-steamers which at present carry the stream of passengers and vehicles between Europe and Asia, but it is a saddening thought that the splendid sweep of that loveliest of water-ways might some day be broken.

Turkey has won for herself a considerable share of the Aegean and Mediterranean trade. Her fast modern passenger and cargo-ships call at Piraeus, Naples, Genoa, Marseilles, Limasol, Haifa and Alexandria. Well over half the ships putting in at Turkish ports are Turkish-owned.

A State Airways organization (*Devlet Hava Yollari*, abbreviated to D.H.Y.) was established in 1935 and, through the deficiencies then obtaining in road and rail transport, acquired an immediate popularity. An Englishwoman, nervous of flying, remarked after her first air-trip in Turkey that whereas a Western airliner, full of smart women and elegant men with brief-cases, must be tempting to the Fates and is obviously potential headline material, there is something that inspires confidence about the unglamorous sight of a Turkish 'plane-load of rough-and-ready Anatolian peasant-farmers, who clearly have every intention of reaching intact the place for which they have bought their tickets. In 1956 D.H.Y. became a corporation with capital subscribed publicly, and was re-named *Türk Hava Yolları A.O.*, abbreviated T.H.Y. There are regular flights between most large towns inside the country, as well as to Athens, Beirut, Cyprus, London and Cairo.

After the hard winter of 1949–50, when several foreign airlines threatened to avoid Istanbul altogether if the alternately water-logged and ice-bound runways of Yeşilköy Airport were not made good, extensive alterations were put in hand and the city can now boast of having one of the most up-to-date aerodromes in the world.

(f) Economic Policy and Overseas Trade

The roots of the perennial crisis in the Turkish economy are threefold: the enormous expenditure on defence, the virtual exemption of farmers from taxation and the irresponsible extravagance of the Democrat regime in the nineteen-fifties. Inflation has been the inevitable consequence.

In the following table, column I shows the value of the note-circulation, column II the total of credits granted by all the banks in Turkey, inclusive of the sums in column III, which represent credits granted to farmers. The unit is one million liras.

Year	I	II	III
1949	893	1,069	337
1951	1,146	1,779	646
1955	2,008	5,062	1,558
1960	4,452	9,640	2,392
1963	5,581	11,984	2,408

In July 1962, the O.E.C.D. set up a consortium to provide aid to Turkey, the members being the Benelux countries, Canada, France, Western Germany, the United States and the United Kingdom. Meanwhile the Turks had been preparing a Five-Year

Plan, under the guidance of Professor Jan Tinbergen of Holland, which began operating at the beginning of 1963. It was to be the first of three plans. It aimed to raise per capita income from around £68 per annum to £130 per annum by 1967. There was an investment programme of just under two thousand million sterling, of which 20 per cent would be spent on housing, 17·7 on agriculture, fisheries and forestry, 16·9 on manufacture, 13·4 on transport, 7·1 on education and 2·2 on public health.

The three great difficulties in the way of the Turks' themselves contributing to the success of the plan are the Turkish tax-structure, the losses incurred by the State industries, especially the railways, and the unwillingness of the private sector to invest on the scale required. Uncertainty about the political future still keeps a vast amount of money under the bed. It is instructive to see how the price of gold rises each year after the harvest when all the farmers have money to spare, and falls later on when they are hard up. On a more sophisticated level, spare cash is devoted to the building of blocks of flats; thus at the beginning of 1964 the planners were hoping that the private sector would invest 1,390 million lira in manufacture, but were expecting it to invest 2,000 million in apartment-buildings.

What is required is easy to say but hard to envisage: a government strong enough to allay investors' fears for the future and strong-minded enough to broaden the basis of income-tax.

The table below shows Turkey's dealings with her principal trading partners in 1963 (in millions of liras).

	Turkey's exports	Turkey's imports
U.S.A.	448,049	1,904,630
Western Germany	556,731	939,980
United Kingdom	423,937	693,691
Italy	390,684	315,149

These dealings constituted 54·9 per cent of her total exports and 62 per cent of her total imports for the year.

The total value of her exports for the year was 3,313 million liras and of her imports 6,216 million.

(g) Education

The Law of Unification of Instruction, of 3 March 1924, did not add only the *medreses* to the responsibilities of the Ministry of Education. The Ministry of *Evkaf* had controlled the religious schools created by private Muslim benefactors. The minorities had their own 'non-provided' schools. There were also schools established and controlled by foreign organizations: the admirable American institution, Robert College, for example, and the excellent schools of the Alliance Israélite, which played a great part in spreading French cultural influence throughout the Middle East. Finally, there were private schools, which were subject to no sort of control; some of these performed a useful service, but many followed the educational pattern set by Mr Wackford Squeers.

By bringing all these institutions under a unified control, the Nationalists were in a position to mould the new generation to the shape they wished. Even in the foreign schools, certain subjects, notably history, must be taught by Turkish-born teachers.

Although education has, after defence, the highest priority in the budget, the educational position is far from satisfactory. The basic trouble is a vicious circle: the villages will never be fit for educated people to live and work in until more educated people go to live and work in the villages. The one way out was the Village Institutes; the sooner they are reopened the better.

The situation in 1963 is shown in this table; the most terrifying fact it reveals is that 30 per cent of children of primary school age were not attending school at all.[1]

Type of school	Population of school age	Actual enrolment	Percentage	Number of teachers
Primary	4,513,000	3,160,000	70	67,900
Middle:	1,786,000			
Technical		68,400	4	8,000
General		333,000	19	5,200
Lycée:	1,505,000			
Technica		46,500	3	8,000
General		86,000	6	2,500
University:	1,816,000			
Technical		10,000	1	1,300
General		51,000	3	2,800

The next table shows how many villages in the east of the country have no school of any kind:

Province	Number of villages	With school	Without school
Ağrı	623	261	362
Bingöl	323	194	129
Diyarbakır	662	240	422
Elâzığ	506	230	276
Mardin	722	220	502

[1] In 1954, however, 31 per cent of children of school age were not attending school. At the end of 1958, when there were 20,773 primary schools, with 48,826 teachers to 2,279,201 pupils, the first goal was still 'to provide schools for every child who is of school age'.

Province	Number of villages	With school	Without school
Tunceli	415	241	174
Urfa	623	261	362

After that, it is not surprising that 60 per cent of the population aged 15 and over are illiterate.

Although the great gate of Istanbul University bears the proud date 1453, this is to be taken as a compliment to the love of learning displayed by Mehmed the Conqueror, and not as the authentic date of the University's foundation. Its oldest Faculty is that of Medicine (1826). Other Faculties were created in the late nineteenth and early twentieth centuries, but the University was not constituted in its present form till 1933.

The oldest Faculty at Ankara is the former School of Law, founded in 1925. The flourishing Faculty of Language, History and Geography, whose title does less than justice to the wide range of subjects covered there, dates from 1935.

The Istanbul Engineering School became the Istanbul Technical University in 1941. By a law promulgated in June 1946 all three Universities were given autonomy and corporate personality, whereas they had previously been under the direct control of the Ministry of Education.

By the end of 1958 the number of universities had risen to six, with the opening of the Ege (Aegean) University at İzmir, the Atatürk University at Erzurum and the Middle East Technical University at Ankara.

(h) Health

From its inception the Republic has carried on a relentless war against disease, and this struggle has been intensified in the last few years.

The number of new tuberculosis cases notified rose steadily from 3,121 in 1948 to 5,181 in 1951; this increase was due not to a rise in the incidence of the disease, but to the growing use of mass radiography. Hospital provision for T.B. patients has been greatly enlarged in recent years; from 1,097 beds in 1950 to 6,357 in 1954. A campaign of mass inoculation began in 1953 and deaths from the disease fell from 1,500 per 100,000 in 1950 to 78 in 1955.

The places where malaria is prevalent are the plains of Antalya and Seyhan and the drained and irrigated valleys of the Aegean coastlands. Modern methods of prevention and treatment are being constantly applied, with no small success. The rate of incidence dropped from 35 per 1,000 in 1950 to 2 in 1954.

The eye-disease trachoma is probably the most widespread ailment in the Middle East. Its incidence in Turkey is far less than in most of the neighbouring countries, but it is still a scourge.

Nor has rabies yet been stamped out. From 1947 to 1951 an average of twenty people died of it annually. In the latter year inoculations were administered at 103 stations, to 10,386 people who had incurred a risk of infection.

There exists a system of sick-benefit insurance for workers. In addition to providing full medical treatment and sick-pay for insured workers, it provides pre- and post-natal care and midwifery services for insured women and the wives of insured men. An allowance is also payable for three weeks before and six weeks after the birth, on condition that the mother does not work during these times. Retirement pensions are also included in the scheme; they will be paid to people aged sixty or over who have been insured for at least twenty-five years.

Four universities have medical faculties: Ankara, Istanbul, İzmir and Erzurum. The last-named was to begin full-scale teaching in 1965; the other three produce a total yearly average of 470 graduates, representing 30 per cent of the annual intake of freshmen.

Although there are over 12,000 doctors registered with the Ministry of Health, 3,000 of them are concentrated in Istanbul and over 1,500 live permanently abroad, mostly in the United States. The average for the whole country is one doctor to 2,800 people; in Istanbul it is one to 561, in Ankara one to 798, in Ordu one to 17,237 and in Gümüşhane one to 22,396. The reasons for this are the same as those for the shortage of teachers in the villages, especially in the east, and the results are comparable. The infant mortality rate for the western provinces in 1963 was 150 in a thousand births; in the east it was 285.

(i) Justice

Trial by jury is as yet unknown in Turkey, although there have been demands for its introduction from those who think that Turkey ought to have all the outward attributes of a Western democracy. Criminal cases are generally decided by a bench consisting of one presiding judge and two assessors, civil cases by a judge sitting alone.

In spite of the rare case where the scales may seem weighted against the foreigner, the courts are, in normal circumstances, just and uncorrupt. Certainly there is nothing in present-day Turkey to match the flagrant injustices of the Capitulations regime. Most important, the judiciary is not, as it is in some neighbouring countries, completely under the thumb of the government, which is why so many judges were compulsorily retired or transferred to the wilds during the Democrat era.

The latest available figure of convictions and sentences are reproduced below. They date from 1948, but there is no reason to suppose that the pattern has changed much since then.

Nature of crime	No. of convictions
Murder	2,348
Robbery	9,816
Other charges	110,529
TOTAL	122,693

To give the reader an idea of what sort of thing may lurk behind the terse 'Other charges', some details are appended of the number of prosecutions for various offences committed by members of the population (totalling roughly 6,000) of eight villages in the vilayet of Manisa, during the years 1936–1941.[1]

Murder	2
Assault, wounding	91
Theft	26
Insult, threat, slander	74
Abduction of girls	14
Rape	10
Damage to property	22
Breaking and entering	5

Miscellaneous offences, including unlawful carrying of arms, unauthorised growing of tobacco, smuggling tobacco, breaches of the Hat Law 151

Over the whole country the following sentences were imposed during 1948:

Death	7
Hard labour	5,437
Imprisonment, long	64,575
Loss of civil rights	1,241
Loss of right to Government employment	1,233
Deportation	123
Heavy fine	55,667
Imprisonment, short	8,390
Small fine	24,418
Other penalties	10,366
TOTAL	171,457

[1] This information is taken from *Toplumsal Yapı Araştırmaları*, by Dr Behice Sadık Boran (Ankara, 1945): one of the few existing scholarly studies of Turkish village life.

Of the 122,693 offenders to whom these punishments were meted out, 112,306 were male and 9,253 female Turkish subjects. The remainder were aliens, 987 men and 147 women. 4,876 of the total were between twelve and fifteen years of age.

The minute number of death-sentences imposed is in striking contrast to the 2,348 convictions for murder. In 1951 only one execution took place in the whole of Turkey.

Chapter 25

Summing-up

TURKEY is a going concern. The reader will understand the force of this remark if he has ever felt the naive wonder one sometimes experiences when visiting certain foreign countries, about whether the policemen ever get paid and whether anyone cares if the ten o'clock train starts before noon or starts at all. Turkish policemen are paid and Turkish trains run on time.

The question is often asked, is Turkey Western? The matter is complicated by the fact that there are manifestly two Turkeys. There is the urban Turkey of the theatres, the smart cafés and the literary revues, and there is the rural Turkey, with its primitive housing, its brutalizing toil and its appalling illiteracy. The importance of this duality can easily be exaggerated. The Turks' resentment of criticism from outsiders (which we shall speak of later) is matched only by their readiness to criticize themselves; the existence of the other Turkey has been frequently discovered by Turkish writers since the First World War.[1] In 1950 a young village schoolmaster named Mahmud Makal published some notes of his observations on village life, under the title of *Bizim Köy* ('Our Village').[2] So startling to the consciences of town-dwellers were the simple truths it contained, that the book speedily became a best-seller, and the author underwent a short term of imprisonment on the mistaken grounds that he was a Communist.

In 1953 a reporter on a leading Istanbul newspaper, *Cumhuriyet*, went to the eastern provinces, from where he sent back harrowing stories of people living in caves; snug caves, admittedly, with carpets on the floors, but caves. Again the townsman was shocked, and these revelations may well have accelerated the pace of rural betterment. But, disturbing though the first sight of a Turkish village may be to those who know only Ankara and Istanbul, its

[1] One of the earliest and most powerful books on this theme is Yakub Kadri Karaosmanoğlu's *Yaban* (first published 1933).

[2] A rather too literary version was made by Sir Wyndham Deedes: *A Village in Anatolia* (Vallentine, Mitchell, 1954). The utility of the annotations, by the anthropologist Paul Stirling, is lessened by his reluctance to give the author credit for saying what he meant.

effect is far less shattering to anyone who has travelled in Auvergne or Calabria. Not for a moment would one wish the Turks to be lulled into a continued neglect of their villages, but it is only fair to point out that the enormous gulf between town and country is not unknown in other lands.

Given then that every country with a large peasant population lives on two distinct levels, is Turkey entitled to be called Western?

One criterion is the position of women. Polygamy has been illegal, and civil marriage compulsory, since 1926. The official Turkish statistics reveal a large gap between theory and practice (and it should be remembered that Turkish censuses are more comprehensive than most, since people are forbidden to go out of their houses at all on census-days). The census of 1945 showed 97,357 more married women than married men, the corresponding figure for 1927 being 177,091. 'Latest statistics' given in the newspaper *Milliyet* for 22 January 1963 (with no source shown) were that there were 3,700,000 married men and 4,200,000 married women; if correct, this is a measure of the growth of free enterprise under the Democrats.[1]

The following table, compiled from the census of 1950, gives the number of marriages in urban centres against total urban population (figures for marriages among the rural population are unfortunately not available) for nine vilayets. The first three are those which contain the three principal cities. The second three are situated in the west of Anatolia, and the last three in the east.

Vilayet	Urban pop.	Urban marriages	Marriages per 1,000
Ankara	346,869	3,019	9
Istanbul	1,018,468	10,057	10
İzmir	362,340	3,599	10
Afyon	65,836	746	11
Aydın	80,326	942	12
Burdur	24,125	331	14
Ağri	21,211	42	2
Bingöl	9,555	35	4
Van	25,825	96	4

There seems no escape from the conclusion that many marriages

[1] 'In a monogamous country it is unnecessary to count both the husbands and the wives in order to ascertain the number of married people. If allowances are made for the few gay Lotharios who do not conform to either custom or statute, it is sufficient to count either the husbands or the wives. There are just as many in one class as in the other. The correspondence between the two classes is one-to-one.' E. Kasner and J. Newman, *Mathematics and the Imagination* (G. Bell and Sons, 1949), p. 29.

in the east are not registered with the civil authorities but are still conducted by the local Imam. The divorce figures are equally informative: in 1950 there were 208 divorces in the vilayet of Aydın, out of an urban and rural population of 337,977. This accords fairly closely with the figures for Istanbul: 929 out of 1,179,666. Van, on the other hand, had only eight divorces out of a total population of 145,803, while Hakâri, another eastern province, with a population of 44,204, had no official divorces at all. It looks very much as though the writ of the sacred law still runs in the east.

In one respect the weight of custom has forced a change in the civil law relating to marriage. The Swiss Civil Code lays down, as the minimum age for marriage, twenty for men and eighteen for women. When this Code was first adopted by the Turks, these figures were reduced to eighteen and seventeen respectively, with the proviso that in special cases a magistrate might give permission for marriage at the age of fifteen, for either sex, if the parents agreed. This was in recognition of the general earliness of maturity among peasant communities. In June 1938 the normal minimum ages were further reduced to seventeen and fifteen respectively, while the absolute minimum age in special circumstances was kept at fifteen for men but was lowered to fourteen for women. The census of 1945 showed that in the age-group ten to fourteen there were 2,132 married women, 120 widows and 23 divorcees. Although Turkish law requires evidence of only three months' desertion before granting a divorce, some of the fourteen-year-olds must have been very quick off the mark.

It must be confessed that, outside the big urban centres, the Republican reforms have so far touched only a minority of women. The visitor to Ankara has only to walk along Anafartalar Caddesi, to the older Ankara, up the hill which rises behind the great equestrian statue of Atatürk, to see women as careful to shroud their faces from the stranger's eye as any of their Arab or Persian or Pakistani sisters. The difference is that a Turkish woman who decides to go unveiled is less likely to be treated by her menfolk as mad or depraved than is a woman in the other Muslim lands. And in every new generation more and more girls are reluctant to shroud themselves as their mothers or grandmothers did.[1]

[1] A minor but significant indication of the Westernizing trend is to be seen in the physical proportions of the girls chosen in the annual competition for the title of Beauty Queen of Turkey. The early ones were quite remarkably plump, but each successive year's winner has approached closer to Western standards of beauty.

An attractive cartoon appeared in the satirical review *Akbaba*, in July 1953. It showed an old-fashioned room containing a divan, on which are seated two black-veiled women, only their noses and eyes visible, and one pretty girl, neatly dressed in Western style, at whom a middle-aged villager is staring in shocked surprise. A younger man by his side is saying, 'You must excuse her, Guv'nor. She's a bit uncouth. She's only just arrived from Istanbul.'

Not that fanatics are wanting, even among young urban Turks. The author was assured by an undergraduate at the Faculty of Law in Istanbul, a man in his early twenties, that the veiling of women was divinely ordained for the good of mankind. 'For if your woman goes unveiled, I may see her and desire her and kill you to get her, which would be displeasing to Allah.' But such an attitude is far from typical—and even in England we still have our share of people who write periodically to the papers to protest that 'nothing's been the same since the women got the vote'.

The propagandists who boast of the fact that all professions are open to Turkish women, are missing the point; other Muslim countries have their few but well-publicized women doctors, teachers and lawyers. But Turkey has women shop-assistants, clerks and telephone operators too: the test of female emancipation is not whether a small number of highly-gifted or highly-placed women can gate-crash one particular masculine preserve, but whether any girl at all who wants a job can get one, of right, and at the same rate of pay as a man. In this respect Turkey is a model to Asia, and perhaps not to Asia alone.

The only fair answer to the question whether Turkey is Western is, 'Potentially, yes'. For well over a century, enlightened Turks, desiring Westernization, achieved only modernization. Now at last there is a real understanding, amongst an ever-growing section of the Turkish people, of the aims and spirit of European civilization. 'Does one find it in the peasantry?' the reader may ask. Yes, one does. Not frequently as yet, but it is there. And this brings us to a characteristic which Turkey has always displayed, in common with other countries of the east; although it is a characteristic which we may like to think of as peculiar to the Western democracies: the absolute lack of class prejudice. It should not be forgotten that most of the great men of the old Ottoman Empire were slaves. The first Grand Vizier of the Köprülü family started life as a scullion. An earlier Grand Vizier, İbrahim Pasha, who held office under Süleyman the Magnificent for thirteen years, had been brought to Turkey as a boy, a captive of the Barbary corsairs. Although his enemies might criticize him for his arrogance, none thought to blame him for being the son of a common Italian sailor. So nowadays the children of villagers can and do rise to high positions in the Republic, and nobody cares who their fathers were. And though their mothers, perhaps their sisters too, may still wear the veil, their wives and daughters do not. Within a generation, if all goes well, the sight of a veiled woman will amuse Turkish children as much as the sight of a man in a fez amuses them now.

Yet although these symbols of the past may disappear, Turkey is still a Muslim land. One is constantly reminded of this, even in the western provinces, even in the great cities. The sleekest fluid-drive taxi, like every cart-horse, carries its little knot of blue beads, to ward off the Evil Eye. The prevalence of berets it due to the facility they afford the wearer of touching the ground with his forehead, just as the old fez did. For mosque-going is on the increase. The more that Western influence spreads in Turkey, the more the Turks' self-respect drives them to be mindful of their inheritance.

At *Kurban Bayramı*, the great religious festival of the Muslim year, many Turks now exchange greeting-cards, decorated with robins, lucky horseshoes, black cats and tinselled crescent moons. Not a few Turkish families have Christmas trees.

Consequently, many thoughtful Turks feel impelled, amidst all these departures from the ways of their fathers, to return to the firm rock of Islam. It may well be that the Republic's best defence against the 'black reaction' is not in maintaining an uncompromising materialism but in encouraging a movement which will worship God in the old way, while recognizing the irrevocability of the disestablishment of Islam. But such a movement requires a leader, and at the moment there seems to be a dearth of outstanding men in Turkish Islam. Indeed, in August 1962 the Minister of State declared publicly that 55,000 out of the country's 60,000 men of religion could not read or write. Of course he may have meant that they knew the Arabic script but not the Latin letters; but even so!

Not all Muslim dignitaries however are *ipso facto* reactionary. The author was shown round the delightful museum at Manisa by the local Imam, who proudly pointed out the various exhibits, displaying absolutely no resentment at the fact that the collections were housed in what had once been the *medrese* of his mosque. 'The people come and learn something; that is all that matters.'

There is a keen interest and pride in Turkey's past, a pride manifested no less by the ploughman who unearths a Greek coin or terra-cotta figurine and takes it to the local museum, than by the devoted archaeologists and administrators who have created, in the old Cloth Market at Ankara, an up-to-date and magnificently displayed exhibition of pre-classical antiquities. They are aware that, with the exception of Athens, Rome and Alexandria, it is no great exaggeration to say that every major city of classical antiquity is in Turkey: Ephesus, Troy, Sardis and Pergamum; Tarsus, Gordium and Halicarnassus and many besides. At Therapia on the Bosphorus, Medea killed her brother; the fiery breath of the Chimaera slain by Bellerophontes still burns in the rocks, west of the Lycian city of Olympus, in what is now the vilayet of Antalya.

And all round them, and a part of their daily lives for the past 500 years, a reflection of their tastes as much as a display of their abilities, are the mosques, with slim minarets and elaborate fountains, cool domes in which the pigeons murmur, expanses of carpet covering the floor, and carved wooden pulpits and inlaid reading-stands. The supreme Muslim art of calligraphy was combined with that of ceramics to produce friezes of vivid colour, along which Koranic verses march, in the intricate majesty of the Arabic script. Elsewhere are walls faced with tiles of tulips and carnations and waving leaves in lovely and luminous colours, of peacock blue and turquoise and tomato red, whose making is now a lost mystery. Supporting the arches and corners is the distinctively Turkish corbelling in the form of tiers of stalactites. The windows, mosaics of stained glass set in plaster, admit a muted light. It is no wonder that the Turks are proud of their past.

We are approaching the end of our survey, and the reader may be wanting the answer to a simple question (and not in terms of an average cranial index): what are the Turks like? Such a question calls for some sweeping generalizations, and here they are.

The Turks' obvious characteristic is dourness; they do not laugh much in public, and the Turkish sense of humour, though real enough, takes a lot of knowing. Their manner is reserved. It is possible to travel by train right across Anatolia with no more risk of being spoken to by the other occupants of the compartment than there would be in England; hence, perhaps, the old appraisal of the Turk as 'the Englishman of the East'.

But once the barriers are down there is a world of friendliness waiting. Turkey is the only country, in the author's experience, where the proprietor of a small hotel utterly refused to present his bill to a departing traveller, whom he had never seen before or was likely to see again, in the words, 'Please! You are our guest.'

Another characteristic is over-sensitiveness. In the Turkish translation of *Macbeth* the witches' cauldron contains neither nose of Turk nor Tartar's lips. 'Turk-disparagement' is an offence in Turkish law.

Indeed, foreign experts often find that their smallest criticism of the Turkish way of doing things is regarded as a studied insult. This attitude is particularly trying to those Americans and Englishmen whose duty it is to teach the use of machinery. Many Turkish farmers tend to begrudge time and effort spent on the maintenance of equipment; they feel that all these wonderful and costly new machines ought to be able to go on working for ever. What is the point of devoting labour to a labour-saving device? The all-too-frequent result of this outlook has been well described as 'unpremeditated sabotage'.

On the other hand, any word of praise for Turks or Turkish institutions, however ill-informed, is sure of the widest publicity. There is actually to be seen on Turkish bookstalls a work entitled *Nice Things that have been Said about the Turks.* All this can only be due to a feeling of insecurity, the time for which has long passed. The Turkish achievement in peace and war does not justify this exaggerated concern with what other people think. Turkey has fought her way up from the pit of defeat and despair, till now she stands in an honoured place amongst the nations. The first successful rebel against the hegemony of the West, she has won the respect of Europe. To the free peoples of Asia she is a guide and an inspiration. She would do well to remember the message of Atatürk: 'Be proud! Work! Be confident! *Öğün! Çalış! Güven!*

Chapter 26

The Turkish Constitution

UNTIL THE 1960 revolution, the Constitution of the Republic was basically the Law of Fundamental Organization, No. 491 of 1340 (in the *Malî* calendar, corresponding to A.D. 1924), as amended in 1928, 1931, 1934 and 1937. The most significant amendment, made on 10 April 1928, was the deletion of the original opening clause of Article 2: 'The religion of the Turkish State is Islam'. For its Fundamental Provisions see p. 150.

On 10 January 1945, an *öztürkçe*, 'pure Turkish', version was promulgated (Law No. 4695), Article 104 of which read: 'This, law, which has been put into Turkish, replaces the Law of Fundamental Organization No. 491, dated 20 April 1340, with no change in meaning and sense'. This version, the *Anayasa*, was disliked not only by opponents of the language reform but also by many lawyers and legislators who felt that the dignity of the Constitution was lessened by the abandonment of the stately Ottoman phraseology. On 24 December 1952, the Assembly approved Law No. 5997, restoring Law No. 491 'together with such of its amendments as were in force up to the date of acceptance of Law No. 4695'.

On 12 June 1960, the National Unity Committee promulgated a provisional law amending the Constitution retrospectively from 27 May, in order to provide a legal basis for its own existence and its assumption of the authority which, constitutionally, was delegated by the nation to the Grand National Assembly. Its most interesting provisions are here summarised.

The 'General Provisions' explain that the G.N.A. had lost its legality as a result of violation of the Constitution by the leaders of the party in power. The Turkish Army, in accordance with its statutory duty to protect the country and the Republic, acted on behalf of the nation, dissolved the Assembly and provisionally entrusted power to the N.U.C.

Article 1. The N.U.C. exercises the right of sovereignty on behalf of the Turkish nation until the date on which it will hand over the administration to the G.N.A., which will be re-established by elections to be held as soon as possible and when the new constitution and electoral law have been approved according to democratic methods. During this period, all rights and powers enjoyed by the G.N.A. in accordance with the constitutional law belong to the N.U.C.

Article 2 laid down the form of the oath taken by members of the N.U.C.: 'I have devoted myself to the Turkish nation without expecting any return, being bound by nothing other than the principles of morality, justice, laws, human rights and my convictions of conscience. I will not pursue any aim contrary to the sanctity of the fatherland and nation and the sovereignty of the nation. I will not depart from loyalty to organizing the democratic community, according to the new constitution, and to the aim of handing over power to the new Assembly. I swear this on my honour and on all things held sacred.'

Article 3 gave the power of legislation to the N.U.C. and executive power to the Council of Ministers appointed by the Head of State.

Article 6 instituted a Higher Judicial Council to try 'the fallen President, Premier, Ministers and Deputies of the former administration and those who participated in their offences.' It would consist of a president, eight regular members and six reserve members, elected by the N.U.C. from the judges of the judicial, administrative and military courts. The prosecutors would be elected by the N.U.C. from the members of a Higher Investigation Committee that would investigate the responsibility of the accused and decide whether to bring them to trial. Members of the N.U.C. could not serve on either of these new bodies.

Article 8. The N.U.C. will cease to exist upon the re-establishment of the Grand National Assembly of Turkey, which will come into existence after general elections. The Committee will dissolve itself or will be automatically dissolved.

Article 24 abrogated a number of Articles of 'the Law of Fundamental Organization No. 491 of 1924'. These included the prohibition of confiscation (as the N.U.C. were determined to deprive the Democrats of whatever profits they had corruptly made in their period of office) and the provision absolving the President of the Republic from responsibility for decrees he had signed; he was to share the guilt, if any, with Menderes and his Ministers.

Over-haste in drafting this provisional Constitution led to one curious consequence, of purely academic interest. As Article 24 abrogated parts of 'Law No. 491 of 1924' and not 'Law No. 491 of 1924 as subsequently amended', and left the remainder of that Law in force, it could be held that until 9 July 1961, the unamended Article 2, *inter alia*, of the 1924 Constitution was in force and that for that period therefore the religion of the Turkish State was Islam.

The new Constitution was promulgated as Law No. 334 of 9 July 1961, this being the date of the referendum which accepted it. It begins with a lengthy preamble:

> Having enjoyed independence and having fought for its rights and liberties throughout history, and having brought about the Revolution of 27 May 1960, by exercising its right to resist a régime which had lost its legality through its unconstitutional and unlawful attitude and actions, the Turkish Nation, prompted and inspired by Turkish nationalism which unites all its individual members, as an indivisible whole sharing alike in destiny, pride and distress, around the national consciousness and ideals, and which has as its goal ever to raise up our nation as a respected member, with equal rights, of the the family of nations of the world, within the spirit of national unity, and with full consciousness of the principle of 'Peace at home, Peace abroad', of the spirit of the national struggle, of national sovereignty and of devotion to the reforms of Atatürk, in order to set up a democratic rule of law based on juridical and social foundations, which will make possible the realisation and guaranteeing of human rights and liberties, national solidarity, social justice and the well-being and prosperity of the individual and society, accepts and proclaims this Constitution prepared by the Constituent Assembly of the Turkish Republic and, with the conviction that its basic guarantee lies in the hearts and wills of the citizens, entrusts it to the vigilance of its children, who love freedom, justice and integrity.

As certain of the Kemalist reforms, for example the Hat Law, could be held contrary to the spirit of human rights and liberties, special provision is made to safeguard them by Article 153: 'No provision of this Constitution shall be construed as rendering unconstitutional the following Reform Laws which aim at raising Turkish society to the level of contemporary civilization and at protecting the secular nature of the Republic. . . .'

The most noteworthy provisions are these. Article 19 permits every individual 'to follow freely the dictates of his conscience, to choose his own religious faith and to have his own opinions.' 'No person shall be compelled to worship, or to reveal his religious faith and belief.' In consequence, the form tourists are given to complete on entering the country no longer has a space for

'Religion'; any tourist who happens to be given an obsolete form and who agrees with the drafters of the Constitution that his religion is his own business might try inserting in the appropriate space 'Anayasa, Madde 19'. This useful Article goes on to prohibit the exploitation of religion for political or personal advantage.

Article 22 establishes the principle that the Press is free and not subject to censorship.

Article 39. 'Where it is deemed necessary in the public interest, private enterprises which bear the characteristics of a public service may be nationalised, provided that the true equivalent value thereof is paid as indicated by law. . . .'

Article 45. 'The State shall adopt the necessary measures so that workers may earn decent wages commensurate with the work they perform and sufficient to enable them to maintain a standard of living befitting human dignity.'

Article 46 entitles employees and employers to establish unions (*sendika*) and federations of unions without having to obtain prior permission, and to become members or to cease to be members of them freely. Article 47 recognizes the worker's right to collective bargaining and to strike 'to protect or correct' his economic and social position.

Article 49. 'It is the responsibility of the State to ensure that everyone leads a healthy life both physically and mentally and receives medical attention. The State shall take steps to provide destitute or poor families with housing that conforms to sanitary requirements.'

Article 54. 'Every individual who is bound to the Turkish State by ties of citizenship is a Turk. The child of a Turkish father or mother is a Turk. The citizenship status of a child of a Turkish mother and a foreign father shall be regulated by law . . . .'

Article 57, on political parties, obliges them to conform to the principles of a democratic and secular republic and to account for their income and expenditure to the Constitutional Court. This is set up in Articles 145–152 and is empowered to review the constitutionality of laws and to try the President of the Republic, the Ministers, members of all higher courts including itself, and the chief law officers of the State.

Articles 63 to 94 deal with the Grand National Assembly, which consists of the National Assembly (*Millet Meclisi*) and the Senate of the Republic (*Cumhuriyet Senatosu*). The National Assembly is composed of 450 deputies elected by general ballot; candidates must have completed their thirtieth year, have done their military service, be literate and have never been sentenced to penal servitude or five years' imprisonment or have been convicted of such disgraceful offences as breach of trust and fraudulent bankruptcy. Judges, officers, military officials and non-commissioned officers cannot be candidates or deputies unless they first resign their position. It is noteworthy that other ranks of the services are not mentioned; as they cannot 'resign their office' they are presumably ineligible. Elections to the Assembly are held every four years but the Assembly may decide to hold them earlier.

The Senate is composed of 150 elected members and 15 appointed by the President of the Republic. The Chairman and members of the N.U.C. as reconstituted in November 1960 and former Presidents of the Republic are *ex officio* members of the Senate, but *ex officio* members who join a political party shall lose their status as Senators on the date of the first senatorial election held thereafter. Elected Senators must be over 40 and have received a higher education. The President's nominees shall be selected from among people distinguished for their service in various fields and must also be over 40. At least 10 of them must be members of no political party. The term of office is six years, one-third of the elected members and the President's nominees being rotated every two years. *Ex officio* members are exempted from this provision.

By-elections to both houses shall be held every two years at the same time as the senatorial elections. Members represent neither their constituencies nor their constituents but the nation as a whole.

Bills and proposals are debated first in the Assembly and then referred to the Senate. If accepted there they become law. If a measure rejected by the Assembly is passed by the Senate, the Assembly reviews the draft approved by the Senate and can reject or approve it. A measure rejected by a two-thirds majority vote of a plenary session of the Senate can become law only if approved by a two-thirds majority vote of a plenary session of the Assembly. Laws must be promulgated by the President within ten days or returned by him to the Assembly for reconsideration. If re-enacted there, the law must be promulgated by the President within ten days.

Article 95 lays down the rules for the election of the President of the Republic: he is elected by secret ballot, at a plenary session of both houses, from among those members who are over 40 and have had a higher education. His term of office is seven years and he is not re-eligible. He must dissociate himself from his party. He is not accountable for his actions connected with his duties (Art.

98) but may be impeached for high treason on the proposal of one-third of the plenary session of both houses (Art. 99). In his absence abroad or through illness, the chairman of the Senate acts for him, as he does in the event of the President's death (Art. 100).

The Prime Minister is designated by the President from among the members of the G.N.A. (i.e. of both houses). The Prime Minister nominates Ministers from among the members of the G.N.A. or from among those qualified for election as deputies.

The members of the Council of Ministers are jointly responsible for the manner in which government policy is implemented.

The office of Commander-in-Chief is 'inseparable from the spiritual being of the G.N.A. and is represented by the President of the Republic' (Art. 110).

No act of the administration is immune from the review of the courts. The administration is liable for damages resulting from its acts (Art. 114).

Article 120 relates to universities; they may be established only by the State and are public corporate bodies enjoying academic and administrative autonomy. They are administered and supervised by bodies consisting of qualified members of the teaching staff elected from among themselves. Neither these bodies nor any member of the teaching staff may be removed from office by authorities other than the universities. University teachers may join political parties but may not assume executive functions outside the central organizations of political parties.

Persons employed in public services shall not carry out any order of a superior if the person receiving the order thinks it unconstitutional or illegal. If the superior insists on the performance of the order he must put it in writing and the subordinate who carries it out is not responsible; but no one can be absolved from responsibility if he carries out an order which by its nature constitutes a crime (Art. 125).

Judges are independent in the discharge of their duties and no one may make recommendations or suggestions to a judge. They may not be dismissed or retired before the age limit of 65 years unless they so desire (Articles 132, 133). Court proceedings are open to all. Cases may be heard in secret only if 'definitely required by public morality or public security' (Art. 135).

For Further Reading

Annotated bibliographies will be found in the two following books:

A Guide to Turkish Area Study, by J. K. Birge (American Council of Learned Societies, Washington, 1949).

British Contributions to Turkish Studies, by Harold Bowen (Longmans, Green and Co., for the British Council, 1945).

There is still no satisfactory English account of Ottoman history to replace Stanley Lane-Poole's *Turkey* (T. Fisher Unwin, 1888). For the early period, this must be supplemented by:

The Rise of the Ottoman Empire, by Paul Wittek (Royal Asiatic Society, 1938), an outstanding work which shows that historical research can be as exciting as any detective story.

The Emergence of Modern Turkey, by Bernard Lewis (Oxford University Press, 1961) is invaluable for the nineteenth and twentieth centuries.

Also warmly recommended are *The Genesis of Young Ottoman Thought*, by Şerif Mardin (Princeton University Press, 1962) and *Reform in the Ottoman Empire 1856–1876*, by Roderic H. Davison (Princeton University Press, 1963).

The Western Question in Greece and Turkey, by A. J. Toynbee (Constable, 2nd edition, 1923), gives an objective account of the Nationalist movement and its struggle for independence. The full story of the triumphant conclusion to that struggle is told in *Lausanne Conference on Near Eastern Affairs* (H.M. Stationery Office, 1923).

Foundations of Turkish Nationalism, by Uriel Heyd (Luzac-Harvill, 1950), is indispensable for the ideological background of the movement. The same author's *Language Reform in Modern Turkey* (Israel Oriental Society, 1954) fully treats the linguistic controversy.

The nature of Islamic Law and the manner of its dethronement in Turkey are brilliantly set out in *The Angora Reform*, by L. Ostrorog (University of London Press, 1927).

The Bektashi Order of Dervishes, by J. K. Birge (Luzac, 1937), is the standard work on the most popular of the *tarikats*.

The reader who wishes to go deeper into the study of popular religion and folklore in Turkey is urged not to be put off by the prosaic title of *Christianity and Islam under the Sultans*, by G. W. Hasluck (Clarendon Press, 1929).

Kātib Chelebi, *The Balance of Truth*, translated, with an Introduction and Notes by G. L. Lewis (Allen & Unwin, 1957), gives information on, *inter alia*, Islamic belief and practice in the Ottoman Empire of the 17th century.

H. C. Armstrong's deservedly famous biography of Mustafa Kemal, *Grey Wolf* (Arthur Barker, 1932; Penguin Books, 1937), is to be taken with a grain of salt; Kemal was not the snarling schizophrene the author would have us think. Incomparably better is *Atatürk: The Rebirth of a Nation*, by Lord Kinross (Weidenfeld and Nicolson, 1964).

A most readable account of the Turkish Revolution is İrfan Orga's autobiographical *Portrait of a Turkish Family* (Gollancz, 1950).

Mary Gough, *The Plain and the Rough Places* (Chatto & Windus, 1954), a charming and informative book by an author who knows, understands and loves the Turkish villager.

The geography of Turkey is adequately treated in W. B. Fisher's *The Middle East* (Methuen, 1950).

Any reader who happens across the two volumes entitled *Turkey*, published by the Naval Intelligence Division of the Admiralty in 1942 and 1943, would be well advised to snap them up.

Index

(For political parties in the Republican period, see under PARTIES, POLITICAL. Treaties, Pacts, etc. are listed chronologically under TREATIES AND INTERNATIONAL AGREEMENTS, except for Lausanne, which is indexed separately.)